# Fiscal Policy in India

PRAMATHANATH BANERJEE

GYAN PUBLISHING HOUSE
New Delhi - 110002

Fiscal Policy In India

ISBN : 9788121200103



Published in 2014 in India by
Gyan Publishing House
23, Ansari Road, Daryaganj,
New Delhi - 110002
Phones : 23261060, 23282060 Fax : 23285914
e-mail : books@gyanbooks.com
website : gyanbooks.com

*Laser Typesetting at :* Vinayak Printers, Delhi
*Printed at :* Salasar Imaging System, Delhi

# PREFACE

This book comprises a series of lectures delivered by the author at the Calcutta University during the last cold weather. An attempt has been made throughout the work to present the different sides to every question in a fair and impartial manner. The historical portion of the book is based mainly on Parliamentary Papers, Blue-books of the Government of India, and other official publications. For the rest of the book the author has tried to avail himself of the most authoritative sources of information. As it is not possible to give references in all cases, he desires to express his gratitude to the authors and publishers of all works from which he has gathered any information. He is especially thankful to Mr. Sudhir Kumar Lahiri and Mr. Dhurjjati Prasad Mukerji, who have helped him with suggestions and in seeing the book through the press.

*Calcutta, September*, 1922

# CONTENTS

# CHAPTER I

## INTRODUCTORY

For nearly half a century, Indian publicists felt keenly, and expressed themselves strongly, on the question of the fiscal policy of India. And the growth of the spirit of nationalism in the country has of late considerably intensified this feeling. But apart from sentiment, the subject has, in recent years, acquired an importance—from the point of view both of the Government and the people—which it never possessed before. With the phenomenal development of the foreign trade of India, the income derived from customs tended continually to grow, and this tendency has been greatly accentuated by the levy of fresh taxes during the last few years. A comparison of the customs figures at different periods is interesting in this connection. In 1793, the customs revenue of India was about 20 lakhs, and, in 1858, the year of the assumption of the direct government by the Crown, it did not go beyond two and a half crores. In 1920-21, however, the customs yielded a sum of no less than 33½ crores. The customs receipts during this year thus exceeded the land revenue which used always to be regarded as the mainstay of Indian finance. The position now occupied by customs in the financial system of India becomes still clearer when the fact is recalled that, in last March, the Finance Member proposed to raise, by a few strokes of his pen, as it were, nearly 15 crores of additional revenue from this source alone.

The subject has had an additional importance lent to it by the fact that, since the introduction of the recent constitutional reforms, land revenue has ceased to be of any benefit to the Central Exchequer. The Government of India is thus compelled to look upon customs as the bulwark of its financial position.

From the point of view of the people the chief interest of the subject lies in the concern which is now being increasingly felt for the economic advancement of the country. The apathy of the people in matters industrial has now given place to a jealous regard for India's economic interests, and the desire is now becoming general to follow in the footsteps of the more advanced nations and use the tariff as a weapon of defence, if not also of offence, in the industrial struggle.

The popular feeling which now prevails in regard to the subject seems to be the natural outcome of the tariff policy which has been followed by the Government in the past. The present can thus be understood only with reference to the past. Besides, the germs of the future are to be found in the past as well as the present. A proper study of the subject must, therefore, begin with its history.

The fiscal history of India divides itself into three fairly well defined periods. The first was the period of the East India Company's rule, when a protective policy was followed in the country. The protection was, however, in favour of Great Britain, and against India. The second period commenced with the transfer of the administration of India from the hands of the Company to those of the British Crown, and ended in 1914. These were the years during which the principles of free trade were applied with the utmost rigour. During both these periods, England carried out in India her own trade policy. The third period was ushered in with the sound of the war-drum, and may be said to be still continuing. The financial stress caused by the great world upheaval led to some modification of the fiscal system of India, but the aftermath of the war has been responsible for the introduction of still greater changes into it. The customs duties of recent years have, it is true, been imposed for revenue purposes, but their protective tendency has, in a few cases at least, been none the less marked. In fact, this period may be said to mark the transition from an absolute adherence to free trade principles to the adoption of a policy of protection.

The second and third chapters of the book have been devoted to a brief historical review of the fiscal system of India. The fourth chapter, also treated historically, will give the reader a glimpse of the state of things as it exists at present. Each of these periods has, again, been divided into sub-periods, in view of their special characteristics.

An adequate understanding of the subject is not possible without a real grasp of the theoretical aspect of the question. There are some people who affect to deride theories. But they forget that facts, by themselves, do not convey any meaning. Facts have to be interpreted. And theory, as has been well said, is the soul of facts. In the fifth chapter, an examination of the theoretic bases of the two rival doctrines of free trade and protection has been attempted, and the main ideas of the different schools have been presented in the words, as far as possible, of their chief exponents.

The question of the future tariff policy of India has been discussed in the sixth chapter. In discussing this question, not only the general principles, but also the special needs and conditions of India, have been kept in view. With the main question are intimately connected many subsidiary questions of considerable importance, and these have been examined in the light, not merely of economic theory, but also of the practice of other nations.

In the seventh chapter, the subject of Imperial Preference has been treated with reference to India's present position and future possibilities. The question of preference within the British Empire has of late attracted considerable attention in all parts of the Empire. But the interests of India have, as a rule, been ignored in these discussions. Besides, the discussions have proceeded mainly upon political considerations.

In India, however, the question has to be approached from the economic, as well as the political, standpoint. A comprehensive view of this question has, therefore, been adopted in this book.

## CHAPTER II

### THE FISCAL POLICY OF THE EAST INDIA COMPANY

The East India Company was, for about a century and a half since its foundation, a trading corporation, pure and simple. Commercial expansion in the East was its only objective during this period. The Company gradually acquired various commercial privileges from the rulers of the different parts of India. In 1716, a *firman* was granted by the Emperor of Delhi, exempting the Company's trade from duties, on the payment of a *peshcush* of 10,000 rupees a year. This *firman* recited, "That Customs on English goods are only payable at Surat; that in Shah Jehan's time these were only two per cent.; in the time of Auranzebe 3½ at Surat, and none at other places; in Bahadur Shah's time they were 2½; that by reason of the government officers' oppressions, it is three years since they have withdrawn their factory.

In Bahar and Orixa they have no customs. In Hughley they give 3,000 rupees a year in lieu."[1]

## §1. (1765—1833)

When the East India Company assumed ruling powers, it developed its own tariff system. But the acquisition of territories by the Company was made piecemeal. For many years, the machinery of administration was very imperfect. Even after a stable form of government had been introduced, the three Presidencies of Bengal, Bombay, and Madras were independent of each other, so far as the regulation of customs was concerned. The Regulating Act of 1773 did, no doubt, give the Governor-General of Bengal some power of control over the other Presidencies, but this power was never interpreted to include interference in matters relating to trade and commerce. The result was that not only did each Presidency administer its own customs department, but had its separate tariff.[2] The Regulations passed by the Presidency Governments were, however, subject to the approval of the Court of Directors and the Board of Control, and this fact helped to introduce some element

[1] J. Macgregor, *Commercial Tariffs*, p. 56.

[2] Report of the Select Committee on the Affairs of the East India Company, 1810. The Customs collections in 1793 in Bengal amounted to £60,000, and in 1806-7 to £2,64,831.

of similarity, though not uniformity, into the tariff systems of the different Presidencies.

The customs in each Presidency were divided into two parts, namely, sea customs and land customs, though both the branches were under the control of the same provincial authority. The customs of the Bengal Presidency (including the Upper Provinces) first claim our attention. This branch of the administration was under the direction of the Revenue Department till the year 1793, when it was transferred to the Commercial Department. A Regulation passed in that year established the principle of collection and the rate of the customs to be collected on imports and exports at the two then existing custom-houses at Calcutta and Manjee. Certain important alterations were made in 1793. when the town duties at Calcutta were abolished, and the government customs, which had been discontinued in 1788, were revived in this city. In 1797, a new duty of 1 per cent. was instituted. In 1801, the Calcutta town duties were re-established, and the government customs on inland imports and exports were revived at the principal cities.[1] Until 1809, the rates of duty prevalent in Bengal on exports and imports were,

[1] Report I of the Customs Committee, 1836.

with a few exceptions, 3½ per cent. customs and 4 per cent. town duty levied generally ad valorem. There were, besides, various other payments to be made, such as stamps on *rowannahs*, commission and fees to customs masters, etc., which were burdensome and vexatious to individuals and increased the cost of collection.[1]

In 1809, a Customs Committee recommended many important changes. The primary object sought by the Committee was two-fold, namely, to improve the revenue, and to afford relief to the people from a system harassing from its complexity and objectionable from the inequality with which its burdens fell on different classes. The Committee, in the revision they proposed, adopted the following principles :

(i) That the burden borne by the inhabitants of the different provinces should be equalized ;

(ii) That trade should be liberated from impolitic restraints, to the extent of permitting merchandize, having once paid duty, to pass free throughout the territories of the Presidency ;

(iii) That the number of customs houses

[1] Report of the Committee on Customs and Post Office Regulations, 1836.

and chowkees should be reduced to the lowest practicable limit ;

(iv) That, in the enumeration of goods liable to inland duty, articles too little in value and too small in quantity should be exempt from duty, and that the duty on enumerated articles should be fixed at such rates as the goods were able to bear ;

(v) That goods of those particular descriptions which were only imported by sea should be allowed free transit throughout the Presidency ;

(vi) That, with certain exceptions especially provided for, goods subject to importation or transit duties should not also be liable to town or consumption duties ;

(vii) That *rowannahs*, fees and commission to customs masters should be abolished ; and that all the duties collected under the various denominations should be consolidated into one tax, to be levied once for all, after which free transit should be allowed to the taxed article ;

(viii) That goods should be rated in the tariff at a fixed valuation in all practicable instances, rather than ad valorem.[1]

These principles were embodied in Regulation

[1] The customs revenue under the new Regulation was estimated nearly at Rs. 57 lakhs, whilst the proceeds of the system which was superseded had amounted to a little over Rs. 51 lakhs. Report, 1836

IX of 1810, which rescinded all previous enactments regarding customs. Export and import duties were fixed ordinarily at 7½ per cent., in some cases at 5, and in others at 10 per cent. A few articles, such as bullion, horses, teak, timber, opium purchased at the Company's sales, etc., were exempted from duty. The general tendency was to raise the rate of taxation. No distinction was made between British and foreign bottoms. Nor were the rates of duty affected by the origin of goods. The administrative provisions of this Regulation related to the time and manner of the collection of export and import duties, and the grant of certificates and drawbacks. In some cases, a drawback was specifically allowed, and all goods imported expressly for re-exportation were declared to be entitled to a drawback amounting to two-thirds of the duty paid on their importation.

The financial results of the system introduced in 1810 were very satisfactory. But while the new system was advantageous to long-distance trade, it became exceedingly burdensome to trade over short distances. Trade with the ports was thus encouraged at the expense of local trade.

Regulation III of 1811 introduced an important alteration into the sea customs law, the object of which was to give a preference to British vessels over foreign shipping by imposing heavier duties on the latter and by securing the carrying trade of India to the former. The duties levied on exports and imports on foreign bottoms were raised to double the rates chargeable on the trade conveyed on British bottoms. The principle that foreigners should be twice as badly off as Englishmen was also followed in regard to drawbacks. Another provision of the Regulation is worth noting. In order to exclude, as far as possible, foreigners from the Indian coasting trade, it was provided that foreign vessels should be cleared out from a British Indian port only direct to their own countries, and they were restrained from proceeding from such port of clearance to any foreign European Settlement in India, or any port belonging to an Indian or Chinese power. Security was also taken for enforcing the delivery of cargo loaded on board a foreign vessel at a British Indian port only at the country to which such vessels belonged.[1]

Many changes of minor importance were introduced in 1812, 1813, and 1814. Regulation IV of 1815 effected very important alterations.

[1] Report of the Committee on Customs and Post Office Regulations, 1836 (House of Commons, 151).

With a view to encouraging the manufactures, trade, and shipping of Great Britain, it was provided that woollens of all sorts, all metals in a manufactured state, and canvas, cordage and marine stores, being the produce or manufacture of the United Kingdom, which were hitherto assessed with duties at 5 and 10 per cent., should be exempted from duty on importation, provided they were brought from Great Britain on British registered or Indian-built ships. It was also provided that all other articles similarly imported and being the produce or manufacture of the United Kingdom should, instead of being subject to the existing duties, be assessed at the rate of 2½ per cent.; wines and spirits only were excepted from this provision, and were subject to the duties already established. Further, it was provided that articles, the produce or manufacture of foreign Europe, if imported in British registered or Indian-built ships, were to pay duty at the rate of 5 per cent.[1] These duties having been once paid at any port in British India, the goods were not to be subjected to any further tax in transit from port to port. With

[1] The Charter Act of 1813 contained some important provisions relating to these matters. The 24th Section subjected the commerce of the East India Company to the payment of the like rates, customs, and duties, as that carried on by private traders. The 25th Section directed that no new or additional duty or tax upon the

regard to exports, the provision was that indigo, cotton, wool, hemp and sunn, the produce or manufacture of British India, should on exportation by sea to Great Britain, on British registered or Indian-built ships trading with the United Kingdom, be entitled to a drawback equal in amount to all duty paid on the articles. All other articles liable to duty under existing Regulations and exported by sea according to the foregoing conditions, were to be allowed to secure such drawback as would leave the amount of duty actually retained at 2½ per cent.[1]

The effect of these modifications was, in reality, to reduce the taxation of the export and import trade with Great Britain to rates of which the maximum was 2½ per cent. A great impulse was thus communicated to British commerce and industry, and the objects of British national policy were accomplished. But their effects on Indian industry and trade were disastrous. The produce and manufactures of India, heavily taxed by the inland system, were placed in an unquestionably disadvantageous

export or import, or transit of any goods, wares, or merchandise whatsover, should be valid in India till sanctioned by the Directors; and the 67th Section declared the whole of the duties, both on the import and export trade, to be a part of the territorial revenue. *Vide* Letter from the Court of Directors of the E. I. Co. to the Governor-General in Council, dated 6th September, 1813.

[1] Report of the Committee on Customs, 1836.

position in coming into competition with free or lightly taxed foreign articles, produced by the most improved machinery. These changes also resulted in a great loss of public revenue, and "caused taxation to operate with a very unequal pressure at the same time that they dried up some considerable sources of revenue."[1]

The exemption from duty, accorded by Regulation IV of 1815 to unmanufactured metals, was extended in 1817 to all metals, whether wrought or unwrought, of British origin. In this as well as the other alterations effected by Regulation XXI of 1817, as was rightly observed by a body of British officials, "the same anxiety to promote British interests which characterised the provisions of Regulation IV of 1815 is observable; but both in that Regulation and in this the effect of such changes on the interests of India seems to have been overlooked, or at least very partially adverted to. If the system of the Sea Customs established in 1810 was one in which due regard was had to the interests of both countries, and there certainly does not appear to be any ground for supposing that the trade of India received more favourable consideration from the Committee than the

[1] Report of the Committee relating to the Customs and Post Office systems, 1836.

commerce of Great Britain; the introduction of modifications, having for their object the especial advantage of one class. was calculated not only to reproduce the inconveniences of inequality and partiality, the remedy of which was one of the chief purposes of the Committee, but it must have tended to work the much more serious injury of depriving one class of interests without benefiting the other to a countervailing extent."[1]

By Regulation V of 1823 the transit and sea import duty leviable on piece-goods (cotton, silk, and mixed), the manufacture of the British Indian territories, was reduced from 7½ to 2½ per cent. It was provided that these descriptions of piece-goods, which had once paid either the transit or the import duty specified, should have free export from any part in the Bengal Presidency, provided they were exported to Europe on British bottom; if exported to Europe on foreign bottom, an export duty of 2½ per cent. was chargeable; if exported to places not in Europe, they became liable to an

[1] Report I of the Committee on Customs and Post Office, 1836.

Regulations XV and XVI of 1817 were enacted for the protection of the salt and opium monopolies. The latter of these duties was entirely prohibitory, and the former was nearly so as respects general trade.

export duty of $2\frac{1}{2}$ or $7\frac{1}{2}$, according as they were exported on British or foreign bottom. "The object of these provisions," as was pointed out by the Committee, "apparently was to place the piece-goods of India on the same footing with those of Great Britain, the latter having, since Regulation IV of 1815 was passed, been favoured by the customs laws to a degree which might have enabled them to drive the former out of their own market, even had the influence of British machinery been less overwhelming than it was. This act of consideration for the manufacturers of Indian piece-goods came too late to do them any service; but the relief, such as it was, was only partial, for there still remained the crying inequality of Indian copper, steel, quicksilver, etc., taxed at the rate of 10 per cent., whilst those of Great Britain were free, and the generality of Indian produce and manufactures, bearing a burthen not only more than double that imposed on the bulk of British imports, but heavier than that borne by the goods of foreign Europe. The no less striking injustice done to India in the heavy taxation which pressed upon her export trade to China, and to other places eastward of the Cape of Good Hope, compared with the burthen imposed on her export trade to Great Britain, remained also unredressed."[1]

But we cannot get a full and accurate view of the whole situation unless we contrast the advantages which were granted to the manufactures of Great Britain by India with the restrictions imposed by Great Britain upon Indian goods. A glance at the tariff schedules of Great Britain will convince any impartial observer of the extreme anxiety felt by the statesmen of that country to exclude Indian cotton manufactures from her shores.[2] In 1787, cotton manufactures from India were subjected to a duty of 50 per cent., except dimity and calicoes which paid 16½ per cent., and muslins which were assessed at 18 per cent. Additions to the rates were subsequently made, and, in 1799, some classes of cotton goods paid duty at the rate of 122 per cent. In 1819, the duty on many descriptions of Indian cotton goods was as high as 67½ per cent.[3] But the injustice did not end with the high duties. The importation into Great Britain of many classes of goods from India, such as embroidered shawls, handkerchiefs,

[1] Report of the Committee on the Customs and Post Office Systems, 1836.

[2] *Vide* Appendix A.

[3] A more favourable treatment was of course accorded to the manufactures of the British colonies.

kingcabs, coloured muslins, velvet, silks, chintz, crape, and calico towels with coloured borders, was absolutely prohibited.[1]

In 1825, the entire customs law of Bengal was recast, but the main provisions of the previous enactments were preserved unaltered. Imports by sea were classed under three heads: first, goods produced in the United Kingdom; secondly, goods of foreign Europe and the United States of America; thirdly, those of places other than Europe and America. Of the imports under the first head, some, namely, metals, woollens, and marine stores, were exempt from duty on importation, and the others were, with scarcely any exception, chargeable with a 2½ per cent. duty. Imports of the second class were, with a few exceptions, subject to duty at the rate of 5 per cent. Imports under the third head were, with two or three exceptions, liable to duty either at 7½ per cent. or at 10 per cent. These were the rates fixed for goods which were imported on British bottoms; when imported on foreign bottoms, double these rates were charged.[2]

In the reigns of George IV and William IV, and in the early years of Queen Victoria, the duties were considerably reduced.

*Vide* Return to an Order of the House of Commons, dated 19th March, 1846.

[1] Accounts and Papers relative to the East India Trade (House of Commons, 1813.)

[2] Thus, goods exported to Europe or America on British bottom must have paid 2½ per cent., and on foreign bottom 5 per cent. Goods destined for other places must, if exported on British

As regards exports, the general rule was that all goods were subject to taxation. The rates varied, as in the case of imports, according to the place to which goods were to be exported and according to the vessel on which the exportation was effected. When goods intended for exportation had paid precisely the regulated rate of taxation in the shape of import or transit duty, they were entitled to free export. When they had paid less than the regulated rate, the difference was exacted as export duty. And if they had paid more, it was refunded in the form of drawback. Here also, a preference was given to British over Indian interests, for the only goods, excepting those specially exempted from duty, which were permitted to leave the country without having been taxed at the rate of 2½ per cent., were the produce or manufactures of Great Britain which had been imported paying 2½ per cent., of which two-thirds were claimable as drawback on re-exportation to Europe or America on a British vessel.

The result of these Regulations was, as the Committee observed, an "unparalled perplexity occasioned by the joint operation of our export

bottom have paid 5, 7½ or 10 per cent., according to the import or transit duty assigned to them in the schedule, and, if exported on foreign bottom, they must have paid double the rates. *Vide* Report on Customs and Post Office Systems, 1836.

and transit duty with the concomitant embarrassments of proportions of drawback or proportions of export duty, according to flag and destination, the whole forming a mass of confusion which has never been equalled in any customs code in the world."[1]

Reference has already been made to the internal duties levied in Bengal. But a few more words must be said about a system which was oppressive to the people, and considerably hampered trade. The inland customs system in the Bengal Presidency (including Agra) was founded on the indigenous method of collecting such taxes which had prevailed from olden times. In 1788, Lord Cornwallis abolished all the internal custom-houses in Bengal and Behar, retaining only export and import duties, which were collected at Manjee on the Benares frontier and at Calcutta and the other seaports. In 1801, internal duties were re-established in these provinces at the rate of $3\frac{1}{2}$ per cent., with a provision that articles which had once paid inland duty should not again be liable to it.[2]

At this period, duties were levied according to

[1] Report of the Committee on Customs and Post Offices, 1836.

[2] In the opinion of the Government of India, the name 'transit duty' was not properly applicable to the impost levied in Bengal, but they regarded it as "in fact a trade duty." *Vide* Extract Separate Letter from India, dated 2nd September, 1835.

various rates in the different parts of the provinces. In 1810, the various systems, as we have already seen, were reduced to one uniform plan. The principle was to consolidate the different duties which were then separately levied, and to realise the consolidated duty once for all on the whole trade of the country by environing the principal marts with cordons of chowkees. For this purpose, customs-houses were established at Balasore, Calcutta, Chittagong, Dacca, Murshidabad and Patna in the Lower Provinces; at Gazipore, Benares and Mirzapore in the Central Districts ; and at Allahabad, Cawnpore, Farrackabad, Bareilly, and Agra, and eventually in each of the five divisions of the Delhi territory, in the Upper Provinces.[1]

A comparison of the two systems of collecting duties is instructive. The indigenous system of transit duties was, in many respects, preferable to the one which was introduced by the East India Company. In olden times, the rate of duty payable for small distances was extremely light. It was increased by the accumulation of new imposts in proportion to the distance over which goods were conveyed. Intercourse

[1] Report of the Committee on Customs and Post Office Regulations, 1836.

between neighbouring places was, therefore, never seriously impeded. The new duty, on the contrary, was fixed at the average amount of the payments to which goods conveyed long distances were before liable, and was thus so heavy as to seriously interrupt commercial intercourse between neighbouring places. Another advantage of the indigenous system was that no passes were required to be taken beforehand. But under the new system they had to be invariably procured before any goods were allowed to pass. The third merit of the old system was that the duties were levied according to such general denominations of quantity and kind that there was no excuse for search and detention. Only in one respect was the new method superior to the old, namely, that large tracts of country on both sides of the river, which had formerly been studded with chowkees, were now entirely free from the presence of customs officers.[1]

The town duties in Bengal were less injurious than the transit duties, because they were far more limited in their operation.[2] Being

[1] Report of the Committee on Customs, 1836.

[2] The Government of India, in a letter to the Directors, after describing the vexatious and unjust character of the town duty, said: "In the Bengal and Agra Presidencies the Town where a Sudder Custom House is established suffers the disadvantage of

confined to particular towns, they did not necessarily interrupt the general course of trade. And as they were levied only on a few articles, and those mostly of a bulky nature, there was not the same necessity for minute search as there was in the case of transit duties, and no rowannahs were required to be taken out. On the other hand, the town duties were extremely partial. A distinction was made not only between town and country, but also between those towns in which such duties were levied, and all other towns. Trade and manufactures naturally deserted places which were so heavily taxed, and hence a perpetual tendency to fluctuations was kept up. The inconvenience of the town duties was daily experienced by the inhabitants. They also seriously interfered with the freedom of manufacture. The most serious evil of all, however, to the inhabitants of the taxed towns was that they were virtually excluded from participation in the general trade. Nor did they bring much revenue into the coffers of the Government. The goods were smuggled into towns enormously, and quite a large percentage of them escaped the payment of any duties.

a separate Consumption Tax, although larger Towns of a more commercial character in its immediate Vicinity may be free from all such Impost". Public Letter from India, 2nd September, 1835.

[1] *Vide* Report of the Committee on Customs, 1836.

So much for Bengal. The territories comprising the Bombay Presidency covered a long sea-board, and contained a large number of ports, some of which, however, belonged to independent States or chiefs, and were free from British interference. The excellent situation of Bombay soon made it the entrepot not only of the commerce of its own territories but of the whole of Western India and of the gulfs of Arabia and Persia.

Originally, duties were levied at Bombay on a low scale, and to this fact was due, to a large extent, the prosperity of the seaport.[1] It is a fact worthy of note that duties were collected on imports only, all export duties having been withdrawn since 1799.[2]

So late as 1805, the rate of duty was 2½ per cent. ad valorem, modified in the case of foreign goods and vessels from certain specified countries by an advance on the prime cost at various rates, thus raising the rate of duty to

[1] In 1793, the customs revenue of the Bombay Presidency was £53,000, and in 1808-9, £137,497. *Vide* Report on the Affairs of the E. I. Company, 1810.

[2] The only exception to this was made in 1813 in the case of goods purchased at Bombay and exported on foreign bottom, which were made liable to 3½ per cent. on the invoice value, making, with the original import duty of 3½ per cent. about 7 per cent., which was probably imposed to equalise the import and export on foreign bottoms. *Vide* Report of the Committee on Customs and Post Offices, 1836.

a certain extent. In that year, an addition of 1 per cent. was made to the rate of duty, raising it to 3½ per cent. In 1813, the rate of duty at Bombay on goods imported or exported on foreign bottom was raised on imports from 3½ to 4½ per cent., with an advance of 60 per cent. in the case of foreign goods and foreign vessels, which made the rate of duty $7\frac{3}{16}$ per cent. On exports, it was fixed at 3½ per cent., which, with the original import duty of 3½ per cent., averaged about the same as the import duty at 7 per cent.

The rates at Bombay were never enhanced beyond those fixed in 1813, and when, in 1815, the import trade of Great Britain was rendered with respect to some articles free, and the duty on others was reduced to 2½ per cent., the port of Bombay shared in the benefit of the reduction. By a special enactment of 1817, the duty on goods coming from foreign Europe on British or registered ships, which was at the three Presidencies fixed at 5 per cent., was at Bombay reduced to 3½ per cent.[1]

The imports from the interior of India, and from all parts or places other than those specified, were charged at 3½ per cent. At Surat and other

[1] Report of the Committee on Customs and Post Office Regulaions, 1836.

ports in the Bombay Presidency, the system and the amount of customs duties differed to some extent, but many of them enjoyed mutual certificate privileges. British goods and goods imported on British bottom were, at all subordinate ports, admitted free on arrival from Bombay.

In 1827, the system of sea customs under the Bombay Presidency was revised by a Committee, when the duties and exemptions on goods from the United Kingdom were retained in their former state, while the duties on foreign produce and goods imported on foreign bottoms were raised.

It was generally the policy of the Bombay Government to retain the sea customs in their own hands. But in 1827-28, the urgent call for the reduction of expenditure led that Government to issue imperative orders for farming the sea customs everywhere except at the port of Bombay and a few other ports. The effect of farming the customs generally proved favourable to the revenue, but oppressive to the people.

The land customs of the Bombay Presidency were based on the ancient system, and were preserved in their original form until the first quarter of the 19th century. An essential feature of the system was to levy transit duties to make the trader pay them by degrees in small sums according to the distance to which they were carried. The duty was levied in each Pargana or Sub-division of a Zila in the shape of a toll on each load of goods passing through or imported into for consumption, or manufactured therein and exported to other places.

The toll was originally computed with some reference to the value of the articles liable to it. But, for the convenience of the trade as well as the revenue, it was fixed upon certain commodities, regulated by the weight which each vehicle was able to carry. The different descriptions of goods were classed in the rate-books with reference to their place and value in the general scale of taxation.[1] The most general rule in regard to the levy was that payment of the dues once in each pargana exempted goods from further charge, but did not exempt them from payment in the next pargana. On payment of the duty at the chowkee, the chowkeedar gave a receipt showing the amount levied and the nature of the goods on which it was paid, which

[1] The first class consisted of "kirana", that is to say, spices, dyes, drugs, condiments, groceries, etc. The highest rate of duty was levied on this class of goods. Grain and pulse held the second place and were generally rated at half the "kirana" rate. Cloths came third. Silk cloths paid about double those made of cotton. Although the articles enumerated were many, the rates were comparatively few. *Vide* Report of the Committee on Customs, 1836.

receipt covered the goods to the frontier of the pargana. The lowness of the duty rendered smuggling or evasion unusual, and the penalty for such an offence was consequently trifling.[1] It is worthy of note that the uniformity of the plans on which the transit duties were levied and the great antiquity of the whole system rendered it easy for the trader to acquaint himself with the rates.

The effect of the transit duties proper upon the trade passing through the Company's provinces to and from the sea-coast was light and not quite so vexatious as might have been expected. But there were irregular additions to the duties made by the establishment of other customs stations on the great thoroughfares and cross-roads, and the vexation of the irregular levy was aggravated by the host of petty exactions it gave rise to on the part of numerous agents employed in the collection of the duty.

Besides the transit duties, there were town or consumption duties which yielded some revenue at the principal towns and most of the larger villages throughout the Presidency. In such places, these duties were levied in the shape and generally at the rate of the transit duty. The

[1] In most such cases, double duty was exacted. *Vide* Report of the Committee on Customs, 1836.

general name of these duties was "Gaum-Ootar".[1]

At all the seaport towns of the Presidency, except Surat, the import customs were held to cover the consumption duties on goods coming in by sea. Goods coming in by land paid a rate of duty different from, and generally lighter than, the sea import duties At Bombay, a town duty was raised since 1803, the amount being 4 per cent. upon the prime cost of goods. Certificates from the other Presidencies exempting goods from sea customs at Bombay did not exempt them from the town duty. Articles for re-exportation were, in some cases, allowed to be warehoused.

The Bombay town duty was abrogated in 1805, but re-imposed in 1810. The evils and inconvenience of the system under which the town duty was levied led to a new arrangement in 1827, which was revised in 1834.[2]

The duties at the other seaport towns were levied at different rates. In 1834, the town duties in the Bombay Presidency consisted of

[1] The meaning of the term is payment for what is unloaded at a village.

[2] In 1834, a law was passed imposing a duty of 1½ per cent. and allowing no drawback except on exportation to the United Kingdom, and then only to such an extent as should reduce the total duty receivable by Government to 2½ per cent.

1½ per cent. at Bombay on spices, luxuries, and cloths; at Surat, of certain duties generally under 5 per cent. upon the same and several other articles of domestic consumption; at Ahmedabad and the principal towns in that district, of 2½ per cent. ad valorem on all but 36 articles.[1] At the other towns in Gujrat and the principal ones throughout the Deccan, a duty on consumption was levied like the transit duty on the load or quantity, without much precision as to the value. The duty in all these cases was light in amount.

In Madras, the revision of the Customs Regulations took place in 1781, and again in 1786. The chief feature of this latter revision was the imposition of a duty on imports into Madras at 5 per cent., at a moderate fair valuation, regulated by the market price of the day,[2] with drawback at 4 per cent. on goods re-shipped. This rate of duty, namely, 5 per cent., was considered too high and was reduced in 1789. In 1794, the Court of Directors sent out instructions to the Madras Government to regulate their tariff

[1] The exempted ones consisted of dyes, of raw material used in manufacture, and of necessaries of life (excluding grains).

[2] This valuation was made after deducting, according to long established usage, 10 per cent. on goods imported by Christians and 20 per cent. on goods imported by any other denomination of merchants.

according to the system prevailing in Bengal. And in 1795, a duty of 2½ per cent. levied ad valorem, with advances of 60 per cent. on foreign goods or goods imported in foreign ships, was fixed. On exports also, a 2½ per cent. rate on all goods, with certain exceptions, was levied. In 1798, the Court of Directors directed the Madras Government to levy an additional duty of 1 per cent. on the imports and exports by sea in order to meet the increased marine charges.

In 1803, a general duty of 6 per cent. was established on articles imported by sea into Madras on British or Asiatic or American vessels, and 8 per cent. on goods imported on other vessels.[1]

In 1812, the customs system of the Madras Presidency underwent a further revision, and a general import duty at 8 per cent. was established on goods imported by sea on British or Asiatic vessels at Madras and the subordinate ports. An export duty of like amount was imposed on goods exported from the subordinate ports; but no export duty was levied at Madras, except on goods exported on foreign vessels.[2]

[1] In 1793, the customs revenue of the Madras Presidency was £22,300, and in 1808-9, it was £152,938. *Vide* Report on the affairs of the E. I. Co., 1810.

[2] Cotton was made liable to an export duty of 8 per cent., whencesoever exported, being, however, at the same time, declared free from all duty on import.

Goods imported or exported on foreign bottoms were subjected to double the amount of duties payable on goods imported or exported on British bottoms, that is to say, a duty of 16 per cent. on their value.[1]

Regulation II of 1816 was framed under the authority of the Court of Directors and the Board of Control, for encouraging the exportation of the staples and the marine stores of Great Britain to the territories of Fort St. George. Its provisions in respect of the import of certain articles from Great Britain free of duty, or at a duty of 2½ per cent. or 5 per cent. (if the produce of foreign Europe,) were similar to those established in Bengal and Bombay. In like manner, it was enacted that if the established duties on the goods should have been paid at any port subject to the British Government in India, no further duty should be levied on their transit from port to port within the same territories. As regards exports, the rules in respect of drawback on exportation to the United Kingdom were also practically the same as in the other Presidencies. Some alterations were made in these Regulations in subsequent years, which, however, did not involve any change in the principles.

The inland customs of the Madras Presidency

[1] *Vide* Report of the Committee on Customs, 1836.

were practically the same as those of Bombay till 1803. In that year, a number of Regulations was passed, which abolished the whole of the anomalous duties of the indigenous system, and substituted the following duties. First, a general duty of 6 per cent. was imposed on goods imported by sea or by land into the town of Madras, or manufactured within its limits: Secondly, a general duty of 6 per cent. was levied on goods exported from the subordinate ports. Thirdly, there was a general duty of 6 per cent. on goods imported or exported across the frontier of the Madras territories. Fourthly, goods imported into certain provincial towns, or manufactured within their limits, paid a duty of 6 per cent.[1] Goods might thus be subjected successively to three distinct 6 per cent. duties, namely, a frontier, a town, and an export duty making an aggregate of 18 per cent.

These duties were more than the external commerce of the country could well bear. The substitution of an ad valorem frontier duty for a toll fell particularly heavy upon cloth which was at that time manufactured largely in the Madras territories for foreign as well as home

[1] Goods belonging to the Company, cotton and cotton thread, and several articles of minor importance, were exempted from duty.

consumption. The duties on all commodities having formerly been regulated by the bullock load instead of the price, they were as high on articles of little as on those of great value; but being now collected upon the cost, and the bullock load of cloth being equal to 5 or 6 times the value of most other articles, the increase of duty upon it was in the same proportion. A great decrease in foreign consumption consequently ensued. Large numbers of weavers were thrown out of employ, and many migrated to other parts of the country. The effect of the duty was gradually to drive traders and manufacturers out of the town into the neighbouring villages, by which they evaded the duty. But no longer having the ready market they had, when residing in towns, they necessarily carried on the trade at greater expense, which expense fell ultimately on the consumer, no advantage accruing to the Government. The inland customs revenue thus gradually declined[1].

In 1808, the town duty, which had been discontinued for two years, but had not been formally abolished, was revived. It was enacted in that year that the town duty, both at Madras and the provincial towns, should be

[1] Report of the Committee on Customs, 1836.

restricted to goods imported into the towns, goods exported from, or manufactured within their limits, being left free. Goods having paid a frontier duty were exempted from the demand of town duty, or having paid the town duty were exempted from the duty on the frontier. These changes, however, did not much improve the productiveness of the inland duties. In 1812, the Customs Regulations were revised. The principal feature of the new system was that a general duty of 5 per cent., on a fixed tariff valuation, was leviable on every article of consumption except such as were necessary to the poorest class of the people, and a few others on articles of trade produced within the country.[1]

The system continued to be the same for many years. In 1826, the Board of Revenue, after giving a highly favourable account of the state of inland customs, concluded by observing that they "are rather an Excise consumption than mere Customs duties upon trade; and it is this consideration which should be borne in mind when the existing Inland Customs, or rather Excise, comes to be regulated anew".

[1] Cotton, grain, and cotton thread were excepted.

Besides the inland duty, a high consumption duty was levied at Madras and the other important towns on betel, tobacco, ganja, bhang, and goduck.

The following comment of the Customs Committee on this expression of opinion was as appropriate as it was true. They said: "The greatest enemy of the general inland duty can say little worse of it than is here voluntarily avowed by its admirers and advocates. A system of universal excise if administered by Government servants, will always be a system of universal fraud on the revenue and exactions on the people; and if administered by farmers, a system of grinding oppression, under which the payment of legal dues will form the lightest part of the burden."

The establishment of a transit duty throughout a vast extent of open territory, and an excise duty at every village of it, required a prodigious body of officers. The great exactions and frauds of these servants were the subject of repeated complaints by the inhabitants and merchants of the country, and the worst of it was that a large portion of the duties actually levied never reached the treasury of the state.[1]

[1] As the Committee on Customs rightly observed, "It was for the power of exaction that the renters paid largely to Government; the limitation of these powers would necessarily reduce the rents. Thus abuse became equivalent to revenue, and the greater the abuse the stronger was the argument, in a financial view, for maintaining the system."

The loss of revenue led the Government to adopt the system of farming the inland duties. This resulted in some increase in the collections, but added immensely to the oppression of the people.

## § 2. (1833—1857)

Such was the state of things when the Charter Act of 1833 established a centralised form of administration in India, and divested the Presidencies of their legislative independence.

Not long after, a Committee consisting of officers of the Government was appointed for the purpose of revising the Customs and the Post Office Regulations of all the Presidencies, with a view to the encouragement of commerce and the increase of revenue.[1] They were asked to consider the method by which an amount of revenue, equal at least to that collected at that time under the general head of customs, might be realised, "on an ameliorated principle". The special attention of the Committee was called to the transit duty, which was "comparatively unproductive to the State, oppressive and vexatious to merchants, and injurious to the people at large". The town duties were also included in the Committee's investigation, which although

[1] This Committee was appointed in the year 1834.

less extensive, were "unavoidably vexatious, bearing indeed a peculiar character of injustice", from the arbitrary manner in which they had been fixed on some places and not on others.[1]

In the meantime, a Report had been submitted by Mr. Trevelyan on the Inland Customs and Town Duties of the Bengal Presidency. In 1835, Lord Ellenborough, President of the Board of Control, invited the attention of the Chairman and Deputy Chairman of the East India Company to this Report, and pointed out some of the evils of the system which then prevailed. Referring to the injury resulting from the system to Indian cotton manufacture, which had of late years been nearly superseded by the importation of British cotton goods, the President remarked, "While the Cotton Manufactures of England are imported into India on payment of a duty of two and a half per cent., the Cotton Manufactures of India are subjected to a Duty on the raw Material of Five per Cent., to a further Duty on yarn of Seven and a Half per Cent., and finally to another Duty of Two and a Half per Cent., if the Cloth should be dyed after the Rowannah has been taken out for it as White Cloth. Thus altogether the Cotton Goods of

[1] *Vide* Extract Separate Letter, 2nd September, 1835.

India may pay Seventeen and a Half per Cent."[1] The efforts made to improve the leather manufactures were counteracted by the heavy duties to which they were subjected. As the President pointed out, the raw hide paid 5 per cent., on being manufactured into leather it paid 5 per cent. more, and when the leather was made into boots and shoes, a further duty of 5 per cent. was imposed; thus in all there was a duty of 15 per cent. Sugar was another instance. On being imported into a town it paid 5 per cent. in customs and 5 per cent. in town duty, and when manufactured, it paid on exportation from the same town 5 per cent. more; in all 15 per cent.

"The effect of these and similar Duties," observed the President of the India Board, "is virtually to prohibit the manufacture in Towns of all Articles not absolutely required for their own Consumption; to confine Manufactures to the place where the raw Material is produced; and by such Restrictions more than any tax actually levied, to depress the productive Industry of the people."

"Not less than 235 separate Articles are subjected to Inland Duties; the Tariff includes

[1] Letter dated the 18th March, 1835. *Vide* Parliamentary Paper, 51.

almost everything of personal or domestic Use; and its operation, combined with the System of Search, is of the most vexatious and offensive Character, without materially benefiting the Revenue."

"The Power of Search, if really exercised by every Custom House Officer would put a Stop to internal Trade by the delay it necessarily occasions. It is not exercised except for the Purpose of Extortion. The Salary of the Officers employed is too small to secure their Honesty. The System gives Advantages to the great Capitalist over the small Trader. The small Trader cannot afford the necessary Bribes: the Capitalist employs an Agent to negotiate the undisturbed passage of his goods."

"The effect upon national Morals is yet more serious than the effect upon national Wealth. Every Merchant, every Manufacturer, and every Traveller, is, as it were compelled, for the security of his property, or the protection of his personal Comfort and not unfreq ently for that of the Feelings of the Females of his Family, to enter into unlawful Collusion with the Officers of Government."

"It is a System which demoralizes our own

People, and which appears to excite the Aversion of the Foreign Traders of Asia."[1]

The revenue actually produced by the internal duties was far from considerable. The total yield in the Bengal Provinces was Rs. 6,81,126. The expenses of collection amounted to Rs. 4,06,986, making the net produce only Rs. 2,74,140. The abolition of these duties was also necessary to redeem the Government from the financial difficulties which beset them, for an increase of taxation being impossible, there was but one course by which revenue could be improved, namely, by giving freedom to internal trade. Lord Ellenborough concluded the remarkable letter with the expression of the confident hope that the time was not distant when the whole of the Indian Peninsula would, as regards commercial intercourse, be "one great Empire".

In 1836, while the Customs Committee were still pursuing their enquiries, the Governor of Agra abolished all the customs-houses established for the levy of transit duties in the interior, except those on the frontiers. The Government of India expressed their disapproval of any steps having been taken without their sanction, but as they found that the effect of these measures was

[1] Letter from Lord Ellenborough to the Chairman and Deputy Chairman of the East India Company, 1835.

beneficial, they decided to extend them to Bengal and Behar. By Act XIV of 1836, all inland transit duties levied within the Presidency of Bengal, except on the Jumna frontier line, were abolished. As this measure entailed a loss of revenue to the Government, a revised scale of import and export duties was adopted. According to the new import schedule, bullion and coin, precious stones and pearls, grain and pulse, animals, ice, coal and coke, and books printed in the United Kingdom or any other British Possession, were free.[1] Marine stores and metals, the produce or manufacture of the United Kingdom or any other British Possession paid 3 per cent.; woollens, 2 per cent., cotton and silk piece-goods, cotton twist, and yarn, 3½ per cent. If any of the articles were the produce of any foreign country, the rates of duty charged were double. Salt was charged at Rs. 3-4 as. per maund; opium, Rs. 24 per seer; spirits, 9 as. per gallon; spices, tea, and some other articles, 10 per cent.; wines and liquors, 10 per cent.; articles not enumerated, 3½ per cent. These were the rates of duty chargeable on goods imported on British bottom; when

[1] An import duty of 3 per cent. was charged on foreign books. The revised scale was calculated to yield an increase of about 8 lakhs. *Vide* Letter from the Court of Directors to the Government of India, dated 7th June, 1837.

they were imported on foreign bottom, they paid at double rates.[1]

As for exports,[2] bullion and coin, precious metals and stores, living animals, books printed in India, opium purchased at Government sales, and cotton wool exported to Europe, the United States, or any British Possession in America, were free. Cotton wool, exported to other places, paid an export duty of 8 as. per maund. Sugar and rum, exported to the United Kingdom or any British Possession were free ; but exported to any other place, paid 3 per cent. Grain and pulse of all sorts paid duty at ½ an anna per maund ; indigo, Rs. 3 per maund ; lac, dye and shell lac, 4 per cent. ; silk, raw filature, 3½ as. per seer ; silk, Bengal wound, 3 annas per seer ; tobacco, 4 annas per maund ; and all articles, not enumerated, 3 per cent. These rates were charged for goods exported on British bottom ; when they were exported on foreign bottom, double rates were charged.[3]

The Customs Committee submitted several

[1] Schedule A, Act XIV of 1836.

[2] Both the Government of India and the Court of Directors regarded the export duties as injurious to trade, but justified them on the ground of financial necessity. *Vide* Separate Letter, dated the 7th June, 1837.

[3] *Vide* Schedule B, Act XIV of 1836. In the case of exports as well as imports, when the duty was declared to be *ad valorem* it was levied on the market value without deduction.

Reports in 1836. In their Fifth Report they recommended the assimilation of the Bombay and Madras tariffs to the revised tariff which had been recently adopted for Bengal.[1] They pointed out that the want of uniformity in the rates of duty prevalent at the different ports of British India involved the injustice of a system of unequal taxation, caused great inconvenience to the public, and entailed much labour which might otherwise be spared to the custom-house officers. They estimated that the "proposed assimilation would result in a total loss of revenue amounting to about Rs. 10½ lakhs, but they thought that such sacrifice was "preferable to the great inconveniences arising from a variety of local and partial laws."

With regard to the town duties of Bombay and Madras, the Committee reported that both these Presidencies, Madras in particular, stood in an immeasurably greater need of relief than did the Presidency of Bengal. They added that the

[1] In a Letter to the Court of Directors, dated the 19th October, 1836, the Government of India urged the assimilation of the tariffs of Bombay and Madras to that of Bengal, on the ground that this step "would be attended with the utmost benefits to the commerce and productive powers of the entire British Indian territory". They, however, remarked that such assimilation was of a secondary importance to granting relief to the trade and industry of the interior from "the very burdensome and oppressive taxation to which these are subject in both the Bombay and Madras Presidencies."

various measures adopted from time to time to improve the system had signally failed Despairing, therefore, of amending these duties, they did not hesitate to recommend their total abolition.

By Act I of 1838, the inland transit duties in the Bombay Presidency were abolished, and duties on imports and exports were revised on the lines of the Bengal tariff. Similar measures were, however, not taken for the Madras Presidency till 1844.

Several Acts were passed between 1836 and 1844, dealing with various matters relating to the customs system of India,[1] but no substantial alteration of the tariff was made till 1845.

Owing to the loss of revenue entailed by the abolition of the inland duties in Bombay and Madras, an addition to the customs tariff became necessary.[2] Therefore, import duties at the following rates were fixed on the different descriptions of goods, being the produce or manufacture of the United Kingdom or of any British Possession: Marine stores, metals, woollens, and cotton and silk piece-goods, 5 per cent.; cotton

[1] The more important of these Acts related to the establishment of warehousing ports, the prohibition of imports of foreign sugar and rum, and an increase in the salt duties.

[2] It was estimated that the loss in Bombay would amount to 18 lakhs, and that in Madras, 20 lakhs.

thread, twist and yarn, 3½ per cent. If any of these classes of goods were imported from foreign countries, double the rates were payable. Porter, ale, beer, etc. paid 5 per cent.; wines and liquors, Re. 1 per gallon; spirits, Re. 1-8 as. per gallon; and all manufactured articles unenumerated, 5 per cent. When goods were imported on foreign bottoms, double the rates of duty were charged.[1]

The principles on which the customs duties in India ought to be regulated were discussed by the Court of Directors in an important Despatch, dated the 22nd April, 1846. These principles were: (i) the abolition of duties on the exportation of the staple commodities of India, with the exception of indigo; (ii) the abolition of the duties on the trade between the several Presidencies of India, commonly called the 'port to port' trade; and (iii) the abolition of double duties on merchandise exported or imported on foreign bottoms. In 1848, it was enacted that "no duty shall be charged on any goods lawfully carried from any port in the territories subject to the Government of the East India Company to any other port in the said territories".[2] Another provision of the same Act was that all goods

[1] *Vide* Schedule, Act IX of 1845.

[2] Act VI of 1848.

exported from or imported into any port in British India on foreign bottoms should be charged only with the same rates of duty as would now by law be charged with, if such goods were exported or imported on British bottoms. Two years later, the last relic of the Navigation Laws was swept off the Indian statute-book when the coasting trade of India was thrown open to vessels of all nations.[1] In 1857, the Government of India recommended to the India Board the adoption of measures for removing from the customs tariff all discrimination between foreign and British goods, but this step was not taken until the administration of India had been transferred from the hands of the East India Company to those of the British Crown.

To summarise: During the greater part of the Company's rule in India, Great Britain protected and encouraged her industries against Indian competition, and treated India as the source of raw materials for her industries and as a compulsory market for her industrial products. British imports were admitted into India practically free, or paid only nominal duties; while Indian goods were penalised by heavy duties within the country, and their entry into Great

[1] Act V of 1850.

Britain was either absolutely prohibited or barred by high duties.[1] The inland trade of the country was discouraged, and her foreign commerce was directed for the benefit of England. Not only was any attempt made to foster the indigenous industries, but also the fiscal policy of India was so shaped as to lead to the destruction of those industries which were then in a flourishing state. The action of the British Government which ruled the destinies of India was so palpably unjust that even Englishmen felt it their duty to condemn it in very strong terms. Montgomery Martin, for instance, said: "For many years, great commercial injustice was done by England to British India."[2] Mr. H. H. Wilson, the eminent historian, wrote: "British goods were forced upon her without paying any duty: and the foreign manufacturer employed the arm of political injustice to keep down and ultimately

[1] In 1810, the Directors of the East India Company wrote to the Governor-General of Bengal: "As far as the Use of those Fabrics is superseded in these Kingdoms by the Cotton Manufactures of this Country, aided by high protecting Duties, there seems little prospect of Recovery." Letter, dated the 20th June, 1810 (Parliamentary Paper, 139.)

[2] Indian Empire, Vol. I, p. 560, foot-note. Mr. Martin added: "The late Sir R. Peel admitted the injustice, and adopted measures for its redress, which merged into the low import system, by a misnomer designated *free trade*, which does not exist in any country."

strangle a competitor with whom he could not have contended on equal terms."[1]

[1] Wilson, History of British India, Vol. I, p. 385, foot-note.

The observations of Wilson deserve to be quoted in full. He said: "The history of the trade of cotton cloths with India affords a singular exemplification of the inapplicability to all times and circumstances of that principle of free trade which advocates the unrestricted admission of a cheap article, in place of protecting by heavy duties a dearer one of home manufacture. It is also a melancholy instance of the wrong done to India by the country on which she had become dependent. It was stated in evidence that the cotton and silk goods of India up to this period could be sold for a profit in the British market at a price from fifty to sixty per cent. lower than those fabricated in England. It consequently became necessary to protect the latter by duties of seventy and eighty per cent. on their value, or by positive prohibition. Had this not been the case, had not such prohibitory duties and decrees existed, the mills of Paisley and of Manchester would have been stopped in their outset, and could scarcely have been again set in motion, even by the powers of steam. They were created by the sacrifice of the Indian manufacture. Had India been independent, she would have retaliated; would have imposed preventive duties upon British goods, and would thus have preserved her own productive industry from annihilation. This act of self-defence was not permitted her; she was at the mercy of the stranger."

# CHAPTER III

## FISCAL POLICY OF INDIA UNDER THE CROWN.

### § 1. (1858-1870).

The financial situation in India was rendered extremely embarrassing by the Sepoy War of 1857-58. And no sooner was the administration of the country transferred from the hands of the East India Company to those of the Crown than the necessity was felt for increasing the resources of the Indian Exchequer. By Act VII of 1859, therefore, the customs duties were largely increased. The duties on imported goods were fixed as follows: Cotton thread, twist and yarn, 5 per cent. ad valorem; tea, coffee, tobacco, spices, haberdashery, grocery, provisions, perfumery, and jewellery, 20 per cent.; porter, ale, etc., 4 annas a gallon; wines and liqueurs, Rs. 2 a gallon; spirits, Rs. 3 a gallon; and articles not included in the above enumeration, 10 per cent. ad valorem. Goods for exportation were made chargeable to the following rates: Grain and pulse of all sorts, 2 annas a maund; indigo, Rs. 3 a maund; lac dye and shell-lac, 4 per cent. ad valorem; and all articles not enumerated, 3 per cent. ad valorem.[1]

It is worthy of note that no discrimination was made in this Act between British and foreign manufactures. This equalization had been recommended by Lord Canning in a letter to the Court of Directors in 1857 In 1859, the proposal received the assent of the Secretary of State, who observed: "The discriminating duties formerly levied on the import into the United Kingdom of goods, the produce or manufacture of foreign countries, have, under the more enlightened legislation of late years, almost disappeared from the British tariff, and it is equally desirable that the same principle should be applied to the commerce of the Queen's dominions in India."[2]

The enhancement of duties gave rise to some opposition in India. A memorial was submitted to the Secretary of State for India by the mercantile community of Bombay in which they urged the "extreme impolicy of placing further imposts upon the trade in British manufactures."

[1] Schedules A. & B., Act VIII of 1859.

[2] Separate Revenue Despatch to India, 7th April, 1859.

They pointed out that competition in the cotton industry had already commenced in India, and added: "England has to oppose superior skill and continuous improvements of machinery to the cheap labour and cheap cotton grown on the spot in India. The result has yet to be seen; but with the heavy burden of 10 per cent. duty imposed upon her production, it is not difficult to foretell what the result will be." [1]

In connection with the revision of the customs duties, Lord Stanley thought fit to discuss some principles which had been urged by the Government of India in 1857. They were: (i) the equalization of the duties on British and foreign manufactures, and the assimilation of the duties on manufactured and unmanufactured goods; (ii) the exemption from duty of all articles producing an inconsiderable amount of revenue; (iii) the abolition of export duties: and (iv) the augmentation of import duties. With the suggestion contained in the first part of (i), Lord Stanley expressed his full and entire concurrence. As for the assimilation of the duties on manufactured and unmanufactured goods, the

[1] This memorial was agreed to at a Town Hall meeting, held at Bombay, and a telegraphic message was sent by the Bombay Government to the Government of India, recommending the exemption from the increased duty of all goods shipped previous to the receipt of the notification. But the exemption was not allowed.

Secretary of State thought that it would throw impediments in the way of indigenous industry which had already suffered much from competition with the British mill industry. The principle involved in (ii) had already been carried into effect in England to a great extent, but it was not thought that there was sufficient reason for extending it to India, as the change would involve considerable sacrifice of revenue. On the question of export duties, Lord Stanley did not defend them in theory, but acquiesced in the opinion that they were so low, and India had so great an advantage over other countries in the production of articles on which the duties were levied, that they could not possibly offer any impediment to exportation. As for (iv), he was of opinion that the rates levied in India were, on the whole, extremely moderate, and he thought an increase might be effected in the import duties on most articles of commerce, and especially on luxuries without the imposition of any serious check on consumption.[1]

The revision of the tariff in 1859 led to the duties on a considerable number of articles being increased from 5 to 20 per cent. This increase was too great, and resulted in the falling off of

[1] Separate Revenue Despatch to India, 7th April, 1859.

imports. Mr. James Wilson, who was appointed Finance Member in 1860, took this as a warning and reduced the rate to 10 per cent. He also abolished the export duties on wool, hemp, hides, flax, jute, and tea.[1] He argued that export duties were impediments in the way of developing the produce of the country, and remarked: "As a general rule, when the products of our soil have to find a foreign market, and in cases in which they enter into competition with those of other countries, the direct effect of export duties must be to place our products in those countries at a disadvantage with their foreign competitors: in point of fact, it cannot be denied that in such cases an export duty falls chiefly upon the producer who cultivates the article."[2] With regard to jute, he expressed the opinion that it was "one of the great raw materials used in England, which competes with the coarse hemp of Russia and the production of which it is much our interest to promote."[3] As for tea, the Government had spent a large sum of money in introducing it as an article of cultivation, and the Finance Member regarded it as one of the few means that existed

[1] These reductions and abolitions involved a loss of £ 82,000.

[2] J. Wilson, Financial Statement, 1860-61.

[3] J. Wilson, Financial Statement, 1860-61.

in India "of attracting European capital and European settlers."[1]

But the Government of India was faced with a large deficit. The Finance Member was, therefore, obliged to make some proposals for the increase of revenue. Saltpetre was at this time produced exclusively in India, and fetched a large price and a high profit. Mr. Wilson thought that this article did not stand in the same position as other articles produced by the cultivators of the soil, and would bear a duty of £ 10 a ton, without any danger of its being interfered with by foreign competition. For some time past, a very small duty had been imposed on the export of this article. Mr. Wilson increased the duty to Rs. 2 a maund as an experiment.[2] Mr. Wilson saw no reason why cotton twist and yarn should be imported at a lower rate of duty than cotton piece-goods. He was not impressed with the argument that it was an earlier stage of manufacture. Nor did

[1] J. Wilson, Financial Statement, 1860-61.

[2] The total quantity of saltpetre exported from India was 8,00,000 maunds. It was, therefore, expected that the increase in the rate of duty would yield £ 180,000, or an additional amount of £164,000. Mr. Wilson proposed to allow the saltpetre refiners to turn to profit the salt which was necessarily made in the process.

He also raised the duty upon unmanufactured tobacco to 8 annas the seer, and manufactured tobacco to Re. 1 the seer. The last change was one which he made with regret, and to which he was driven by sheer necessity. "Necessity," he said, "has no law." Financial Statement, 1860-61.

he attach much importance to the view that a low duty on yarn and a higher duty on cloth encouraged the indigenous weaving industry. He, therefore, raised the import duty on yarn and twist to 10 per cent. The result of these changes was a tariff imposing one uniform ad valorem duty of 10 per cent. on all articles subject to duty, except beer, spirits, wines, and tobacco. A considerable net gain to the exchequer was estimated. And there was another source from which an increased revenue was looked for, viz., tariff valuations. Mr. Wilson thought that the then existing tariff valuations were too low, and he took steps to revise them and also to apply a uniform system of valuation to all India. An increase in the export duty on indigo had been suggested in some quarters, but Mr. Wilson refused to accept the suggestion, because, in the first place, a rival production was supposed to exist in Mexico, and, secondly, it was not desirable to place any impediment in the way of the extension of an industry which was one of the few cultivations in India which attracted "British capital and skill to direct Native labour."[1]

[1] Financial Statement, 1860-61. Mr. Wilson added: "The value of the European gentlemen settled in our country districts cannot, in our opinion, be over-estimated, and it will be the

Next year, the Government of India was faced with a deficit of £6 millions. But this did not prevent the new Finance Member, Mr. Samuel Laing, from proposing the reduction of the duty on imported twist and yarn to 5 per cent. on the ground that it "might not be maintained at a rate which might stimulate the growth of a protected interest."[1] He expressed the wish that he could at once reduce the duty on piece-goods and other manufactures from 10 to 5 per cent, but, unfortunately, the amount of sacrifice was too large to enable him to propose it without imprudence. In the case of yarn, however, the amount was small, the failure of the high duty palpable, and the matter was urgent, because parties were "actually building mills and importing machinery on the strength of the high duty."[2]

So, even in this year of deficit, a revenue of £40,000 was sacrificed in order to maintain what were called the principles of free trade, while an addition was made to the duty on salt, an article of necessity for the poor.

The financial position of the Government

steadfast policy of the Government to encourage it in any fair way it can."

[1] Financial Statement, 1861-62.

[2] Financial Statement, 1861-62.

improved considerably in 1862, and the Finance Member estimated a surplus of £900,000. It was then proposed to reduce the duties on imported cotton goods from 10 to 5 per cent. Some eminent persons, among them the then Lieutenant-Governor of Bengal, thought that a 10 per cent. duty on imported manufactures was one of the most legitimate sources of Indian revenue. But the Government of India were of a different opinion, and their reasons were thus explained by the Finance Member:

"Firstly, the duty applies exclusively to British manufactures. Now as long as England and India remain parts of one great Empire, it is impossible to apply precisely the same rules as if they were separate and independent countries. I have opposed, as sharply as any one, any attempt to ease English finance unduly at the expense of India: but I cannot deny that England, having founded the Indian Empire, and being ready to sustain it, and having given up all pretensions to exact a tribute, as Holland does from Java, or Spain from Cuba, and all claim on a monopoly of the Indian market and carrying trade, may, with some reason, ask India so to levy the necessary revenue as not to interfere injuriously with trade between the two countries... A heavy import duty, therefore, on trade between England and India comes very near in principle to a transit duty between different parts of the same Empire. But secondly, there is another argument, even more conclusive, against the permanent retention of a 10 per cent. duty. Either the clothing of the people is a proper subject for taxation or it is not; if it be so, on what principle can we impose a considerable duty on clothing which comes from abroad and levy no duty at all on clothing produced at home?"[1]

The Finance Member was not, however, prepared to extend the policy of reduction to the other articles of the tariff, and he did not consider a moderate duty, such as 10 per cent., as an objectionable mode of raising revenue. He placed paper on the free list,[2] and reduced the duty on beer, which was "to many European constitutions almost a necessary," by one-half, and the duty on tobacco from Rupee 1 per seer to 20 per cent. ad valorem.[3]

The year continued to be one of financial

[1] Financial Statement, 1862-63. It is worthy of note that memorials had been sent by the Chambers of Commerce at Calcutta, Bombay and Madras urging a reduction of the duty.

[2] Mr. Laing refused to be drawn into the controversy namely, whether a tax on paper was a 'tax on knowledge,' but he, thought while books were on the free list, a duty on paper was indefensible.

[3] It was estimated that the total effect of the reductions proposed in customs duties was £ 475,000.

prosperity, and, in 1863, some other reductions were made in the rates of duty.[1] No reduction was made on the duty on piece-goods, because the 5 per cent. ad valorem duty, charged on a valuation which was fixed when prices were about half of what they were at this time, really amounted to $2\frac{1}{2}$ per cent., and the so-called protective duty had utterly failed to give protection. The hand-loom weavers, as Sir Charles Trevelyan stated in the Council, had been "prostrated by the blow which staggered Manchester. They had gone down before the excessive price of the raw material and had migrated or gone upon the Railways or other public works or had given themselves up entirely to agriculture." The Finance Member prophesied that when Manchester set to work again, she would "find her rival local manufacturers converted to an unexpected extent into ready-money customers.[2]

A few years ago, the plan had been adopted

[1] Duties on beer and wine were further reduced. Iron, which was regarded as a material of industry essential to the development of great works in India and which had been charged with a duty of 10 per cent., was now subjected only to a registration fee of 1 per cent. Machinery continued to be on the free list.

[2] Financial Statement, 1863-64. He added: "There has been occasional severe distress, particularly where the manufacture was carried on for general sale at marts, but, on the whole, it is a remarkable proof of the healthy, progressive state of India, that the transition has been got through with so little difficulty." Discussing the causes of the trouble, the Finance Member remarked that "the 40, 50 and even 60 per cent. advance of price paralysed trade, and not the nominal 5 per cent. duty."

in England of confining customs duties to a limited number of principal articles of import. It was suggested in many quarters that a similar system might with advantage be extended to India. But Sir Charles Trevelyan held the view that, under the special circumstances of India, "our policy should be to levy a wide-spread but moderate duty, so as to give free scope to trade in time of peace, and to cherish the increase of a fund which would be our first financial reserve in time of War."[1]

In 1864, the finances of the Government of India showed further improvement, and the general import duty of 10 per cent. was reduced to 7½. The duty on tobacco was reduced to 10 per cent. The loss of revenue arising from these reductions was sought to be balanced by increased receipts from the re-adjusted valuations of piece-goods.

Next year, some important alterations were made in the customs tariff in view of the growth of expenditure and the cessation of the revenue derived from income-tax. The Finance Member

[1] His reasons were as follow: "Whether duty be levied on many articles or on few, all must undergo the usual examination. Nothing, therefore, is gained by limiting duties to a few articles either in saving expense of collection or in exempting the trade from interference....India is such a vast and imperfectly developed country that articles which hardly appear in one part exist in abundance in another, and entirely new staples occasionally spring into life in answer to some unexpected demand or discovery."

expressed the opinion that Indian exports had in general such a hold on foreign markets that they could easily bear some duty without being seriously checked.[1] He showed, by reference to the trade figures, that the exports of jute, wool, tea, and coffee had increased considerably during the last four years, and he proposed to levy an export duty of 3 per cent. on each of them. Hides, sugar, and silk, which had not increased in the same proportion, were subjected to a duty of 2 per cent. On the other hand, the duty on saltpetre—which was now in a decadent state—was reduced from Rs. 2 to Rupee 1.[2]

There were no changes of any importance in 1866, except that the duty on saltpetre which had been unable to compete with the new manufacture in Europe, was reduced from one Rupee a maund to 3 per cent. ad valorem. The relief, however, came too late.

During this year, the tariff was revised by a Committee with a view to the better classification of the articles, to a re-adjustment of value and charges, and to the removal of duties which

[1] Sir C. E. Trevelyan said: "The old policy of the East India Company was to levy low rates of duty upon exports and imports. However contrary this practice may have been to some received maxims of political economy it was suited to the circumstances of the country." Financial Statement, 1865-66.

[2] An additional duty of 4 annas a maund was also levied on salt in the Bombay Presidency.

were not so valuable to revenue as they might be obstructive to trade. The new classification was far more simple and intelligible than the one it superseded. The Committee adopted the plan of enumerating the articles which were to pay customs duties, any article not enumerated being free. They removed from the column of charge in the tariff schedule upwards of 40 articles, leaving only 97 articles, further reduced to 65 classes of articles upon which duty in future was to be collected. Further, they suggested the abolition of export duties on 88 articles, retaining only 9 classes of articles on the export list. In 1867, the Government accepted most of the recommendations of the Committee. The loss of revenue resulting from the adoption of the new system was met by an increase in the export duty on grain from 2 to 3 annas per maund[1] and an alteration of the wine duties. The Committee had advocated the raising of the duty on grain not only as a legitimate mode of improving the revenue, but also on the ground of its tendency to check the exportation of a staple article of food during a period of famine.[2]

[1] The Right Hon'ble Mr. Massey pointed out that, in 1857, in the prospect of scarcity, a prohibitory duty on the exportation of grain had been proposed, but not adopted; in 1859, however, the duty had been raised from half anna to two annas per maund. *Vide* Financial Statement, 1867-68.

[2] Some of the grain merchants of Burma memorialised the

## § 2. (1871-1882.)

The customs tariff was again carefully revised by a Committee in 1869, and, in accordance with their recommendations, the tariff valuations of cotton yarn and piece-goods and other articles were largely reduced in 1871.

In 1873, the Committee of the Bengal Chamber of Commerce suggested, for the consideration of the Governor-General in Council, the expediency of revising the tariff. In January, 1874, the Manchester Chamber of Commerce addressed a memorial to the Secretary of State for India, complaining—

That the duties of 3½ per cent. on yarns and 5 per cent. on British cotton manufactures imported into India were assessed on tariff rates fixed many years ago, when values ruled much higher than at present;

That the tax was found to be absolutely prohibitory to the trade in yarn and cloth of the coarse and low-priced sorts;

That the Chamber were informed that it was proposed to import Egyptian and American cotton (no duty being charged thereon) to manufacture the finer yarns and cloth which would

Secretary of State against the increased duty, basing their opposition "not on the ground of its tendency to check the trade but in the prospect of its decreasing their profits."

thus compete with goods received from England on which duty was levied;

That a protected trade in cotton manufacture was thus springing up in British India to the disadvantage both of India and Great Britain; and

That the duties increased the cost to the native population or at least to the poorest of the people, of their articles of clothing, and thereby interfered with their health, comfort, and general well-being.[1]

The Manchester Chamber of Commerce, therefore, prayed that early consideration might be given to the subject of the duties with a view to their abolition.

In reply to the memorial, it was pointed out by the Government of India that tariff valuations had been revised only a few years ago, and an expectation was held out that another Committee would be convened soon for the purpose. Thereupon, the Manchester Chamber of Commerce reminded the Secretary of State that, in their memorial, they had only incidentally referred to the valuations, and that their main object was the total and immediate repeal of the duties themselves. They added, "A large number of new mills are now being projected,

[1] *Vide* Resolution of the Government of India, Financial Department, 12th August, 1875.

and the revenue from import duties will be consequently diminished. The impost is, therefore, defeating its own object, as well as inflicting an injustice on the consumer and importer."[1]

In November, 1874, a Committee was appointed by the Government to consider the whole question of the tariff. In the Report submitted by the Committee, they recommended a lower scale of tariff valuations. They also recommended the abolition of the export duties on cotton goods, grain and pulse (except rice and paddy), seeds, oils, and spices.[2] As for the import duties, their suggestion was that the duty on some of the metals should be reduced from 7½ to 5 per cent., while the duties on luxuries, wines and iron should be raised, and a 2½ per cent. duty on machinery should be levied. With regard to the duties on cotton manufactures, they observed: "The demand that, because one class of goods, represented by 4 lakhs of duty in all India, has in one part of India, to meet a local competition, the Government shall remit the remaining 77 lakhs which competition

[1] *Vide* Resolution of the Government of India, Finance Department, 12th August, 1875.

[2] Two members of the Committee recorded their dissent from the decision to remit the export duties on the ground that "the substituted taxation would be worse." *Vide* Report, dated 27th February, 1875.

cannot affect, appears to the Committee quite unreasonable, and it is unnecessary even to enquire whether the finances could afford the remission." They also rejected the alternative of an excise duty on Indian mill products as they saw "no need for establishing a cumbersome and expensive excise machinery."[1]

The Government of India accepted, in the main, the recommendations of the Committee in regard to the valuations. They also concurred with the majority of the Committee in the opinion that it was of primary importance to relieve, as far as possible, the export trade of India from taxation and "to stimulate the growth of Indian produce, whether raw or manufactured, for exchange with other countries." They went further, and decided to remit the export duty on tanned hides and skins.

Thus, the entire export trade was freed from all fiscal burdens, except three articles, namely, indigo, rice, and lac. The Government of India did not think it necessary to increase the duties on luxuries as proposed by the Committee. On the other hand, they decided to reduce the general rate of import duty from 7½ to 5 per cent. Of course, the cotton manufacturers of Manchester

[1] Resolution, dated 12th August, 1875.

shared, along with others, in the benefit of this reduction, and the lower scale of valuations represented a considerable gain to them[1]. A further concession to the sentiments and fears of Manchester was the decision of the Government of India to impose an import duty of 5 per cent. on long-stapled cotton. But they declined to abolish the cotton duty altogether, being of opinion that a duty of 5 per cent. could not "practically operate as a protection to native manufacture." [2]

These decisions of the Government of India were embodied in a Bill which was passed on the 5th August, 1875. A cable was sent to the Secretary of State on the same day, informing him of the substance of the changes. To this message the following reply was received :

"Provisions of Act very important. Some objectionable. Please explain, by mail, grounds on which you have withdrawn it from operation of Legislative Despatch 9 of 1874".[3]

[1] The actual relief to cotton goods was no less than Rs. 8,80,000, or nearly 11 per cent. of the whole duty paid. *Vide* speech of Mr. T. C. Hope in introducing the Tariff Bill. Legislative Council Proceedings, 1875.

[2] Resolution, dated 12th August, 1875. They expressed their agreement with the view held by Mr. S. Laing in 1861, who had said : "Free trade does not mean that there shall be no taxes, but that taxes shall be levied solely with a view to revenue, and not partly for revenue and partly for protection."

[3] This Despatch is one of considerable importance as showing the relations which existed between the Secretary of State and the

In their reply by letter to this telegram, the Government of India explained that it was a matter of considerable urgency, and pointed out that it had not been the practice, on former occasions, "to refer alterations of customs duties for the opinion of Her Majesty's Government previously to their being introduced and passed in the Legislative Council." They also observed that in Despatch 9 of 1874, the degree of importance which would necessitate the reference of a measure to the Secretary of State before its introduction into the Legislative Council had been left to be determined by the judgment of the Governor-General in Council.

A few days later, a Despatch was received from the Secretary of State in which Lord Salisbury strongly urged the Government of India to abolish the import duty on cotton manufactures as soon as the condition of the finances should enable them to part with it. He thought that the duty was open not to economic,

Governor-General in Council. In it, Lord Salisbury criticised the action of the Government of India in taking the entire responsibility for many important measures which had been recently passed by the Legislative Council. This practice he regarded as a departure from older precedents, and he desired that in future whenever the Governor-General in Council, should decide to submit any important measure to the Legislative Council, a Despatch should be addressed to the Secretary of State, stating at length the reasons which were thought to justify the step intended to be taken, and the mode in which the intention was to be carried out.

but political, objections. "The gradual transfer", he wrote, "of the Indian trade from the English to the Indian manufacturer, which appears likely to take place, will be attended with much bitterness of feeling on the one side, and with the keen anxiety for the security of an unexpected success upon the other. The English manufacturer will press with increasing earnestness for the abandonment of the duty to which he will impute his losses; and in proportion to his urgency the Indian manufacturer will learn to value it. It is impossible that, under these conditions, the duty can be permanently maintained. The entire acceptance of free trade by England is incompatible with the continuance cf an exception apparently so marked. Parliament, when its attention is drawn to the matter, will not allow the only remnant of protection within the direct jurisdiction of the English Government to be a protective duty which, so far it operates at all, is hostile to English manufacturers".[1]

On the 30th September, Lord Salisbury sent

[1] Separate Revenue Despatch, No. 6, dated 5th July, 1875. Regarding the possible effect of the proposal, Lord Salisbury remarked: "Some soreness even now will be felt, and more will be expressed, by persons who will trace such a policy to a preference of English over Indian claims. But the irritation will only extend over a wider surface if action is delayed, and may, if the delay be too far prolonged, become a serious public danger".

a telegram to the Viceroy expressing his disapproval of the Tariff Act and practically enjoining the removal of the cotton duties. Sir E. Perry, a member of the Council of India, in his note of dissent to the telegram, said: "It is a violation of the fundamental principles of good government for India that fiscal measures should originate with the local authorities there".

In a Despatch, dated the 11th November, 1875, Lord Salisbury again urged upon the Governor-General in Council the necessity for the speedy removal of the duty on cotton goods which, in his opinion, offered "a false encouragement to the Indian manufacturer," and was "a matter of serious importance both to Indian and Imperial interests."[1] He refused to sanction the import duty of 5 per cent. on long-stapled cotton. Minutes of dissent were recorded by Sir E. Perry and Sir H. Montgomery to the Despatch,[2] but Lord Salisbury was obdurate. A few weeks later, Sir L. Mallet, Under-Secretary of State for India, was sent out to this country

[1] Legislative Despatch No. 51 of 1875. He suggested that the abolition should be gradual for the entire removal of the duty within a fixed term of years.

[2] Sir E. Perry wrote: "I am as strong an anti-protectionist as any of my colleagues, but I am clearly of opinion that the small duty of 5 per cent. which has been imposed for purposes of Revenue should not be remitted until the state of the Indian finances permit the operation."

to discuss the whole subject with the Government of India.

In their reply to the Despatch of the Secretary of State, Lord Northbrook and his colleagues pointed out the financial difficulties which were likely to arise from any measure for reducing the customs duty on cotton manufactures, and they made the significant observation: "After carefully examining the records of the Government of India since the year 1859, we can find no precedent of a measure so seriously affecting the future of Indian finance as the prospective removal of a tax which brings in a revenue of £ 800,000 per annum having been directed by the Home Government." They concluded the letter with the remark that the duty could not be removed "without danger to the Indian finances, and that the imposition of new taxes in its stead would create serious discontent"[1].

Other Despatches to and from India followed. The Secretary of State continued to insist on the abolition of the cotton duties, while the Government of India adhered to their position of reluctance to agree to the

[1] Letter dated 25th February, 1876. Parliamentary Paper (House of Lords) No. 3 of 1876. The whole attitude of the Government of India was thus described in one sentence: "It is our duty to consider the subject with regard to the interests of India; we do not consider that the removal of the import duty on cotton manufactures is consistent with those interests".

proposal. In these Despatches, the question of the relations between the British and Indian Governments was discussed with enthusiasm on both sides[1]. The resignation of Lord Northbrook, however, helped to smooth matters over. And when Lord Lytton became Viceroy, the Secretary of State was able to have his own way. The new Viceroy, soon after his appointment, publicly declared his view in favour of the abolition of the cotton duties. In 1877, the Finance Member, Sir John Strachey, made his attitude towards this question clear in these words: "We are often told that it is the duty of the Government of India to think of Indian interests alone, and that if the interests of Manchester suffer, it is no affair of ours: for my part, I utterly repudiate such doctrines: I have not ceased to be an Englishman because I have passed the greater part of my life in India, and have become a member of the Indian Government. The interests of Manchester, at which some foolish people sneer, are the interests not only of the great and intelligent population engaged directly

[1] The opinion of the Council of India was often divided on this question. For instance, Sir B. H. Ellis and Sir F. Halliday submitted Notes of Dissent to the Despatch of the 23rd May, and Sir E. Perry and Sir H. Montgomery expressed their dissent from the view of the majority regarding another Despatch of the same date.

in the trade in cotton, but of millions of Englishmen: I am not ashamed to say that, while I hope that I feel, as strongly as any man, the duties which I owe to India, there is no higher duty in my estimation than that which I owe to my own country."[1] Financial embarrassments, however, prevented the Finance Member from giving effect to his views at this particular moment.

In the same year, the Secretary of State again called the attention of the Government of India to the customs tariff generally, and to the duties levied on cotton goods in particular, in several Despatches. In forwarding a copy of a memorial from the East India Association[2] protesting against the proposed abolition of cotton duties, and a reply thereto by Mr. R. Jackson on behalf of the Associated Committees of Employees and Workmen in the cotton manufacturing districts, Lord Salisbury observed: "Your Excellency is well aware of the great importance attached by Her Majesty's Government to the gradual reduction of these duties at the earliest

[1] Speech in the Governor-General's Legislative Council on Financial Statement, 1877.

[2] In this memorial it was pointed out that there was no appreciable competition between the cotton goods of Manchester and those of India and it was urged that an impartial Commission be appointed to institute a full and searching enquiry into the whole subject.

period that is not inconsistent with the financial requirements of your administration."[1] On the 30th August, 1877, a Resolution was adopted by the House of Commons without a division in the following terms:

"That, in the opinion of this House, the duties now levied upon cotton manufactures imported into India, being protective in their nature, are contrary to sound commercial policy, and ought to be repealed without delay as soon as the financial condition of India will permit".

In March, 1878, the Finance Member said in the Governor-General's Legislative Council that the Government of India was bound to give effect to the principles on which the customs legislation of Great Britian was based. These principles were:

"As regards imports,—

(1) that no duty should exist which affords protection to native industry, and as a corollary that no duty should be applied to any article which can be produced at home, without an equivalent duty of excise on the home production; also that no duty should be levied except for purely fiscal purposes;

(2) that, as far as possible, the raw materials

[1] Despatch No. 124, dated 22nd August, 1877.

of industry and articles contributing to production should be exempt from customs taxation:

(3) that duties should be applied only to articles which yield a revenue of sufficient importance to justify the interference with trade involved by the machinery of collection.

As regards exports,—

that duties should be levied on those commodities only in which the exporting country has practically a monopoly of production." [1]

He added: "These principles are of general application, but, in the case of India, they possess a peculiar significance. India is a country of unbounded material resources, but her people are a poor people. Its characteristics are great power of production, but almost total absence of accumulated capital. On this account alone, the prosperity of the country essentially depends on its being able to secure a large and favourable outlet for its surplus produce. But there is a special feature in the economic conditions of India which renders it a matter of yet more, and even of vital importance,—this is the fact that her connection with England and the financial results of that connection, compel her to send to Europe every year about 20 millions sterling

[1] Financial Statement, 1878-79.

worth of her products without receiving in return any direct commercial equivalent. It is this excess of exports over imports which, in the language of the economists, is described as tribute."[1]

As a first step towards giving effect to the policy enjoined by Parliament and the Secretary of State, the Government of India exempted those coarser qualities of cotton goods with which the Indian manufactures were likely to compete successfully. This involved considerable financial sacrifice, and that in a year of deficit when the imposition of fresh taxes was found necessary. The duty on foreign raw cotton which had not only been regarded as objectionable in principle, but had proved entirely unproductive, was removed. A number of minor articles, which produced inconsiderable revenue, together with railway materials, were also removed from the tariff schedules.

The relief thus granted to the imported cotton goods failed to give satisfaction, and an official Commission was appointed to enquire into the grievances complained of. In accordance with the recommendations of this Commission, Lord Lytton, in 1879, decided to exempt from duty all

[1] Financial Statement, 1878-79.

cotton goods containing no yarn of a higher number than 30s. At the same time, the valuations were reduced, and it was decided to prevent subjection to octroi duty of cotton or other goods on through traffic. The majority of members of the Viceroy's Executive Council were opposed to this reduction. But the extraordinary step was taken by the Viceroy to overrule the Council under the power vested in him by law for use on emergent occasions.[1] The objections of the dissenting members were based mainly upon financial considerations. This was a time when the finances of the Government were in a most deplorable state owing to the combined effects of war, famine, and loss by exchange. Mr. Whitley Stokes, a member of the Executive Council of the Governor-General, in the course of an admirably written Note of Dissent, urged seven very cogent reasons against

[1] Sec. 41 of the Government of India Act runs thus: (1) "If any difference of opinion arises on any question brought before a meeting of the Governor-General's Executive Council, the Governor-General in Council shall be bound by the opinion and decision of of the majority of those present."

(2) "Provided that whenever any measure is proposed before the Governor-General in Council whereby the safety, tranquility, or interests of British India, or of any part thereof, are or may be, in the judgment of the Governor-General, essentially affected, and he is of opinion that the measure ought to be adopted and carried into execution, or that it ought to be suspended or rejected, and the majority present at a meeting of the council dissent from that opinion, the Governor-General may, on his own authority and responsibility, adopt, suspend or reject the measure, in whole or in part".

the measure. One of his principal objections was that the people of India would be convinced that the step had been taken "solely in the interest of Manchester and for the benefit of the Conservative party." "Of course," he added, "the people of India will be wrong: they always must be wrong when they impute selfish motives to the ruling race.[1] Nevertheless, the evil political results likely to follow from this popular conviction should not be ignored and should, if possible, be avoided." He also objected to the way in which the proposed change in the law was effected, namely, by an executive order. The power vested in the executive to exempt goods from customs duties was merely intended to relieve the Government from the useless and troublesome formality of coming from time to time to the Legislature to make petty alterations in the tariff. But the adoption of such an important measure as the exemption of cotton goods by a mere executive order would, Mr. Stokes wrote, "thus resemble what lawyers call a fraud on the power; and there is, unfortunately, no court of equity to relieve the people of India against it."[2]

[1] Mr. R. C. Dutt's comment on this passage is very appropriate. He says: "The keen satire of the last sentence quoted is not excelled by anything I have ever seen in official literature". *India in the Victorian Age*, p. 413.

[2] Sec. 23 of the Sea Customs Act, 1878 provides: "The Governor-General may, from time to time, by notification in the Gazette of

Another dissentient Note was written by Mr. R. Thomson, who afterwards became Lieutenant-Governor of Bengal. He opposed the measure on various grounds, and specially deprecated it because it had "all the appearance of subordination of the reasonable claims of the Indian administration to the necessities of English politics." Sir Alexander Arbuthnot thought that the circumstances of the case were of extreme gravity, and expressed the view that the adoption of such a course was as "unwise and ill-timed" as it was "destructive of the reputation for justice" upon which the prestige and political supremacy of the British Government in India so greatly depended. Sir Andrew Clarke concurred in the Minute of Sir Alexander Arbuthnot.[1]

It is thus clear that the action of the Government was not supported even by all the officials. It is needless to say that it was strongly opposed by the entire Indian community. This feeling was also shared by the leading representatives of the European mercantile community in

India, exempt any goods imported into, or exported from, British India, or into or from, any specified port therein, from the whole or any part of the customs duties leviable on such goods".

[1] Return to an Address of the House of Commons, dated 8th May, 1879.

India. The Madras Chamber of Commerce was of opinion that this was a "most unsuitable time for thinking of sacrificing any of the State's resources under pressure from interested and imperfectly informed foreign manufacturers." The Chamber of Commerce of Calcutta concluded a letter addressed to the Governor-General with the following words: "It will be a source of mortification and disappointment if it be now shown that the opinions and wants of sections of the people of England have more influence in determining the character of the financial legislation in India than the interested and expressed wish of the people under the Government of Your Excellency."

It is worthy of note in this connection that the Finance Member showed by reference to the trade figures that, although there had been a large increase in the importation of goods of finer quality, the imports of the coarser goods had fallen off considerably. He expressed his satisfaction at the great expansion of local industry which had taken place, but he added, "Such facts as those which have been stated show very plainly the duty incumbent on the Government of taking care that the great increase attained in the manufacture of cotton goods by the Indian mills is not fostered by defiance of the fundamental principles of British commercial policy, or by improper restrictions on other classes of Her Majesty's subjects."[1]

This reduction was, of course, heartily approved by the Secretary of State, but no less than seven members of the Council of India were opposed to it.[2] Sir B. H. Ellis contended that "the remission devised by the Viceroy in opposition to the majority of his Council was not justified by the circumstances of India at the time," and he observed that "virtually the remission has been effected by taxing the people of India." Sir E. Perry wrote: "I think the remission of cotton duties at that period was most inopportune, and that the overruling of his Council by the Governor-General was unconstitutional and a dangerous precedent for the future if allowed to pass unnoticed."

On the 4th April, 1879, the House of Commons passed the following resolution:

"This House accepts the recent reduction in those duties as a step towards their total abolition

[1] The Bombay Mills had, during the last four years, not only increased their exports of yarn and piece-goods to foreign countries by 26 per cent. and 51 per cent. respectively, but had more than doubled their exports to other parts of India.

[2] The Council of India was equally divided on this question, and it was carried only by the casting vote of the President.

to which Her Majesty's Government are pledged."

An important step was taken during this year to free the internal trade of the country from restrictions. The Inland Customs Line, which was one of the greatest reproaches against British administration in India, and which had often been likened to the Great Wall of China, was abolished[1]. The primary object of the erection of the barrier was to safeguard the levy of the duty on salt. But it was also used to safeguard the heavy export duty imposed on sugar produced in British territories. The duty on sugar had been abolished in 1878, and now the salt duty was equalised throughout India with some minor exceptions. The retention of this barrier was thus no longer necessary.

In 1880, the Committee of the Bengal Chamber of Commerce, in a letter to the Government of India, pointed out the anomaly involved in admitting free certain kinds of cotton goods, while levying a duty on large quantities of goods of almost precisely the same character in everything but name, and the hardship which was caused

[1] This Customs Line was first formed on the frontier of the North-Western Provinces in 1843. It was gradually extended until it stretched beyond Attock in the extreme north-west, right across the continent of India over a distance of about 2,000 miles to near Cuttack. It consisted of thick rows of hedges, and was an almost impenetrable barrier.

not by competition between Lancashire and the Indian mills but "by competition amongst Lancashire manufacturers themselves, to secure the full benefit of the Government of India's last act." Sir John Strachey admitted that the state of things was anomalous and objectionable, and he expressed the hope that the time was not hopelessly distant when the ports of India would be thrown open freely to the commerce of the world.[1] But as this would involve considerable loss of revenue, some other source of income had to be found. He rejected in this connection the proposal of a reciprocity between England and India as "unsound in theory, and impossible in practice."

On the question of the export duty on indigo, the Finance Member held a reasonable view. He was warned by the fate which had overtaken the trade in saltpetre, and he considered the danger of competition from indigo of Central America and chemically prepared substitutes as real. This duty, as well as the one on lac, the trade in which had been in a depressed condition, was abolished.

In 1882, the financial position of the country improved, and the opportunity was taken to

[1] Financial Statement, 1880-81.

abolish the whole of the cotton duties and of the general import duties. Only the special duties, namely, those on wine, spirits, and liquors, remained; and so did the duties on arms and ammunition, salt and opium. This, according to Sir E. Baring, was the form which a remission of taxation might "most beneficially assume." The net loss of revenue involved in this abolition amounted to £ 1,108,000. But he regarded the measure as most beneficial to India, and observed: "As an incident of her connection with England, India has a right to profit from English experience and English economic history. That experience and that history show that by the adoption of free trade a country benefits, indeed, all the world, but more specially benefits itself."[1] If there be people who would feel inclined to read English history in a different light and refuse to accept the dictum of the Indian Finance Member, they would, of course, deserve the severest censure for their perversity.

In the course of the discussion of the matter in the Legislative Council of the Governor-General, Maharaja Jatindra Mohan Tagore, an ultra-loyalist, and one who was proud to wear the decorations bestowed on him by a benign

[1] Financial Statement, 1882-83. Sir Evelyn Baring afterwards became famous as Lord Cromer.

Government, regretted that the interested cry of Manchester carried greater weight with the Government than justice to the millions entrusted to their care. He also observed: "As to free trade, it might be all very well in theory, but it must be borne in mind that England, with her advanced notions in commercial matters, had not yet been able to introduce it in practice. In the trade of the country with Great Britain, while Indian goods should continue to pay duties to swell the large revenue of the latter, that this poor country should sacrifice any portion of her limited resources for the sake of a theory was what, he must frankly confess, did not commend itself to Native thoughts and ideas."[1]

Thus closed an important chapter in the fiscal history of India. As regards the actual effect of this abolition on local industry, Major Baring said in 1883 that it did not "in any way affect Indian mills." But Indian opinion was almost unanimous in holding that the remission of the duty helped to check the speedy development of the cotton industry in India.

## § 3. (1883-1896.)

There were no changes of any importance in the tariff for several years after 1883. The

[1] *Vide* Proceedings, Viceroy's Legislative Council, 1882.

improvement which had shown itself in the financial position of the country did not last long. A deficit occurred in 1884, and there were several other deficits in subsequent years. The Government were only enabled to make their two ends meet with the help of additional taxation. Besides other taxes, there was a duty on petroleum in 1888. The salt duty was enhanced in the same year, and, next year, the duty on imported spirits was raised. The financial difficulties of the Government were due to the combined effects of war and the fall in the gold value of silver. After a short spell of buoyancy, the situation became again acute in 1892. In 1893-94, there was a deficit of 1¾ crores, and in the following year, Sir James Westland was faced with a deficit of no less than 3½ crores. He, therefore, proposed to suspend the Famine Insurance Grant for the time and to call upon the Provincial Governments for contributions. But as these measures were not likely to meet the full amount of the deficit, he was obliged to bring forward a proposal for levying general import duties at the rate of 5 per cent. The Secretary of State accepted the proposal, but refused to sanction the inclusion of cotton yarn or cotton fabrics among the articles declared liable to duty. Six members of the Council of India, however, expressed their dissent from this decision of the Secretary of State[1]. Sir Charles Lyall wrote in his minute of dissent: "Hitherto, whenever import duties have been generally imposed in India, the schedule has included cotton goods, and I do not think that their special exclusion can be defended on economic grounds, having regard to the existing situation of the Indian finances. The cotton duties have never been imposed in India for protective purposes." During the debates in the Legislative Council, several members including Mr. Patrick Playfair, Dr. Rash Behary Ghosh, Sir Griffith Evans, Mr. Fazulbhai Vishram, Mr. G. Chitnavis, the Maharaja of Darbhanga, and the Maharaja of Ayodhya urged the inclusion of cotton goods in the list of articles subjected to duty.[2] Mr. Playfair voiced the unanimous opinion of India when he said: "It is impossible to deny that there is a growing feeling in this country that India's interests are being subordinated to Lombard Street on the one hand and Manchester on the other. It is believed that

[1] The dissenting members were A. J. Arbuthnot, A. Alison, D. M. Stewart, H. Rawlinson, C. A. Turner, and A. C. Lyall.

[2] *Vide* Proceedings of the Indian Legislative Council, March 10, 1894. It is interesting to note that the exemption was opposed by all the Indian members together with two European members.

through the influence of the former the Empire has been made to feel, to the full, the effects of the fall in the value of the silver, without being accorded the liberty to deal with the situation as appears to be in her best interests, and that through dictation on the part of the latter, she is now forbidden to find for herself a way out of a difficulty by imposing taxes upon herself." Even Mr. C. C. Stevens, a high Government official, who not long afterwards rose to the position of Acting Lieutenant-Governor of Bengal, expressed his disappointment that a "just, impartial and reasonable method of increasing the revenue" was not adopted.[1] Sir Griffith Evans considered the matter "so scandalous" that he thought it his duty to protest against it in the strongest terms.[2]

But the Government were unable to accept

[1] Mr. Stevens added: "The opposition is practically universal and most thorough and sincere, and cannot be disregarded with safety." Proceedings of the Governor-General's Legislative Council, March, 1894.

[2] He described the position of the Finance Member in these words: "When we find the Financial Member—when we see a man of his grasp and power—grovelling in the dust heaps of the third schedule for 'fish maws' and 'sharks' fins' to meet a deficit of $3\frac{1}{2}$ crores, we feel very much like what the ancient Assyrians must have felt when they saw Nebuchadnazar going on all fours and eating grass under the compulsion of the Higher Powers. It is a pitiable spectacle." Ibid.

On the occasion of the discussion of the Financial Statement for 1894-95, Sir Griffith Evans described the exemption of cotton goods as "inequitable in action as well as inadequate in result." Proceedings, March 27, 1895.

the suggestions of the members in view of the attitude of the Secretary of State and the British Parliament. Various public bodies, representing both Indians and Europeans, and including the Chambers of Commerce, made representations to the Government, protesting against such exclusion. Public meetings were also held in various parts of the country with the same object. But the Tariff Bill was passed in the form in which it was introduced. Agitation, however, continued, and the financial situation of the Government showed no signs of improvement. On the 31st May, 1894, the Secretary of State sent a Despatch to the Governor-General in Council, in which he observed: "If, however, your Government should be forced again to consider the question of imposing duties on cotton manufactures, it will be requisite to ascertain what classes of imported cotton goods came into competition with Indian manufactures of the same kind. Among imported cotton goods, there will probably be some classes of goods which directly compete with goods produced in India, some which partly compete, and some which practically do not compete at all. It would be for your Government, after full enquiry, to decide how far you could distinguish between these three classes of imported cotton goods; and then to consider by what measures you could deprive any duties, that might be imposed, of a protective character. This object would be obtained either by exempting from duty those classes of imported goods which clearly and directly compete with Indian manufactures, or by levying on the latter an excise duty equivalent to the import duty on corresponding goods from abroad."[1]

In their reply to this Despatch, the Government of India expressed their readiness to accept an excise duty as a solution of the difficulty, and forwarded a Minute by Sir. J. Westland in which he recommended the imposition of import duties at the rate of

*(a)* 5 per cent. ad valorem on all cotton piece-goods;

*(b)* 3½ per cent. ad valorem on all cotton yarn of counts above 24;

and *(c)* an excise duty of 3½ per cent. ad valorem on all machine-made cotton yarn, produced at mills in British India of counts above 24.

Indian-made piece-goods would thus pay excise duty on the yarn of which they were woven, whenever such yarn was finer than 20.

[1] Parliamentary Paper, 7602.

Sir Henry Fowler accepted these proposals with two amendments, namely, that the rate of import duty on yarn should be 5 per cent., and that the duty on yarn should begin with counts above 20. These proposals were embodied in Bills and placed before the Legislative Council of the Governor-General in December, 1894.

The proposal to levy an excise duty was opposed by the Bombay Mill-Owners' Association and the Bengal Chamber of Commerce and other public bodies. Sir Griffith Evans, Sir Patrick Playfair, Mr. Fazulbhai Vishram and several other members protested against the levy of an excise duty[1]. But Sir James Westland told the Council that the measure "was recommended to us by superior orders and orders which we are obliged to obey."[2]

[1] Proceedings of the Governor-General's Legislative Council, 1894. Sir Griffith Evans regarded the excise duty as "onerous, unprofitable, and harassing to trade", and he thought "no sufficient case had been made out for the imposition of this excise." Sir P. Playfair said ; "In itself it will be regarded as pernicious, or to take the mildest view, not promotive of revenue or economy", and as a principle "it may take away from this Council all independence and its representative character".

Mr. Fazulbhai Vishram moved an amendment to substitute '24' for '20', and though it was supported by all the Indian members and two European members, it was lost. Mr. C. C. Stevens spoke in favour of the amendment, but refrained from voting.

[2] Sir James Westland added : "I freely admit that it is because the Secretary of State, or rather Her Majesty's Ministers, have laid upon us the condition of accompanying that measure with a measure for excise duties, that we have brought forward this bill."

The duties of the members of the Legislative Council were incidentally discussed on this occasion. Sir Griffith Evans remarked that when the Legislative Council met, all members were at liberty to look at any matter from a purely independent point of view.

The concession of a duty on yarn did not satisfy the cotton manufacturers of Manchester, but only egged them on to further demands. On the 21st February, 1895, during a debate in the House of Commons concerning Indian cotton duties, the Secretary of State gave the pledge that, if the duties could be proved to have had any protective character, Her Majesty's Government would, in concert with the Government of India, consider the matter with a view to avoiding "protective injustice." Several representations were made to the Secretary of State, and in December, 1895, an influential deputation of Lancashire operatives, employees, and M.P.'s, and of the Scotch dyers and printers, waited upon Lord George Hamilton. The new Secretary of State showed himself even more sympathetic than his predecessor to the claims of Manchester, and he assured the deputation of his firm resolve

But Sir James Westland said: "That may be the case with members of the Council who are not also members of the Government, but I do not know any foundation for the theory that, when your Excellency calls together the additional members of Council to advise the Government, the Government thereby acquires an authority which, in other respects, it does not possess. The orders of the Secretary of State, though they may not be a sufficient excuse for the additional members of this Council voting against what is recommended to us, yet are sufficient for us who are members of the Executive Council, and who exercise our power not by any authority of our own, or in our own name, but in the name of Her Majesty." Proceedings of the Legislative Council, 20th and 27th December, 1894.

to accord to them "perfect equality of treatment." Telegraphic communications between the Secretary of State and the Viceroy followed, and, in February, 1896, two Bills were passed in the teeth of non-official opposition both in and outside the Council, by which a direct excise duty of 3½ per cent. was levied on all cotton piece-goods woven by the Indian mills, the import duty of 5 per cent. was reduced to 3½ per cent., and all duty on yarn, whether imported or manufactured, was abandoned.[1]

It is worthy of note that, when the matter went to the Council of India, two of its members took strong exception to the measures that had been just enacted. Sir James Peile protested against the subjection of the whole of the Indian mill cloth to excise. He did not think that this excise was countervailing, for the Indian mill cloth co-existed, but did not compete, with the Lancashire fine goods, and he concluded his Note with the significant observation: "I desire to relieve myself from all responsibility for leaving to their operation Acts which I regard as not logically defensible, and therefore politically

[1] Proceedings of the Indian Legislative Council, January and February, 1896. The views of the various Chambers of Commerce and other public bodies and the opinions expressed at public meetings are to be found in Parliamentary Paper No. 807[8] (of 1896).

unwise."[1] Sir Alexander Arbuthnot expressed his entire concurrence in the opinion of Sir James Peile.

Thus ended the second stage in the controversy over duties on cotton goods. But it was not the final solution of the question. The bitterness of public feeling did not subside with the lapse of time. So far, however, as the Government was concerned, the matter was not re-opened till twenty years had elapsed from this date.

§ 4. (1897-1914.)

No further alterations were made in the tariff till 1899, when Sir James Westland proposed to open an entirely new chapter in the fiscal history of India[2]. The object of the Bill, which he introduced, was to confer on the Government the power to impose countervailing duties in the case of bounty-fed sugar imported from European countries. These duties were to be in addition to the ordinary tariff, and the rates were to be equal to the amounts of bounties which were granted by foreign nations[3]. With regard to

[1] Parliamentary Paper 229 of 1896.

[2] Mr. P. Ananda Charlu welcomed the bill, and said: "I consider it to mark a very important epoch by way of a departure in the fiscal legislation of this country." *Vide* Proceedings of the Governor-General's Legislative Council, 1899.

[3] As Sir James Westland pointed out, the Bill was copied in its wording from the United States Act of 1897. There was, however, a difference. In the United States, the Act imposed the duty, but

the principle of the Bill, Sir James Westland said that it was not a measure which condemned the action of foreign countries in putting bounties on their sugar. He added: "We only wish to protect our own industry, and we claim the same right to preserve our industry in this country as foreign nations no doubt claim to preserve and encourage the sugar industry and sugar cultivation in their own territories."

This was really a measure of defence, but the acceptance of the principle of protection was, indeed, a marked departure from the policy so far pursued by the Government of India. Of course, there was in this case no conflict of interests between England and India. On the other hand, here was an opportunity not only for benefiting some of the English Colonies but also opposing, in an indirect manner, the economic policy of two of the most powerful continental nations. It has also been a matter of doubt whether the initiative in this measure was taken by the Government ot India or whether the policy was enjoined by the Government of England "with Imperial, rather than Indian, objects in view."[1]

the Executive was given the power to prescribe the rules. In this case the Indian Legislature gave power to the Executive Government to impose the necessary duties as well as to lay down the rules and regulations.

[1] *Vide* J. W. Root, Trade Relations of the British Empire, p. 162.

The imposition of the duty, however, did not produce the expected result, and the imports of beet-sugar continued to increase. The reason was that, in addition to the bounties granted by the Governments, sugar produced in Austro-Hungary and in Germany enjoyed other bounties created by the operation of the kartel system. These kartels made large profits on the sugar sold at home, which enabled them to export the surplus produce at very low prices, even below the cost of production.[1] In 1902, therefore, additional duties on German and Austro-Hungarian sugar, at Rs. 2-13-9 and Rs. 3-3-9 per cwt. respectively, were imposed.[2] It was originally intended that this provision was to expire on the 31st August, 1903, but the period was subsequently extended.

During the next few years, no changes were made in the tariff, except increases in the duties on liquors and reductions in the salt tax. In 1910, the shrinkage in the opium revenue and the necessity for aiding the bankrupt Government of Eastern Bengal and Assam compelled Sir Guy

[1] Mr. M. C. Turner pointed out, in the course of the debate on the subject in the Legislative Council, that there were other indirect bounties, such as preferential rates in the matter of sea and rail carriage. *Vide* Council Proceedings, 1902.

[2] These rates were in accordance with the principles laid down in the Brussels Convention of 1901.

Fleetwood Wilson to propose fresh taxation. The customs duties on liquors, tobacco, silver, and petroleum were raised. The Finance Member disclaimed the slightest inclination towards a protective customs tariff. He also expressed the hope that he would not be "charged with framing a Swadeshi budget." But a very vigorous agitation was started, immediately after the passing of these measures, on behalf of the tobacco trade in England with the result that, in the following year, the Finance Member was compelled to reduce the duty on imported tobacco by one-third. In order to make up for the loss of revenue, the duty on petroleum, an article of necessity for the poorer classes of the population, was further increased.[1]

During this period of over fifty years, India was compelled to follow the principle of free trade, ostensibly on the ground of theory, but really for the benefit of England, and in opposition to the wishes not only of the people, but, sometimes, of the Government of India. She was not allowed to develop any industrial enterprise if it happened to come in competition,

[1] These proposals were strongly opposed by the non-official members, particularly by Mr. M. Haque and Mr. G. K. Gokhale, but they were carried by an official majority. *Vide* Proceedings of the Indian Legislative Council, 1912.

even in a remote and indirect way, with any English industry. This unjust treatment accorded to India, while she was in a position of helpless political dependence upon England, was often the subject of adverse comment at the hands of fair-minded Englishmen. Dr. Cunningham, for instance, wrote, "Ireland and India have been forced, under compulsion, to submit to free trade without being consulted, and for the sake of English interests; in both these cases, economic dissatisfaction is associated with political unrest."[1] Nor did it escape the observation of foreigners. Fuchs, a German economist, said: "It is King Cotton—the industry of Lancashire—whose interests have been most to the front."[2]

[1] The case against Free Trade, p. 87.

[2] Trade Policy of Great Britain, p. 272.

# CHAPTER IV

## THE FISCAL SYSTEM OF THE WAR PERIOD AND AFTER

### § 1. (1914-1919.)

On the eve of the European War of 1914, India was in a fairly satisfactory financial position. But no sooner did hostilities commence than the impact was felt in India, situated though she was many thousand miles from the theatre of operations. The Government were able, however, to meet the financial strain without resort to fresh taxation for the first year and a half of the war. But as the deficiency in the revenue tended to assume a more or less abiding character, additional taxation became necessary. In 1916, an augmentation of revenue was sought to be obtained from various sources, including customs. The general import duty was raised from 5 to 7½ per cent. *ad valorem*, the duty on sugar was increased to 10 per cent., that on iron and steel to 2½ per cent., and on other metals to 7½ per cent.

The free list was considerably curtailed, and some of the articles which had previously been imported free were now subjected to a duty of 2½ per cent., while others were taxed at 7½ per cent. The special duties on arms, liquors, tobacco, and silver manufactures were also considerably enhanced. The salt duty was raised from Re. 1 to Rs. 1¼ per maund. Finally, an export duty was levied on two important staples, namely, jute and tea. The duty on cotton goods, however, was left untouched. Anticipating an adverse comment on this policy of partial treatment, Sir William Meyer said: "Well, the Government of India have not failed to represent their view that there should be a material increase in the cotton import duties, while the cotton excise, which has formed the subject of such wide-spread criticism in this country, should be left unenhanced, subject to the possibility of its being altogether abolished when financial circumstances are more favourable. But His Majesty's Government, who have to consider the position from a wider stand-point, felt that the raising of this question at the present time would be most unfortunate, as it would provoke a revival of old controversies at a time when they specially desired to avoid all contentious questions, both here and in England, and might prejudice the ultimate settlement of the larger issues raised by the war. His Majesty's Government feel that the fiscal relationship of all parts of the Empire as between one another and the rest of the world must be reconsidered after the war, and they desire to leave the question raised by the cotton duties to be considered then, in connection with the general fiscal policy which may be thought best for the Empire, and the share, military and financial, that has been taken by India in the present struggle."[1]

The proposals for increasing the customs duties met with the approval of the Indian Legislative Council. The only objection which was taken was with regard to the salt duty. As for the exclusion of cotton goods from the additional burden, although the action of the Government gave rise to keen disappointment, the explanation offered by the Finance Member went some way towards disarming criticism. Almost all the non-official members of the Council gave expression to the sense of injustice which had been done to India by the partiality shown to the cotton manufacturers of England. Many of them, however, were unwilling to embarrass the

[1] Financial Statement, 1916-17.

Government at a critical moment. But Sir Ibrahim Rahimtoola moved an amendment for raising the 3½ per cent. import duty on cotton goods to 6 per cent. In the course of his speech on the subject, he said: "It appears to me that it is rather hard that when the Government of India want the revenue, when the country is willing to agree to give them that additional revenue from a source which is agreeable to themselves, that they should be debarred from doing so, and in that way necessitate the proposal for the increased salt tax."[1]

In May, 1916, an Industrial Commission was appointed by the Government of India, but, strangely enough, the tariff question was especially excluded from the scope of its enquiries. In the following year, the financial stress of the war increased, which necessitated further taxation. Various steps were taken to improve the revenue, and customs came in once more for their share in the scheme. The export duty on jute, both raw and manufactured, was doubled. The import duty on cotton goods was fixed at 7½ per cent., which was the general tariff rate, but the excise duty on cotton was left at 3½ per cent. Of course, this last measure was taken with the

[1] Proceedings of the Indian Legislative Council, 1916.

sanction of the Government of England, which was accorded to enable India to make an adequate contribution towards the expenses of the war. The proposal was welcomed by the non-official members of the Indian Legislative Council.[1]

§ 2. (1919-1922).

In September, 1919, the Government of India introduced a Bill which sought to impose an export duty of 15 per cent. on hides and skins, exported to any part of the Empire. The object was to ensure that the hides and skins of India should be converted into fully tanned leather or articles of leather so far as possible in India, and failing this in other parts of the Empire, instead of being exported in a raw state for manufacture in foreign countries. In the course of his speech introducing the Bill, Sir George Barnes, the Commerce Member, said that, before the war, the hide trade had been monopolised by the Germans, and the tanning industry of India had been of comparative insignificance, but great changes were brought about by the war. "We want," Sir George added, "to keep this industry alive,

[1] One member said: "The principles of taxation devised in the Bill is a distinct indication of the sign that the Government is more and more in touch with the popular opinion, and that it has come to the conclusion that its future policy in the matter of taxation shall be, as far as practicable, in the direction of a well considered system of protective tariff."—*Speech of the Hon. Mr. M. B. Dadabhoy in the Legislative Council, 7th March, 1917.*

and we believe that in this case protection in the shape of a 15 per cent. duty is justifiable and effective". But, in reality, the Government wanted to kill two birds with one stone. The second object which the Government had in view was described by the Member in charge of the Bill in these words: "Though Indian tanneries have enormously increased in number during the past three years, they can only deal with a comparatively small proportion of the raw hides and skins which India produces, and it is to the advantage of India and the security of the Empire generally that this large surplus should, so far as possible, be tanned within the Empire, and with this end in view the Bill proposes a 10 per cent. rebate in respect of hides and skins exported to any place within the Empire."[1] Sir George Barnes did not, however, make it clear how the manufacture into leather of hides in a country within the Empire but outside of India could be of advantage to India herself. Nor did he say which of the two objects mentioned by him was regarded by the Government as the more important.

The first part of the Bill was welcomed by the Indian, as well as the European, members of the

[1] Proceedings of the Indian Legislative Council, September, 1919.

Council. Mr. W. E. Crum supported the Bill on behalf of the Bengal Chamber of Commerce, and, in doing so, he reminded the Council that, as long ago as 1917, a Conference of the Chambers of Commerce had recommended that "any industries which can be regarded as key industries should be supported."[1] Pandit Madan Mohan Malaviya, while supporting the export duty of 15 per cent., saw no justification for the other proposal, namely, the grant of a rebate of 10 per cent. Another non-official member of the Council, Mr. B. N. Sarma, congratulated the Government most heartily upon the departure from the economic policy which had so far been pursued by it, but moved an amendment to delete the second part of the Bill on the ground that it raised, in an indirect manner, a large and important question, namely, the question of preference between the various parts of the Empire. To this objection Sir George Barnes replied that the rebate was not proposed as part of any general scheme of Imperial Preference.[2]

In their Report on Indian Constitutional Reforms, Mr. Montagu and Lord Chelmsford incidentally referred to the question of Indian

[1] Proceedings of the Indian Legislative Council, March, 1919.

[2] *Ibid.*

fiscal policy. They said, "Educated public opinion ardently desires a tariff. It rightly wishes to find another substantial base than that of the land for Indian revenues, and it turns to tariff to provide one. Desiring industries which will give him Indian-made clothes to wear and Indian-made articles to use, the educated Indian looks to the example of other countries which have relied on tariffs, and seizes on the admission of even free traders that for the nourishment of nascent industries a tariff is permissible . . . He believes that as long as we continue to decide for him we shall decide in the interests of England and not according to his own wishes; and he points to the debate in the House of Commons on the differentiation of the cotton excise in support of his contention."

The Joint Select Committee appointed by Parliament to consider the Government of India Bill of 1919 recommended the question of the tariff as a "special case of non-intervention." "Nothing," they said, "is more likely to endanger the good relations between India and Great Britain than a belief that India's fiscal policy is dictated from Whitehall in the interests of the trade of Great Britain. That such a belief exists at the present moment there can be no doubt. That there ought to be no room for it in the future is equally clear. India's position in the Imperial Conference opened the door to negotiation between India and the rest of the Empire, but negotiation without power to legislate is likely to remain ineffective. A satisfactory solution of the question can only be guaranteed by the grant of liberty to the Government to devise those tariff arrangements which seem best fitted to India's needs as an integral portion of the British Empire. It cannot be guaranteed by statute without limiting the power of veto which rests in the Crown; and neither of these limitations finds a place in any of the statutes in the British Empire. It can only, therefore, be assured by an acknowledgment of a convention. Whatever be the right fiscal policy for India, for the needs of her consumers as well as her manufacturers, it is quite clear that she should have the same liberty to consider her interests as Great Britain, Australia, New Zealand, Canada and South Africa. In the opinion of the Committee, therefore, the Secretary of State should, as far as possible, avoid interference on this subject when the Government of India and its Legislature are in agreement, and they think that his intervention, when it does take place, should be limited to safeguarding the international obligations of the Empire or any fiscal arrangements within the Empire to which His Majesty's Government is a party." [1]

Lord Curzon endorsed this view when, speaking in support of the third reading of the Bill in the House of Lords, he observed: "For the first time a responsible and representative British Committee, charged with shaping a government for India, have conceded to India almost absolute freedom of fiscal policy. They have laid down the policy and the principle that she ought to be free to exercise, in respect of her tariffs, and so on, the same degree of liberty as is enjoyed by the great Dominions of the Crown. This is a change so fundamental and fraught with such stupendous consequences that I am amazed at the little attention it has attracted in this country."[2] These expressions are so clear and emphatic that there could not be the slightest doubt as to the intentions of Parliament as well as of the

[1] Report of the Joint Select Committee of Parliament, p. 11.

[2] Lord Curzon added: "It is a starting-point to a future career in the growth of self-governing institutions in India the importance of which cannot be exaggerated. I am the last to complain of it, because in all the controversies about these Cotton Duties, and so on, I have always fought the battles of India. Therefore, I am delighted to see my views and theories prevail." Debate in the House of Lords, Dec. 19, 1919. *Vide* P. Mukherji, *Indian Constitution.*

Executive Government of England in regard to this subject.

In 1921, the Government of India were faced with a large deficit.[1] The Finance Member was thus obliged to bring forward fresh proposals for taxation. Among other measures, he proposed a large addition to the customs tariff. In the first place, he proposed to increase the general *ad valorem* duty of 7½ per cent. to 11 per cent., except in the case of matches and certain articles of luxury, but inclusive of cotton manufactures. The excise duty on cotton was to be left at 3½ per cent. He estimated that this measure would produce an additional revenue of Rs. 384 lakhs. This measure was, of course, proposed after a previous reference to His Majesty's Government in order to make it clear to them that the sole object of the Government of India was the production of additional revenue, and that they had no ulterior motive of a protective or any other kind. "It would," said Sir Malcolm Hailey, "ill become this country, at a time when the senior partner of the Empire, upon whom fell by far the severest burden of the war, both in blood and money, is anxiously endeavouring

[1] This was due to various causes, the principal ones being the exchange difficulty and increased military expenditure.

to face the most acute problems of unemployment and trade distress, to requite the services which Great Britain has rendered to the rest of the Empire, including India, by taking the first opportunity to introduce a measure of protection against her manufactures. We made it clear, therefore, that it is solely our financial necessities, and no new departure of fiscal policy, which have obliged us to propose to the legislature this particular measure. We trust that our fellow-subjects in the United Kingdom will appreciate this and will acquit the Indian Government and Legislature of any desire to use their newly conferred liberty of action to injure the country which only a year ago conferred that liberty upon them."[1]

In view of the advantage which was thus to be gained by the weaving and spinning mills, the concession of the free import of machinery and stores required for use in these mills was withdrawn, and most of such articles were made liable to duty at 2½ per cent.

The second customs measure proposed by the Finance Member was the levy on matches of a specific import duty of 12 annas per gross boxes in place of the *ad valorem* duty of 7½ per cent.

[1] Financial Statement, 1921-22.

His third proposal was an increase of duty on liquors. The fourth measure was the raising of the general *ad valorem* duty of 7½ per cent. to 20 per cent. in the case of certain articles of luxury, such as motor-cars, motor-cycles and tyres (excluding lorries), silk piece-goods, fire-works, umbrellas, clocks and watches, musical instruments, cinematograph films, etc. Fifthly, the import duty on foreign sugar was proposed to be raised from 10 to 15 per cent. The Finance Member's last tariff proposal was that duties on tobacco, other than manufactured, be raised to 50 per cent.

While strong objection was taken to the other proposals for taxation, almost all the tariff proposals were accepted by the Legislature.[1]

The action of the Indian Government and the Indian Legislature gave rise to much consternation in Lancashire. The Manchester Chamber of Commerce appointed a deputation to wait upon Mr. Montagu, Secretary of State for India, who, in the course of his reply, at the outset, disposed of the impression that the Government of India had taken the first chance of a new-found liberty to pay off an old score and to impose a

[1] It should be noted that the composition, powers, and responsibilities of the Indian Legislature were different at this time from what they had been a few months before.

duty with the main object of protecting Indian cotton goods and of injuring the Lancashire trade. He then pointed out that the expenditure of the Government of India fell short of their revenue by 18½ crores. After examining the other sources of increased revenue, and showing their inadequacy, Mr. Montagu continued: "Now when we come to customs, again they have not singled out cotton. There is to be a general rise in the whole customs duties right away through the gamut of them, from 7½ per cent. to 11 per cent., with a special rate on luxuries, which goes up to 20 per cent. You are here to complain to-day of a very small proportion of the Indian Budget—something which produces $\frac{1}{15}$th of the total increase, and that what really you are asking is either that cotton should be left out of the general increase of customs, which it has been absolutely necessary to impose, or in the alternative, that a corresponding excise should be put upon cotton, whereas it is not put on any other of the goods on which there is going to be an increased customs duty. It is only about cotton that we have this question raised."

Mr. Montagu added: "It would be theoretically impossible for me to veto the Bill, in which these duties are contained, when it comes home for sanction. Actually it is, I would submit, absolutely impossible. I cannot veto part of a Bill, I must veto the whole Bill; and I should, therefore, leave the Government of India with none of their increased revenue to meet their increased charges." He then referred to the opinion of the Parliamentary Joint Committee and Lord Curzon's speech in the House of Lords, and observed: "After that Report by an authoritative Committee of both Houses and Lord Curzon's speech in the House of Lords, it is absolutely impossible for me to interfere with the right—which, I believe, was wisely given and which I am determined to maintain—the right of the Government of India to consider the interests of India."[1] A little later, the Secretary of State sent an important despatch to the Government of India, in which he said that His Majesty's Government had accepted the recommendation of the Joint Committee on the question of fiscal autonomy for India.

[1] Addressing the Labour members of the deputation, Mr. Montagu said that the Labour Party gave valuable support to the passage of the Bill but they always protested that they took it because they could not get anything better—that they wanted more liberty for India, that the time had come to concede to her, if not complete self-government, something very near it. "Now when, despite the limitations of the Bill, you concede to her the right to mould her own fiscal destinies, a section of the Labour Party feels that those rights and liberties which she has achieved are even too large for the well-being of the interests that they are here to represent to-day."—*The Times, 26th March, 1921.*

In October, the Government of India announced the appointment of a Fiscal Commission, with Sir Ibrahim Rahimtoola as Chairman, "to examine with reference to all interests concerned, the tariff policy of the Government of India, including the question of the desirability of adopting the principle of Imperial Preference, and to make recommendations."

During the financial year which closed on the 31st March last, the revenue of the Government fell short of their expectations, while the expenditure largely exceeded the estimates. And another large deficit was expected to occur in the current year. The Finance Member, being unwilling to budget for a deficit, made various proposals for increasing the revenue, and his first thoughts naturally turned towards the customs. In view of the fact that a Fiscal Commission was sitting, he would have preferred to await the decisions of that body before proposing any further alteration of the tariff. But the needs of revenue were urgent, and there was no escaping the conclusion that "the pressure of financial necessity must in any case inevitably involve the raising of our customs duties, purely for revenue purposes, irrespective of what the effect may be in the case of any particular tariff-head in the direction of protection, Imperial Preference, or free trade." Sir Malcolm Hailey was careful also to add that he had endeavoured to limit his proposals in such a way "as not to involve any important change of principle in the existing fiscal arrangements."[1]

The proposals of the Finance Member were the following: To raise the general import duty on all articles including cotton goods to 15 per cent.; to increase the cotton excise duty from 3½ to 7½ per cent.; to raise the duty on machinery, iron and steel to 10 per cent.; to increase the duty on foreign sugar to 25 per cent.; to double the duty on matches; to increase the duty on petroleum; to increase the salt tax from Rs. 1¼ to Rs. 2½ a maund; to levy a duty of 5 per cent. on imported yarn; to raise the duties on luxuries to 30 per cent.; and lastly, to enhance the duties on alcoholic liquors except wines, by approximately 20 per cent. The Finance Member estimated that the total of revenue obtainable from the proposed increase in customs would amount to Rs. 1,490 lakhs.[2]

Some of the proposals of the Finance Member did not find favour with the Indian Legislature.

[1] Financial Statement, 1922-23.

[2] *Ibid.*

The two most important modifications introduced into the budget both related to cotton goods. The Legislative Assembly refused to give its sanction to the increase in the excise duty on cotton manufactures, and, on the motion of Mr. Rhodes, President of the Bengal Chamber of Commerce, the import duty on cotton goods was left at 11 per cent.[1] A few days later, that is to say, on the 29th March, 1922, a deputation of Members of Parliament and others representing cotton textile interests, headed by Sir John Randles, M.P., was received at the India Office by the Secretary of State and the Parliamentary Under-Secretary for India. Lord Peel welcomed the deputation, but was obliged to leave the meeting in consequence of a sudden Cabinet engagement. He asked Lord Winterton to take charge of the proceedings in his absence.

Representations were made by the deputation that the terms of the convention recommended by the Joint Select Committee of Parliament of the Government of India Bill of 1919 to the effect that the Government of India, acting in agreement with the Legislature, should be conceded the same fiscal autonomy as is possessed by the

[1] The proposals for the enhancement of the salt tax and the duty on kerosine were also objected to. *Vide* Proceedings of the Indian Legislative Assembly, March, 1922.

Dominions, travelled beyond the intentions of the Government of India Act of 1919, to which alone Parliament was committed. It was further argued that the indigenous cotton industry of India had been able to make headway against competition even in the days when the import duty on cotton was balanced by a countervailing excise duty of the same amount, and therefore the industry itself did not stand in any need of protection. It was also stated that whereas Indian politicians of all classes were admittedly protectionist, the cotton duties were bound seriously to affect the poorest class of the population. The suggestion was made that the revenue derived from the cotton import and excise duties would be equally secured if the import duty were lowered from 11 per cent. to 6 per cent., and the excise duty raised from 3½ per cent. to 6 per cent. In general it was urged that the Government should recognise the grave dissatisfaction caused in Lancashire by the suspicion that the Indian cotton duties were dictated by a clique of wealthy mill-owners in India, and that the Government should ensure that a true balance was held between all parties interested and should undertake that the representations made to them should receive their close attention in co-operation with the Government of India.

Lord Winterton, replying on behalf of the Secretary of State, indicated as regards the convention recommended by the Joint Select Committee that ultimate self-government must contain fiscal autonomy as an essential feature, and that, therefore, if and when, as was hoped, India attained self-government, the right of fiscal autonomy must then be unreservedly conceded. He expressed his wish, however, not to press this argument too closely for the moment, and he assured the deputation that there was no doubt that the ultimate responsibility for India's financial measures must in present circumstances rest with the Secretary of State.[1] He was not in a position to promise definitely that the Secretary of State would undertake to re-examine the whole position on the lines suggested by the deputation; but he expressed his full agreement with the view

[1] Lord Winterton pointed out that the actual position as regards cotton import and excise duties had by virtue of the vote of the Indian Legislative Assembly been left as it was twelve months ago, *viz.*, the figure of the import duty remained at 11 per cent., and that of the excise duty at 3½ per cent. He added that in one respect the British cotton trade was better off than other trades, since the general import duty had been raised in the recent Indian budget from 11 per cent. to 15 per cent., whereas by the vote of the Indian Legislative Assembly the import duty on cotton had been left at its former figure.

that close co-operation between the Home Government and the Government of India in this matter was essential in the interests of both countries, and he promised that the fullest consideration should be given to the representations made, which he would charge himself with conveying to the Secretary of State.[1]

The opinion expressed by Lord Winterton, on behalf of the present Secretary of State for India, seems to indicate a significant change in the attitude of the British Government towards India on this important question. Lord Winterton's words are in direct contrast with the clear and emphatic language—without any 'if' or 'when'—in which Mr. Montagu defined the constitutional position of India in respect of her tariff. And no wonder that this change of attitude has given rise to a keen and intense feeling of dissatisfaction among all classes of people in the country. It is, however, to be earnestly hoped, in the interests of the future good relations between India and England, that no attempt will be made to go back upon the definite assurance of fiscal freedom which was given by a responsible Parliamentary Committee, and endorsed by the King's responsible Ministers.

[1] Report published in the *Englishman*, April, 1922.

# CHAPTER V

## THE THEORETIC BASES OF FREE TRADE AND PROTECTION

Mercantilism was the accepted economic creed of the nations of Europe in the seventeenth and eighteenth centuries. Control of trade and industry in various shapes and forms was the essential feature of the mercantile theory and practice. The Physiocrats were the first to lead a movement of revolt against the system of exclusions and prohibitions by which the mercantilists sought to advance the industrial and commercial interests of their respective countries. The doctrine of free trade grew out of certain principles advocated by the Physiocrats. Adam Smith was the prophet—though not the father—of this theory.[1] He held that all restraints were bad, and urged the removal of

[1] Several writers had advocated freedom of trade and industry before Adam Smith. He must have been largely influenced by the writings of Quesnay, Gournay, and Turgot of France, and David Hume of England. But to Adam Smith belonged the credit of having first presented this doctrine in a precise and intelligible form.

restrictions on trade in order that the "obvious and simple system of natural liberty" might establish itself.

Natural liberty was thus the most important basic principle of free trade. The duties of the State would, in this view, be limited only to protection of the community from external invasion, the preservation of internal peace, and the maintenance of a few works of public utility. "Every nation," said Adam Smith, "which endeavours, either by extraordinary encouragements, to draw towards a particular industry a greater share of the capital of the society than what would naturally go to it; or by extraordinary restraints, to force from a particular species of industry some share of the capital which would otherwise be employed in it, is in reality subversive of the great purpose which it means to promote. It retards, instead of accelerating, the progress of the society towards real wealth and greatness; and diminishes, instead of increasing, the real value of the annual produce of its land and labour."[1]

Every individual, in this view, was a better judge of what species of industry was likely to be of greater value to him than any statesman or

[1] Wealth of Nations, Bk. IV, Ch. IX.

lawgiver. Regulation by the State, therefore, was either useless or hurtful. And natural liberty would promote the welfare not only of the individual, but also of society. "Every individual", according to Adam Smith, "is continually exerting himself to find out the most advantageous employment for whatever capital he can command. It is his own advantage, indeed, and not that of the society, which he has in view. But the study of his own advantage, naturally, or rather necessarily, leads him to prefer that employment which is most advantageous to society."[1]

Another important principle on which the free trade doctrine was based was international division of labour. Just as a prudent master of a family, argued Adam Smith, never attempted to make at home what it would cost him more to make than to buy, so if a foreign country could supply us with a commodity cheaper than we ourselves could make it, it would be an advantage to buy it with some part of the produce of our own country. Such purchase would not lead to any diminution of the general industry of the country, for industry was always in proportion to the capital employed. Left to

[1] Wealth of Nations, Bk. IV, Ch. IX.

itself, therefore, the industry of the country was always able to find out the way in which it could be employed with the greatest advantage; but artificially regulated, it was turned away from a more, to a less, advantageous employment, and the exchangeable value of its annual produce was diminished.

Originally, it seems, Adam Smith's view rested on the question of natural advantage. "The natural advantage", he said, "which one country has over another in producing particular commodities are sometimes so great that it is acknowledged by all the world to be in vain to struggle with them". But he perhaps felt disinclined thus to limit the theory, and extended it to advantages of other sorts.

Freedom of trade and industry ought, therefore, in Adam Smith's opinion, to be the general rule for all countries. But he recognised certain exceptions to this rule. In two cases, he thought, it might be advantageous to lay some burden upon foreign industry for the encouragement of domestic industry. First, when some particular industry was necessary for the defence of the country. The Navigation Laws of England were justified on this ground. Secondly, when some tax was imposed upon local produce, an equal tax might reasonably be imposed on the like produce of foreign countries. Besides these, there were two other cases in which it might sometimes be a matter of deliberation. The first was when some foreign nation restrained by high duties or prohibitions the importation of manufactures of a particular country into its own, retaliation might be a good policy, if there was any probability that it would procure the repeal of the high duties or prohibitions. Then again, when particular manufactures, by means of high duties or prohibitions upon all foreign goods, had been so far extended as to employ a great multitude of hands, humanity might require that freedom of trade should be restored only by slow gradations, and with a good deal of reserve and circumspection.[1]

Adam Smith was certainly on firm ground when he condemned the abuses which resulted from the acceptance of Mercantilism. But the theory of natural economic liberty, as formulated by him, has not stood the test of experience, for every civilised nation, not even excepting England, has found it necessary to impose restrictions in some form or other on commercial and industrial activity.[2] Adam Smith's

[1] Wealth of Nations, Bk. IV, Ch. II.

[2] Sidgwick adopted a moderate attitude towards the question of economic liberty. He said, "Complete laissez faire is not to be

narrow conception of the functions of the State has now given place to a more enlightened view. His belief in the absolute identity of the economic interests of the individual and the community, and of the nation and humanity, under all circumstances, has now been found to have been based on wrong hypotheses. His failure to draw a distinction between natural and acquired advantages is a very regrettable omission. Lastly, Adam Smith's vision was limited to the static side of economic activity, which prevented him from considering national economy in its more important—namely, the dynamic—aspect. The main thesis of the great economist, therefore, can be accepted as true only within certain well defined limits.

The doctrine of free trade, as expounded by Adam Smith, was followed by Ricardo and developed by J. S. Mill. Ricardo, like his predecessor, thought that under a system of perfectly free commerce, each country would

taken as a political ideal; the problem for the statesman is to balance its advantages against the disadvantages of extending the sphere of government."

As for the application of the theory of individual freedom to economics, a contemporary writer says: "The case for Free Trade is thus essentially a part of the general case for individual liberty. It does not, of course, follow that those who accept individual liberty as a general rule of policy are bound to accept Free Trade, but it does follow that they will be inclined to do so, until they are proved to be wrong". H. Cox, Economic Liberty, p. 99.

naturally devote its capital and labour to such employment as would be most beneficial to it. And this pursuit of individual advantage would lead to the universal good of the whole. "By stimulating industry", he said, "by rewarding ingenuity, and by using most efficaciously the peculiar powers bestowed by nature, it distributes labour most effectively and most economically: while by increasing the general mass of productions, it diffuses general benefit, and binds together by one common tie of interest and intercourse, the universal society of nations throughout the civilised world."[1]

John Stuart Mill expressed similar views with his usual precision of thought and language. He laid great stress on the fundamental idea of mutual benefit, which was believed to underlie international trade. "The importation of foreign commodities", wrote Mill, "in the common course of traffic, never takes place, except when it is, economically speaking, a national good, by causing the same amount of commodity to be obtained at a smaller cost of labour and capital to the country. To prohibit, therefore, their importation, or impose duties which prevent it, is to render the labour and capital

[1] Ricardo, Principles of Political Economy and Taxation, Ch. VII.

of the country less efficient in production than they would otherwise be; and compel a waste of the difference between the labour and capital necessary for the home production of the commodity and that which is required for producing the things with which it can be purchased from abroad. The amount of national loss thus occasioned is measured by the excess of the price at which the commodity is produced, over that at which it could be imported. In the case of manufactured goods, the whole difference between the two prices is absorbed in indemnifying the producers for waste of labour, or of the capital which supports that labour. Those who are supposed to be benefited, namely, the makers of the protected articles, (unless they form an exclusive company, and have a monopoly against their own countrymen as well as against foreigners,) do not obtain higher profits than other people. All is sheer loss to the country as well as to the consumer."[1]

Mill ridiculed the "specious plea of employing our own countrymen and our national industry, instead of feeding and supporting the industry of foreigners". "The alternative", he added, "is not between employing our own people and

[1] J. S. Mill, Principles of Political Economy, Bk. V, Ch. X.

foreigners, but between employing one class and another of our own people. The imported commodity is always paid for, directly or indirectly, with the produce of our own industry: that industry being at the same time rendered more productive, since with the same labour and outlay, we are enabled to possess ourselves of a greater quantity of the article."[1]

If each country devoted itself to the production of those goods for which it had the best advantages, no doubt productive costs would be reduced to the lowest possible limits, and all countries would reap the benefit. It would be impossible to dispute the correctness of Mill's view, provided it was assumed that the advantages which one country possessed over another in the production of any article were of a permanent character. But this assumption is not always true, and, therefore, there may be conditions to which his argument would not apply.

Mill himself, like Adam Smith, was quite prepared to make exceptions, though the exceptional cases mentioned by him were not exactly the same as those of his predecessor. In the interests of national defence, restrictions might, in his opinion, be "though economically

[1] J. S. Mill, Principles of Political Economy, Bk. V, Ch. X.

disadvantageous, politically expedient". But the only case in which he would regard protective duties as defensible on mere economic principles was when they were "imposed temporarily (especially in a young and rising nation) in hopes of naturalising a foreign industry, in itself perfectly suitable to the circumstances of the country". Mill thus went further than Adam Smith in the direction of limiting the doctrine. He drew a distinction between natural and acquired advantages. "The superiority of one country", said Mill, "over another in a branch of production often arises only from having begun it sooner. There may be no inherent advantage on one part, or disadvantage on the other, but only a present superiority of acquired skill and experience. A country which has this skill and experience to acquire, may in other respects be better adapted to the production than those which were earlier in the field. ... But it cannot be expected that individuals should, at their own risk, or rather to their certain loss, introduce a new manufacture and bear the burthen of carrying it on until the producers have been educated up to the level of those with whom the processes are traditional. A protecting duty, continued for a reasonable time, *might* sometimes be the least inconvenient mode in which the nation can tax itself for the support of such an experiment."

Mill was careful, however, to add a word of caution. He said, "But *it is essential that* the protection should be confined to cases in which there is good ground of assurance that the industry which it fosters will after a time be able to dispense with it; nor should the domestic producers ever be allowed to expect that it will be continued to them beyond the time necessary for a fair trial of what they are capable of accomplishing."[1]

Another significant admission, which was characteristic of the sense of fairness which distinguished Mill from the other advocates of free trade, was that "there is a great foundation of reason" for the belief "that a nation all engaged in the same or nearly the same, pursuit—a nation all agricultural—cannot attain a high state of civilisation and culture."

The concession made by Mill in favour of

[1] Mill, Principles of Political Economy, Bk. V, Ch. X. As Sir William Ashley points out, the "will" of the original text was changed into "might" in the 7th edition, and the words "it is essential that" were inserted.

It is worthy of note that Adam Smith himself concedes that "by such (Mercantile) regulations a particular manufacture may sometimes be acquired sooner than it could have been otherwise, and after a certain time may be made at home as cheap as or cheaper than in the foreign country". *Vide* Marshall, Industry and Trade, Appendix D.

'infant industries' was regarded as a heresy by the other followers of Adam Smith.[1] These latter lacked Adam Smith's breadth of view and moderation and Mill's scrupulous regard for truth.[2] When Adam Smith and Mill made reservations or exceptions, they suggested that certain conditions were implied for the validity of their theory. But other supporters of free trade made "simple sweeping statements of broad scope without the necessary limitations and conditions." They bolstered up the doctrine as an absolute truth which was applicable to all circumstances. One reason of this narrowness of view was perhaps to be found in the deductive method of reasoning which was exclusively employed by some economists. Another reason was the limited knowledge of the world possessed by them, which tempted them to generalise from the circumstances with which they were familiar. But the most important reason was patriotic bias. These

[1] Sir William Ashley points out that, writing to a correspondent in 1869, Mill expressed an intention to withdraw the opinion, and remarked: "Even on this point I continue to think my opinion was well grounded, but experience has shown that protectionism, once introduced, is in danger of perpetuating itself, and I, therefore, prefer some other mode of public aid to new industries though in itself less appropriate." But he subsequently changed his mind and allowed the opinion to stand.

[2] In France, the chief advocate of the classical doctrine was J. B Say, who also was prepared to make some concession in favour of young industries for the purpose of development.

economists looked to the needs and interests of their own country, and failed to appreciate those of other countries. As has been rightly expressed by a great economist, "It was clearly to the interests of England that her manufactures should be admitted free by other countries. Any Englishman who attempted to point out that there was some force in some of the arguments which were adduced in favour of Protection in other countries was denounced as unpatriotic."[1] The evil was further aggravated when the theory was put to polemical use by politicians who made all sorts of overstatements and exaggerations.

The free trade theory came thus to be looked upon with suspicion by statesmen in other countries, and was for a time discarded by economists—with a few notable exceptions—outside England. About 1860, the doctrine of free trade was triumphant. But not long after, a reaction began to set in. In recent years, however, a more sober and moderate view of this doctrine has been adopted by its supporters amongst economists. Prof. Marshall does not hesitate to point out that "the wording of these doctrines was often so narrow and inelastic that, when applied under conditions of time and place

[1] Marshall, Industry and Trade, p. 760.

different from those in which they had their origin, their faults became obvious and provoked reaction." He adds: "Looking back, then, it is easy for us to see that English economists made a grave error of judgment as to the proportions of one leading problem of their own age, though not of their own country. They misjudged the needs no less than the potentialities of backward countries, and specially of new countries. They took little account of the fact that, though any county of England, which had latent resources and faculties for an advanced industry, would attract that industry to itself from other counties; yet what is true of counties is not true of countries."[1]

The most formidable critic and opponent of Adam Smith's theory was Frederick List, the father of modern economic nationalism and the intellectual founder of the German Zollverein. He was, in reality, more a critic of the popular notions on free trade than of the exposition of the doctrine by the great classical economist himself. The necessity which List felt for "energetically contradicting" a great writer like Adam Smith often led him—though unconsciously—to misunderstand or misinterpret him.

[1] Marshall, Industry and Trade, Appendix E.

The main characteristic of List's system, as distinguished from that of Adam Smith and others—which he understood to be cosmopolitanism—was nationality. List was not wholly opposed to a system of free trade. But he saw that all nations were not equal in wealth or productive power. He argued, therefore, that "in order to allow freedom of trade to operate naturally, the less advanced nations must first be raised by artificial measures to that stage of cultivation to which the English nation has been artificially elevated." The most effectual means for this purpose was, in his view, protection which should be resorted to by "all nations which feel themselves to be capable, owing to their moral, intellectual, social, and political circumstances, of developing a manufacturing power of their own."[1]

List laid great emphasis on productive power. He held that the power of producing wealth was "infinitely more important than wealth itself; it insures not only the possession and the increase of what has been gained but also the replacement of what has been lost." The prosperity of a nation was not greater in proportion in which it amassed more wealth (*i. e.*, values in exchange)

[1] List, National System of Political Economy.

but in the proportion in which it developed more its powers of production. The distinction which List drew between present and future advantage is of fundamental importance. A nation, according to him, must sacrifice some present advantages to secure future ones. List did not overlook the fact that protective duties tended at first to increase the price of goods but this loss he believed to be only temporary. When, in the course of time, the nation was enabled by this means to build up a completely developed manufacturing power of its own, these goods would be produced more cheaply at home than could be purchased from foreign countries. If, therefore, a sacrifice of value was caused by protective duties, it was made good by the gain of a power of production.

List laid great stress on the necessity for developing manufactures as well as agriculture. These two kinds of industry, he thought, depended mutually upon one another, and he called this relation "the balance or the harmony of the productive powers." He regarded the value of manufacturing industries, from the point of view of civilisation, as very great. Without them a nation must remain relatively unprogressive. "In a condition of merely agricultural industry," he wrote, "caprice and slavery, superstition and ignorance, want of means of culture, of trade, and of transport, poverty and political weakness exist. In the merely agricultural State only the least portion of the mental and bodily powers existing in the nation is awakened and developed, and only the least part of the powers and resources placed by nature at its disposal can be accumulated." And from the national stand-point, he considered the exclusive pursuit of agriculture a source of weakness. "A nation," said he, "which only carries on agriculture, is an individual who in his material production lacks one arm. Commerce is merely the medium of exchange between the agricultural and the manufacturing power, and between their separate branches. A nation which exchanges agricultural products for foreign manufactured goods is an individual with one arm, which is supported by a foreign arm." On the other hand, manufactures not only helped to secure the material prosperity of a nation but also its industrial independence in time of war.

List did not reject the idea of an international division of labour, but he believed that this was determined by climate and nature herself. Evidently, he did not favour a permanent territorial division of labour based on acquired advantages. List was not entirely opposed to free trade. According to his system, protection would always be of a temporary character, and it was to be limited to the educational or young industry stage of development. Protective measures were considered by him justifiable only in the case of nations which possessed an extensive territory, large population, and natural resources. Universal free trade was his ideal, but it could be realised only when the industrially backward nations were educated up to the level of the more advanced nations by means of protection[1].

Frederick List was the founder of 'scientific protectionism' as distinguished from 'mercantile protectionism.' But he was a protectionist only in a qualified sense of the term. There were, however, other advocates of protection who went very much further than List. They were not content to limit protective measures to young industries, or to articles required for national defence, but wanted to extend them as widely as possible. And in their disputations they used arguments which were not only untenable, but sometimes appeared ludicrous. Thus their

[1] List, National System of Political Economy, Bk. II, Ch. XXVI.

attitude furnished grounds for censure and condemnation. One of the most brilliant economists who attacked the protectionist doctrine was Frederic Bastiat. He employed not only all the fruits of his observation and study, but all the resourses of his wit and humour, to demolish the position of his opponents. In his famous satire on the Candle-makers' Petition he poured ridicule and contempt on the protectionists.[1]

Bastiat, however, did not present the protectionist case in a fair and impartial manner. The chief arguments in favour of protection may be briefly discussed here. In the first place, it is claimed that protection secures diversity of industries. This is true only of countries which are, economically speaking, young. Agriculture is exposed to the freaks of the seasons, while

[1] The imaginary petitioners are made to say: "We are suffering from the intolerable competition of a foreign rival...This rival, who is none other than the sun, wages war to the knife against us, and we suspect that he has been raised up by perfidious Albion... What we pray for is, that it may please you to pass a law ordering the shutting-up of all windows, skylights...by or through which the light of the sun has been in use to enter houses, to the prejudice of the meritorious manufactures with which we flatter ourselves we have accommodated our country—a country which, in gratitude, ought not to abandon us now to a strife so unequal." In anticipation of the possible objection that the grant of their prayer might be hurtful to the consumers, the petitioners are made to reply: "You have ceased to have any right to invoke the interest of the consumer, for, whenever his interest is found opposed to that of a producer, you sacrifice the former. You have done so for the purpose of encouraging labour and increasing employment. In the same reason you should do so again."

manufactures are dependent more upon human effort than upon the gifts of nature. The development of manufacturing industry is also necessary for the social progress of a people. But it takes long to develop manufactures in a country which has been accustomed only to the cultivation of the soil, unless some special encouragement is offered to a portion of the population to change their occupations. But this argument does not hold good of countries which have already succeeded in establishing manufactures.

Secondly, it is argued that protection by encouraging various branches of home industry, makes a community much less dependent upon foreign countries. It is possible that, in time of war, the imported supplies of a country may be cut off by its enemy, and to guard against such a contingency, it may be desirable to encourage the production of all the essential kinds of goods within its own borders, even though it may be more expensive to produce than to buy them in normal times. But this is really a political, and not an economic, argument. Its validity, however, has been admitted by even ardent free traders. The only question is whether or not the premium which has to be paid for such national insurance is too high. England, perhaps, finds it less costly to maintain a large navy which enables her to obtain her food supplies from the most distant parts of the world than to produce the entire quantity of her food at home.

Thirdly, it is asserted that a protective duty falls ultimately on the foreign producer, and, consequently, protection secures the double advantage of taxing the foreigner and of fostering home industry. This argument is valid only in part. It is true that, very often, the foreign manufacturer bears a part of the burden of an import duty in order to retain his market in the importing country. But this is not a matter for rejoicing to the consumer who has to pay a higher price for the article on which the duty is levied. The real test in such a case is, not whether the foreigner suffers, but whether it is worth compelling the home consumer to pay a higher price in order to develop the productive power of the country; in other words, whether an immediate sacrifice is desirable in order to secure an ultimate gain.

The fourth argument in favour of protection is that when a country produces commodities for itself, instead of obtaining them from abroad, the cost and labour of transportation are saved. This argument is wholly fallacious, for goods would never be conveyed from one country to another, unless such conveyance was more profitable than local production.

The fifth argument is that protection helps to raise the wages of labour. The real cause of high wages is the large productiveness of labour, and so far as protection helps to establish successful industries, it does certainly tend to raise wages. It, very often, happens, however, that only nominal wages are raised. In many cases, a rise in wages is accompanied by a rise in prices. How far protection results in a rise of real wages is a matter not entirely free from doubt.

Sixthly, it is argued that protection, having been once established, cannot be removed without causing great loss to employers and employed in the protected industries. While there is a great deal of force in this argument, it is, in fact, an argument against initial protection. It cannot be denied that industries, which have enjoyed protection for a long series of years, suffer considerably when it is withdrawn. But all changes are attended with suffering to some classes of people. When it is found necessary to withdraw protection, the intensity of the suffering may be greatly minimised by making the withdrawal gradual, instead of sudden.[1]

The last and most important argument in favour of protection is the 'infant industry' argument. This, as has already been said, was the main ground on which Frederick List based his theory, and the support lent to it by J. S. Mill added immensely to its value. As an eminent economist puts it, "the really sound arguments in favour of protection are various presentations of the case for aiding infant industries, and unborn infants along with the rest"[2]. Evidently, the applicability of the argument is confined only to countries which are still in the earlier stages of industrial development. But two essential conditions are implied in it. First, the industries selected for protection should be suitable to the country, and secondly, protection ought to be withdrawn as soon as the protected industries are able to stand on their own legs. The first of these conditions is comparatively easy of fulfilment. But the case is quite different with the second. Once protection is established, it is always extremely difficult to abandon it.[3]

[1] *Vide* Fawcett, Free Trade and Protection, Ch. IV.

[2] Flux, Economic Principles, p. 261.

[3] This, in fact, was one of the principal objections urged by Sidgwick against a policy of protection. He said: "I agree, indeed, with these writers in holding, as a conclusion of abstract

This tendency towards the perpetuation of specially favoured interests is an evil of the protective system. Another objectionable feature of the system is that the original object of protection is often lost sight of, and when protection is afforded to one industry, the contagion spreads, and many other industries claim special treatment. Thus industry and trade are diverted from their natural channels, and the remumeration of labour and capital diminishes. Protection also tends to discourage industrial enterprise by weakening the feeling of self-reliance. The encouragement which undesirable combinations like trusts and kartels often receive from protection is another evil of the system. But the worst evil of all is that it fosters political corruption. "There are also to be apprehended,"

economic theory, that Protection, in certain cases and within certain limits, would probably be advantageous to the protecting country,—and even perhaps to the world—if only it could be strictly confined to these cases and kept within these limits; but I am nevertheless strongly of opinion that it is practically best for a Government to adhere to the broad principle of 'taxation for revenue only'—at any rate in a free community where habits of commercial enterprise are fully developed. My ground for this opinion is that I do not think we can reasonably expect our actual Governments to be wise and strong enough to keep their protective interference within due limits; owing to the great difficulty and delicacy of the task of constructing a system of import duties with the double aim of raising revenue equitally and protecting native industry usefully, and the pressure that is certain to be put upon Government to extend its application of the principle of protection if it is once introduced."

Principles of Political Economy, Second Edn., pp. 488, 489.

observe a body of distinguished Professors, "those evils other than material which Protection brings in its train,—the loss of purity in politics, the unfair advantage given to those who wield the power of jobbery and corruption, and the growth of the 'sinister interest."[1]

According to Prof. Smart, the following are the chief evils of a system of protection: It is impossible to devise a tariff which does not permit all manner of anomalies and inequities; it tends to political immorality; it tends to commercial immorality; it raises costs and checks exports; it is bad as judged by the canons of taxation.[2]

A well-known continental economist distinguishes between three groups of protectionist theories, namely, the developmental, the compensatory, and the defensive theories. "The developmental theories," says he, "look upon

[1] The Fourteen Professors' Manifesto, 1903, quoted in Pigou, Protective and Preferential Duties, p. 82. Prof. Sumner describes the evils of protection in the United States in these words: "The continual law-making about industry has been prolific of industrial and political mischief. It has tainted our political life with log-rolling, presidential wire-pulling, lobbying and customs-house politics. It has been intertwined with currency errors all the way along. It has erected privileged classes in the free American community, who were saved from the risks and dangers of business to which the rest of us are liable. It has controlled the election of congressmen, and put inferior men in office, whose inferiority has reacted upon the nation in worse and worse legislation."

[2] Smart, Return to Protection, Chs. X & XII.

world economy as an ideal, but one which cannot be reached immediately, but only by way of a transitional stage of development through protective duties. The compensatory theories seek a solution of the conflicts which arise from the existence side by side of national economy and world economy without concerning themselves with the question of the ultimate goal of the development. The defensive theories, finally, see in national economy itself the permanent form of organisation which on political and economic grounds must defend itself against injurious tendencies originating in the world-economy sphere. According to the last view, the national economy is an organism, while the world economy is merely a community of commercial relations serving the interests of this organism."[1]

While this writer is intensely national in his economic ideas, he is not absolutely hostile to internationalism. In fact, he argues that protectionism is an aid to a proper understanding among the nations of the world : He concludes a well-ordered and properly-balanced study of the subject with the following words : "The protective policy embodies a permanent principle which

[1] J. Grunzel, Economic Protectionism, pp. 141, 142.

varies only in its application, and one which in general must be so manipulated that national economy and world-economy development must be brought into the closest harmony. National economy and world-economy do not stand in a relation of hostile opposition, but rather condition each other. In the economic sense also the truth holds good that he most benefits the world who best serves his own people."[1]

Fair trade, reciprocity, retaliation, and colonial preference are modifications of the system of protection. The supporters of fair trade aim at placing home and foreign producers on an equal footing, with regard to the artificial conditions of production, while leaving undisturbed the natural conditions. Reciprocity is the system under which one nation grants to another certain concessions in respect of the tariff in exchange for similar concessions granted by the other nation. Retaliators hold that free trade is the best system, provided that all countries adopt it. If, however, tariff-walls are raised by foreign countries, they consider it necessary to retaliate in order to convert them to the policy of the 'open door.' The main object of an advocate of colonial preference is to

[1] J. Grunzel, Economic Protectionism, p. 351.

give some economic advantage to his own kith and kin over foreigners in order to draw the former closer to the mother country.[1]

The German Historical School stands midway between the two principal schools of free trade and protection. Knies, one of the chief exponents of this school, said many years ago, "No more the present than any previous economic organisation of society is to be regarded as absolutely good and right, but only as a phase in a continual historical evolution, and that in like manner the more prevalent economic doctrine is not to be received as complete and final, but only as representing a certain stage in the unfolding or progressive manifestation of the truth."[2] Prof. Schmoller, another prominent representative of the school, held the view that neither free trade nor protection was wholly true, but each was true according to circumstances.[3]

While it must be admitted that this view is perfectly sound in substance, the opportunist style of argument adopted by some followers of

[1] Dietzel, Retaliatory Duties.

[2] *Vide* Ingram, History of Political Economy, p. 203.

[3] In regard to the adoption of a policy of free trade by a nation, Prof. Schmoller says, " That age could begin to think and act in the spirit of free trade which had left so far behind it the toilsome work of national development that it regarded its best results a matters of course." P. Ashley, Tariff History.

the Historical School is hardly satisfactory. They go too far in their disregard for theory, and their absolute faith in expediency may often lead to harmful consequences.[1]

The practice of the nations of the world shows something like a consensus in favour of protection. And, strangely enough, the largest countries, with only one exception, are the strongest supporters of the protective system. Even England, which stood fast by free trade for more than three quarters of a century, has now found it expedient to modify its policy to some extent. The key to this situation is to be found in the intermingling of economic and political considerations. Economic protectionism thrives on national sentiment.

Thus we find that, although the theoretic basis of protection is comparatively weak, its hold on the sentiments of nations is strong. On the other hand, in economic science, free trade is still the prevailing idea. The present position of the theory is correctly described by Professor Taussig in these words: "The essence of the

[1] Prof. Taussig says, "I have little patience with this attitude It assumes to be large-minded and judicial, and a certain tinge of contempt for the old-fashioned theories often goes with it. Yet in truth it usually rests on inability or unwillingness to follow the threads of severe reasoning." Free Trade, the Tariff, and Reciprocity, pp. 26-27.

doctrine of Free Trade is that *primâ facie* international trade brings a gain and that restrictions on it presumably bring a loss. Departures from this principle, though by no means impossible of justification, need to prove their case; and if made in view of the pressure of opposing principles, they are matter for regret. In this sense, the doctrine of Free Trade, however widely rejected in the world of politics, holds its own in the sphere of the intellect."[1]

A reconciliation of the two doctrines has recently been attempted by Professor Nicholson. In his opinion, the need of the hour is to combine the best of both systems and to avoid the worst in both. "The real strength of free trade," he says, "lies in the stress laid on the character and initiative of the individual. Its great danger is that unlimited competition may destroy the ideas of nationality and national welfare. The strength of the opposing system is in organisation and in the stress laid on the power of good government. Its great danger is that too much government will destroy the character and force of the individual.[2]

[1] Free Trade, the Tariff, and Reciprocity, p. 27.

[2] War Finance, p. 417.

## CHAPTER VI

### THE RIGHT FISCAL POLICY FOR INDIA

An examination of the theories of free trade and protection has brought us to the conclusion that the tariff problem admits only of relative solution. In other words, the fiscal policy which ought to be adopted by a country at a particular moment should be appropriate to its peculiar circumstances at that moment. Let us now consider the circumstances in which we find India at the present day.

A cursory glance at the foreign trade returns of India brings home to the mind of the observer the significant fact that the bulk of her imports consists of manufactured goods, while raw materials constitute much the greater part of her exports.[1] This is an unnatural state of

[1] The classification adopted in the Government returns is illogical and misleading. In order to form a correct estimate of the character of India's imports and exports, the bulk of the goods shown under the head "Food, Drink, and Tobacco" ought to be added to the list of manufactures in the former case, and to the list of unmanufactured products in the latter. Thus calculated, manufac-

things, and its consequences are extremely harmful. The imports are what are technically known as consumers' goods, while the exports consist mainly of producers' goods. This distinction is a matter of great importance. As things are, the imported goods are consumed exactly at the value shown in the importation statistics. If, on the other hand, the imports were to consist of unfinished articles, their value would be greatly enhanced by the industry of the country before they became fit for consumption.[1] The present situation has another drawback. The exportation of agricultural products means the sending away of the soil. This tendency towards the diminishing fertility of the soil can only be checked by the development of local manufactures.[2] The growth of manufactures is also necessary for affording a greater diversity to the occupations of the people. A purely agricultural country, dependent on the mercy of the monsoons, must always remain subject to periodical visitations

tures represent over 90 per cent. of the total imports; while manufactures and raw produce represent about one-third and two-thirds respectively of the total exports of India.

[1] *Vide* Grunzel, *Economic Protectionism*, p. 133.

[2] J. S. Mill admits that this argument deserves attention on account of the physical truth on which it is founded but he is of opinion that it is not relevant to the question of Protection.-*Principles of Political Economy*, Bk. V., Ch. X., 1.

of the spectre of famine.[1] Besides, agriculture is not a sufficiently remunerative occupation, and a people devoted almost exclusively to it can never hope to make any great progress in material civilisation.[2]

But the worst evil of the present system is to be found in its effect on the character of the people. A community engaged in agriculture is generally found to lack breadth of outlook and to suffer from conservativeness and stagnation. Industrial and commercial occupations, on the other hand, have a tendency to widen the vision of those engaged in them, to develop initiative and enterprise, and to foster a spirit of freedom. Besides, as Ranade said many years ago, "the political domination of one country by another attracts far more attention than the more formidable though unfelt domination, which the capital, enterprise and skill of one country exercise over the trade and manufactures of another. This latter domination has an insidious influence which paralyses the springs of all the activities which

[1] The Famine Commission of 1880 observed, "The failure of the usual rains thus deprives the labouring class, as a whole, not only of the ordinary supplies of food obtainable at prices within their reach, but also of the sole employment by which they can earn the means of procuring it."

[2] The authors of the Report on the Indian Constitutional Reforms correctly appreciated the situation when they remarked, "The economics of a country which depends to so great an extent as India on agriculture must be unstable." P. 210.

together make up the life of the Nation."[1] The magnitude of the evil becomes apparent when the fact is recalled that the political status of a country depends very largely on its economic position.

The solution of the problem can only be found in industrial development. But in order that the trouble and expense involved in industrial effort may not go in vain, it is desirable, at the outset, to consider whether or not India satisfies the conditions essential for the successful development of manufactures. Such conditions are of two kinds, namely, natural and acquired. As for the natural conditions, India has an abundance of natural resources and a large population. The former is the most important requisite of production, and the latter not only ensures the supply of labour, but affords a market for the goods produced by industry. In respect of the acquired factors, however, India is in great defect. Skilled labour is scarce, and industrial expansion is considerably hampered by the absence of technical knowledge on the part of the children of the soil. The supply of capital is inadequate. The people lack enterprise, and business organisation is far from

[1] *Essays on Indian Economics*, Second Edition, p. 105.

perfect. These defects, however, are not irremediable. Technical knowledge and skill can be acquired by education and practical training. Indigenous capital has already begun to overcome its shyness, and development of banking facilities will go a long way towards removing this deficiency. Educated men are now beginning to engage in commerce and industry, and experience will before long enable them to develop the proper sort of business organisation.

Artificial conditions are in the present age becoming more and more decisive as factors in production. But acquired advantages are not the monopoly of any race or nation, and in her possession of natural advantages India has a great superiority over many other countries. The industrial backwardness of India is due, however, in part, to the causes mentioned above, and partly to her political environment. The State in India has in the past not only failed to foster industries, but has actually hindered their development. Even now, the people believe, rightly or wrongly, that, in the industrial struggle the forces of the State are arrayed against them. A feeling of helplessness has thus been induced in the community. To remove the feeling of despair from the minds of the people and to restore their confidence in their own selves, it is absolutely necessary for the Indian Government to adopt a policy of active encouragement of industries. Such a policy will give a feeling of security to the industrialist, afford a stimulus to individual enterprise, and call into being the necessary capital and organisation.

In every civilised country, the industries receive the fostering care of the State. The economic greatness of the United States and Germany has been due, in no small measure, to the efforts of the State. In England also, industry and trade received considerable assistance from the State in the earlier stages of their development. It is true that when these had become well developed, they were able to do without the help of the Government. But now that some difficulty has arisen, State aid is being once more invoked and ungrudgingly offered[1]. What is needed most in India at the present moment is an enlightened system of protection, by which should be understood all those measures which will tend to promote the economic interests of the country.[2]

[1] *Vide* Report of the Committee on Commercial and Industrial Policy after the War.

[2] The authors of the Montagu-Chelmsford Report observed, "English theories as to the appropriate limits of the State's activity

These measures may be either positive or negative. Of the positive measures, the most important appear to be the granting of bounties, subsidies and concessions in suitable cases, the establishment of technical colleges, the provision of credit facilities, the proper regulation of railway and steamship freights, the collection and dissemination of useful information regarding industry and trade, and the local purchase of stores.

A tariff is only one form of protection. Although it is merely a negative measure, it is regarded in most countries as the most effective means of promoting a national economic policy. Freedom of trade and industry ought surely to be the ultimatel goa for India, as for all other nations. But, in the abnormal circumstances in which she finds herself at the present moment, India cannot be expected to derive the same advantage from free trade as the industrially advanced countries. A departure from the present economic policy thus seems to be not only justifiable, but absolutely necessary. Competition of the right sort, no doubt, is good for

are inapplicable to India." And again, "We are agreed therefore that there must be a definite change of view; and that the Government must admit and shoulder its responsibility for furthering the industrial development of the country. . . . Though these are serious difficulties they are not insuperable; but they will be overcome only if the State comes forward boldly as guide and helper". P. 213.

industry and trade in a state of health and vigour. But it would be extremely difficult, if not impossible, for the immature and undeveloped industries of India to stand and survive the competition of the mature and fully-developed industries of countries which have had a long start. The most advanced nations often impose restrictions in the interests of children and weak persons. Freedom of contract, in the case of young children, is described by political philosophers as 'another name for freedom of coercion'. On the same analogy, it would be unreasonable to expect the young industries of India to be able to make proper use of their freedom.

If success is to be achieved, industrial conditions in India must adjust themselves to modern requirements. In fact, the industrial structure in India will have to be built anew. But this cannot be accomplished in a day. The transition from the agricultural to the industrial stage will take time. Some amount of tariff protection is, in the meanwhile, indispensable to offset the temporary lead of the older industrial countries. But there should be discrimination in the application of the principle of protection An "all-round, all-inclusive" protective system cannot possibly be advantageous or beneficial to the country. It is argued by some enthusiastic supporters of a protective policy that an indiscriminate use of protection is necessary in order to create an atmosphere favourable to industrial development.[1] But they forget to count the cost of such a policy or to estimate its probable ultimate gain or loss. The creation of an atmosphere is certainly desirable, but this object can be best attained through some form of voluntary effort, such as the *swadeshi* movement. The difference between such a movement and Government action lies in the element of compulsion always involved in the latter, which may, unless proper safeguards are adopted, produce as much harm as good.

While, therefore, infant industries should be maintained at public expense during the period of their education or apprenticeship, adequate care must be taken so as not to allow protection to run riot. Protection ought to be afforded only to such industries as have a reasonable chance of successful development. When the raw material required for a particular industry is available within the country or can be easily obtained from abroad, when there is an adequate supply of labour, and when there

[1] See Mr. M. Subedar's Evidence before the Indian Fiscal Commission.

is also a ready market at home, there is *primâ facie* ground for believing that the industry is suitable to the circumstances of the country. In this view, protection will be required in two sets of circumstances, namely, first, when an existing industry is struggling against foreign competition, and secondly, when a new industry is established for the sake of an experiment. In the former case, if it is found that the difficulty which the industry encounters does not arise from any natural or inherent disadvantages and that the superiority of the foreign rival consists only in acquired skill or experience, it ought to be assisted by the State. As for a new industry, it is hardly likely that individuals will take the risk attending such an experiment, unless they are guaranteed against possible loss.

The primary object of a tariff is to equalise the conditions of production. But it is not possible to equalise conditions in all industries. It will thus be necessary to discriminate. And great care must be taken in selecting the industries to be protected. The most important among the large-scale manufactures which may be encouraged in the beginning appear to be the following: Steel and iron manufactures, sugar, glass, paper, leather, rubber goods, vegetable oils, silk and woollen goods, and cotton fabrics of the finer sorts.

Iron and steel goods now occupy the second place in order of importance in the list of India's imports. In 1920-21, the total value of imported goods of this description was 31⅓ crores. There is no dearth of raw material for these industries in the country. Steel of a good quality is now being turned out by the Tata Iron and Steel Company. During the war, the Company made great strides, but, at present, foreign competition is beginning again to hit the industry rather hard. A few years ago, it was hoped to establish no less than seventeen subsidiary industries in the vicinity of Jamshedpur, but this has not yet been found possible. The Company is, however, still negotiating for the establishment of plants for the manufacture of railway wagons and locomotives, agricultural implements, wire products, tin-plates, enamelled ironware, cables, and special steel for reinforcement.[1] Two other Companies are also doing good business, and several more have been projected. The manufacture of steel bars, billets, plates and sections of all kinds is increasing. The

[1] Ainscough, *General Review of the Conditions and Prospects of British Trade in India*, 1920-21, p. 60.

engineering workshops in India are trying to compete with foreign manufactures in structural steel work and simple steel engines of all kinds. Jute mill machinery will shortly be produced at Jamshedpur and tea machinery at Agarpara[1]. As steel is a 'key' industry, it fully deserves to be placed on a sound footing by means of protection.

Sugar, during the war period, used to rank second in the list of India's imports. In 1920-21, however, there was a fall in the quantity, which was due to high prices. But, even then, the total value was no less than 18½ crores. India is the largest sugar-producing country of the world. The methods of extraction and preparation are, however, extremely primitive, and the competition of foreign sugar has resulted in a progressive decline of cane cultivation. Sugarcane is one of the most paying crops, and it occupies an important position in maintaining agricultural prosperity. In order that the industry may thrive, it will be necessary to replace the antiquated and wasteful methods which now prevail by up-to-date and scientific processes. But as some time must elapse before this can be done, tariff protection and other measures of

[1] Ainscough, General Review, 1920-21, p. 75.

encouragement must be afforded. A high rate of duty will, of course, prove a hardship to consumers, but as refined sugar is not an article of necessity for the poorest classes of the population, its incidence will not be very widespread. In the opinion of the Sugar Committee, it is perfectly practicable to produce the whole amount of sugar required for consumption in India, and she may even look forward to the time when she will again become an exporting country [1]. The suggestion of the Committee that a Government Pioneer Factory should be established in Upper India deserves consideration.

There is a great demand for glassware in the country. Glass is a bulky article, but the value of the imports was no less than 4 crores in 1920-21. The raw material of glass is nothing but clay of a particular kind, which is available in abundance in the country. There is no reason, therefore, why this manufacture should not prove a success in India.

The raw material for making paper is available in the country in various shapes, such as sabai grass, bamboo, and several varieties of wood. In 1920-21, the imports of paper and paste-board amounted to over 7¼ crores. About

[1] Report of the Sugar Committee, pp. 9 and 10.

one-third of the total consumption is now produced by the Indian mills. If the industry is properly encouraged, it will be quite possible for India to produce not only the whole quantity of paper required for use in the country but also for export to foreign countries.

In the pre-war year 1913-14, the value of exports of raw hides and skins was over 12½ crores. It dwindled down to 5¼ crores in 1920-21. This fall was due in part to the growth of leather manufactures in the country, but mainly to the preference of 10 per cent. granted to the United Kingdom and the Dominions over foreign countries in the rate of the export duty. The chemicals required for the industry are mostly produced locally. With a proper organisation, India ought to be able to convert large quantities of her hides and skins into leather and also to manufacture boots, shoes, and various other kinds of leather goods which are now obtained from abroad.

The importance of rubber manufactures is rapidly growing in India. In 1920-21, the value of imports of this class of goods was no less than Rs. 2½ crores. During the same year, India exported raw rubber of the value of over 1½ crores. The production of rubber can, however, be vastly increased. If rubber manufactures are started in India, there will thus be no lack of raw material, and the home market for the finished product is sure to grow steadily in future. A rubber factory has recently been started in Ceylon, and it is hoped some factories will soon be started in India. But without protection, they will hardly be able to stand on their legs.

Vegetable oils are a species of industry which deserves to be fostered. India's consumption of vegetable oil and cake is large, and is likely to increase with the growth of industries like soap, paints and varnishes. She exports huge quantities of oil seeds every year. In 1913-14, the value of the exports of oil seeds was 24¼ crores, but in 1920-21, it declined to 16⅓ crores. The entire quantity of oil seeds ought to be converted into oil and cake, and the oil should be refined, before any portion of it is exported. It is a strange anomaly that India, with her great resources of this commodity, should obtain vegetable oils from abroad.

Silk and woollen goods require some assistance from the State. At present, considerable quantities of both these kinds of goods are imported into India. In 1920-21, the value of the imports of silk piece-goods was Rs. 4 crores, the bulk of which came from Japan. There are a few silk factories at present working in India, but many more may easily be started. The imports of woollen fabrics amounted last year to over 5½ crores. Before the war, Germany used to supply the bulk of the cheaper kinds of woollen goods, while England sent the finer qualities. For a few years, England was almost without a rival in this trade, although Japan contributed a small proportion of the total supply. But German goods are likely again to flood the Indian market before long. The Indian mills are turning out excellent qualities of woollen goods of various sorts. The most important of these mills are the Lalimli of Cawnpore and the Dhariwal mill in the Punjab. Carpets and rugs of excellent qualities are also produced in different parts of the country, while the hand-made shawls have still retained their excellence. The chief difficulty experienced by the woollen industry is the want of raw material of a good quality. But wool is being imported from other countries, and the industry seems to have a great future before it.

Lastly, we come to cotton manufactures, the largest mill industry of India. The natural conditions in India are quite favourable to the growth of the cotton industry. The local supply of cotton is abundant, and there is a ready market close at hand. Although a considerable part of the demand for cotton goods is met by the local produce, yet their imports amount to nearly one-third of the total imports of the country. In 1920-21, imported cotton goods were valued at Rs. 102 crores, and exceeded any other three classes of imported goods taken together. It is small wonder that in men's minds protection has thus come to be identified with the use of *swadeshi* cloths[1]. As a matter of fact, only a small percentage of the imported goods competes with local produce of a similar character.[2] The coarser kinds of cotton goods are thus able to withstand the competition of Manchester. If the owners of existing mills show greater enterprise, and if some more mills are started, it will be quite possible in the near future to manufacture, within the borders of the

[1] This was an abnormally large figure, and, in 1921-22, the value of imported cotton goods decreased to Rs. 60 crores, which is about the normal figure. Even in this year of boycott and trade depression, the imports of cotton goods exceeded any other single import head.

[2] Mr. A. C. Coubrough points out that, in 1920-21, "the total quantity of piece-goods consumed in India was 400 crores of yards. The amount of piece-goods of similar character to those produced in India was less than 40 crores of yards". He also shows that 75 per cent. of imported piece-goods are non-competitive. See *Notes on Indian Piece-Goods Trade* (Bulletin No. 16).

country, the entire quantity of wearing apparel required by the poorer classes of the population. The absence of a local supply of long-stapled cotton at present offers an obstacle to the manufacture of the finer fabrics, but the successful experiments which have been made in certain parts of the Punjab lead us to hope that this difficulty will soon disappear. This branch of the cotton industry fully deserves to be encouraged. While no protection is required for the coarser kinds of cotton goods, the finer qualities will perhaps need protection for some time to come.

The question of yarn is not free from difficulty. It is highly desirable that Indian mills should produce yarns of the higher counts, and a protective duty would be helpful in this regard. But, on the other hand, as yarn is an earlier stage of manufacture, a duty levied on this article, is likely to prove harmful to the later stage, namely, the manufacture of cloth. On the whole, the balance of advantage would seem to lie in admitting yarn free or in levying only a small duty on yarns of the higher counts, until the mills in India are fully equipped to take advantage of a comparatively high rate of duty.[1]

[1]Mr. Ainscough points out that, although there has been a steady increase in the production of yarn during the past three years, the amount of raw cotton consumed has steadily decreased.

Jute manufactures stand on a footing different from other industries. They have already proved a success in India. There are at present seventy-five jute mills in Bengal, and exports of manufactured jute amount annually to over Rs. 50 crores in value. Before the war, more than one-half of the total exports of jute consisted of the raw material. But the proportion has now considerably diminished. If more mills are established, it will be possible to manufacture the whole of the raw jute within the country. This industry, therefore, does not seem to stand in need of State assistance.

Industries of a comparatively small size ought also to be protected. Cement, pottery, soap, paints and varnishes, cutlery, matches, and stationery articles are classes of goods of which the raw material is available in the country, either wholly or in part, and which have a ready market at home. If they are properly aided, these industries will add to the productive power and wealth of the country. As the industrial

This he takes to be a clear proof that the mills are tending to spin finer counts. (Report for 1920-21, p. 57). But Mr. Ainscough does not apprehend a serious loss in the whole of the cotton goods trade of England. He says, "My personal opinion is that, on balance, our trade with India will continue to increase. The trade we lose in coarse grey goods will be more than made up by increased shipments of the finer cloths due to the steady advance in the prosperity of the country." (P. 99.)

development of the country proceeds, many new industries will also claim the attention of the State.

Chemicals, machinery, and railway plant present some difficulty. The growth of chemical industries is of the greatest importance to the general industrial advancement of the country. They thus deserve encouragement at the hands of the State. But as the price of chemicals enters largely into the production of various kinds of manufactures, these latter are sure to be adversely affected by any import duty that may be imposed on chemicals. A bounty in such a case would seem to be a more suitable form of assistance than tariff protection. Any way, the question will require very careful handling. The same thing may be said of machinery. It would be hardly right for India to continue to depend for an indefinite period on foreign countries for the supply of machines for her manufactories. If she has to take her place among the industrial nations of the world, India must manufacture her own machinery. For such a purpose, India has ample raw material. But a duty on machinery will increase the equipment charges of a factory, and thus prove a handicap to the growth of industry generally.

As for railway plant and stores, any duties levied on them will fall on the entire community, and will, besides, tend to retard the development of transport which is so essential to industrial expansion. This difficulty can, however, be partially solved by the local purchase of stores to the utmost extent possible.

These, indeed, are instances of the possible conflict of interests, which may arise from time to time between different industries. It is not unlikely to happen, on some occasions, that producers of a raw material or of an intermediate product will ask for protection, while manufacturers will oppose them. It is even possible that tariff protection afforded to some industries may result in the crippling of others. The danger of unintelligent interference with industry is always present in a protective system. The details of a policy of protection will thus be no easy matter to settle. But if the earnestness and independence of the Legislature and the honesty and foresight of officials can be ensured, the difficulties will not prove insurmountable. Of course, the general principle which will guide the fiscal authorities in deciding between the rival claims of different industries, will be the balance of advantage to the community as a whole.

The question of rates is important. Some of the classes of goods mentioned above are already subject to duty. But as the present rates were fixed with sole regard to revenue, a reconsideration of the whole matter will be necessary when a protective policy is decided upon. And the determination of the rates will require the exercise of great care and caution. They should be high enough to afford protection, but not so high as to unduly or unnecessarily add to the cost of living. The existing general rates may continue for revenue purposes, unless it is found desirable, on financial grounds, to enhance or reduce them. But special rates should be fixed for purposes of protection. As a rule, a protective duty of 20 or 25 per cent. ought to be sufficient. In exceptional circumstances, however, higher rates may be justifiable. In this connexion, a serious drawback, which is characteristic of high duties, must not be lost sight of. They always have a tendency to encourage smuggling and put a heavy strain on the honesty of officials. In the interests of protection, it will perhaps be found necessary to expand the free list. All raw materials of industry should be allowed to enter the country duty-free.

Market is one of the most important requisites

for the successful development of industry. The primary aim of the future tariff policy of India will thus be to secure the home market for the home produce. A carefully adjusted protective system will enable her to put an end to the present abnormal state of things. But an indiscriminate increase of customs duties will produce harmful consequences. It will not only destroy India's external commerce, but prove harmful to her social as well as her economic life.

While it is necessary to modify the present position of too great dependence of India upon England, it is neither possible nor desirable for her to attain absolute economic independence. We cannot wall ourselves in with high protective tariffs, and the attempt to do so is sure to end in disaster. This will be neither economically good, nor morally justifiable. Isolation would lead to stagnation, which in its turn, would result in degeneration. Besides, inter-dependence of all nations is a higher ideal than economic self-sufficiency. If we look at the question from the practical stand-point, we cannot resist the conclusion that the days of self-containment are gone, and are not likely to return. With the rapid development of means of communication, the world is fast becoming one economic unit.

It should also be remembered that the substitution of domestic production for imports is not necessarily a national gain. The fostering of some industries may entail an unnecessarily heavy burden on the community without securing a corresponding advantage to it. In such cases, protection would mean sheer loss to the nation. The best thing for India to do will, therefore, be to concentrate her energies on the production of such articles as she will find it possible to make, under the changed circumstances, at less cost and with greater efficiency than other countries, and to import those articles which she can buy cheaper than make at home. It is not likely that, for at least some time to come, she will find it advantageous to embark upon the production of goods involving secret processes, or requiring exceptional technical skill or the use of highly specialised machinery, such, for instance, as synthetic dyes, delicate scientific instruments, and watches.

Each industry seeking protection must thus establish the validity of its claim. Protection should begin only when a particular industry is fully equipped to take advantage of it. And it should be continued only for a reasonable period, and not indefinitely. As soon as the protected industry is able to stand on its own legs, or it is found that it has no chance of proving a success, protection should be withdrawn. The exact period for which protection may be afforded will, of course, depend upon the nature of the particular industry and other circumstances. But fifteen years would seem to be a reasonable period in most cases. If, after the lapse of the specified number of years, it is found, as the result of careful examination, that the industry has made satisfactory progress, but that some more time is needed to place it on a footing of stability, the period may be extended. At the end of the term of apprenticeship, every protected industry should be allowed to breathe the vitalising air of freedom. Competition will then give it strength and vigour. To continue protection after the need for it has ceased will be to encourage indolence and inefficiency A policy which seeks to keep the industries of the country in perpetual tutelage can only result in decadence and retrogression. The danger, which Prof. Smart points out,—" once an infant, always an infant ",—is real, and must be guarded against. We want in India strong, healthy industries, not perpetual infants. The great evil of a protective system is the growth of

M

vested interests. This can only be prevented or checked by the formation of a wide-awake public opinion from the very beginning.

The temporary character of a protective duty should be particularly emphasised when the article protected is one of the necessaries for the poorer sections of the community. The immediate tendency of protection is to affect in almost entirely opposite directions the interests of producers and consumers, although, in the long run, their interests are identical. Of course, producers are also consumers, and consumers, generally speaking, are producers of some sort or other. Both these classes are thus, ultimately, benefited equally by an improvement in the general well-being of the community. But in regard to particular commodities, it may frequently happen that, while the producer will derive an unconscionable gain from a protective duty, the consumer will suffer an undeserved loss. It will be the duty of the State always to hold the balance between all parties. On some occasions, it may even be necessary to take into special consideration the interests of the consumers, who are generally the weaker party. It is of the utmost importanee to ensure that the tariff policy of the country is determined for the good of the community as a whole, and is not dictated either by the manufacturers of England or by the mill-owners of India.

While protection should be temporary in most cases, it would be wrong to regard protective policy as a "necessary evil."[1] Most people would rather be inclined to consider it as a necessary good, for protection is advocated in India chiefly as a means of national reconstruction. This, however, is a more or less academic question.

The arguments which have been advanced in favour of withdrawing protection at the earliest possible moment do not, of course, apply to industries which are essential for purposes of defence, or which are of vital importance to the economic life of the people. Such 'pivotal' or 'key' industries will require continued assistance.

Special protection may sometimes be necessary against foreign goods favoured by such measures, as dumping, bounties, subsidies, or transport concessions. Measures like these often have for their object the supplanting of local produce by

[1] It is interesting in this connexion to recall the opinion of Kobatsch, who held that protective measures "are a suitable means of guarding the interests of a particular national economy; they are a necessary evil of historic origin which will disappear as it has come when it has lived its day."

foreign produce with the aid of an artificial advantage. In order to equalise the conditions of production, it may be desirable in such cases to levy a duty on the imported product. But the mere fact that a particular country affords protection to its industries will not be enough to justify the imposition of prohibitory duties in India. These measures may, in fact, be either benignant or malignant. When the object is merely to encourage a young industry, there is no cause for complaint. A case of dumping arises when goods are sold in the Indian market below their cost prices or at prices lower than those at which the goods are currently offered in the country of manufacture. Dumping may, however, be accidental. When the surplus goods of a foreign country are sold at low prices at a time when the home market is in a depressed condition, no objection can reasonably be taken to such sale. When, however, a policy of dumping is resorted to with the deliberate and persistent object of killing an Indian industry, a protective duty would be justifiable as a measure of defence. Such dumping, as has been rightly observed, produces a feeling of insecurity in the corresponding industry of this country, which diminishes the incentive to development.

Anti-dumping measures have been adopted in various countries. In the United States, it is unlawful for any person to import dumped goods into the country. The Tariff Act, 1907, of Canada provides for the levy of a special duty on dumped goods.[1] In India, a special 'anti-dumping' duty, equivalent to the difference between the selling price of the article in this country and its fair market value in the country of origin, may very properly be imposed in order to counteract the evil effects of a foreign dumping policy.

The influence of a protective policy on prices is a matter which should be carefully considered. It is mainly through prices that a protective duty affects the foreign, as compared with the local, produce. The principal use of a tariff is, in fact, to secure differential advantages in markets. But it is extremely difficult to estimate beforehand the possible effect of an import duty on the price of the article on which it is levied. A very small duty may sometimes have no effect on prices at all. But, as a rule, when an import duty is imposed on a commodity, the tendency of the price is to rise by the full extent of the duty. But the actual rise

[1] *Vide* Report of the Committee on Commercial and Industrial Policy After the War, pp. 44—46.

in price is seldom equal to the amount of the duty. The imposition of the duty disturbs the equilibrium of demand and supply, and the price at which a fresh equilibrium is established depends, first, upon the elasticity of the demand, and, secondly, upon the elasticity of the home production as compared with that of the foreign production. If, as a result of the duty, there is no fall in the demand, or if the home production fails to increase, the whole of the duty appears in the price, and, consequently, the entire burden falls on the consumer. If, on the other hand, the demand tends to decrease, or the supply of the home produce shows a tendency to increase, the rise in the price of the article is less than the amount of the duty. In such a case, the burden is borne in part by the foreign producer who, in order to retain the market, is compelled to curtail his profit. Prof. Pigou is right in expressing the view that "a part of the direct burden of import duties is, in general, shifted permanently on to the foreigners."[1]

[1] According to Prof. Pigou, this takes place because the ratio of interchange is altered in favour of the taxing country. Vide *Protective and Preferential Duties*, p. 23.

Prof. Marshall is of opinion that a part of such burden is borne by the foreign producers in the following cases: (1) if one country is the chief consumer of a thing for which another has special natural advantages, a tax on it may cause the exporters to work at barely remunerative prices; (2) when producers in one country

Prof. L. V. Birck, a Dutch economist, draws attention to another side of the question. He says, "The duty, which increases the price at home, will often depress the world-price. The consumers of the importing country, who must now pay import duty, are not able to pay as much for the goods, duty unpaid, as they were before, while the duty has further caused an increase in the quantity in the country itself, which again means a smaller demand on the world market."[1]

The main object of a protective duty is to secure an increase in the price of the commodity protected, and if the price fails to rise, this object is partly frustrated. It is not, however, wholly frustrated, because the fact that the foreign producer is compelled to work under less advantageous conditions is an indirect gain to the home producer. But whether the rise in

have set themselves to cater for the special requirements of another, they will go a long way towards meeting any import duty that is suddenly sprung upon them, until they have made other arrangements for utilising their resources; (3) when a particular brand yields monopoly profits high above the normal, such profits can be annexed in part.

Mr. J. A. Hobson, on the other hand, holds that "the ordinary notion that 'the foreigner will pay' the import duty, is void of substance. The circumstances under which he would bear some portion of the duty are so rare and so incalculable that no government officials could be safely entrusted with the adjustment of such a tariff." *Taxation in the New State*, p. 134.

[1] *The Theory of Marginal Value*, p. 257.

price is large or small, there is, as a rule, some rise. Moreover, the increase is not always limited to the prices of the dutiable goods alone. A change in the price of one commodity influences the consumption and, therefore, the prices of other commodities. It is also necessary to determine the effect of protective duties on production-costs. If the costs of production of protected articles rise along with the rise in their prices, no advantage is gained. But profits can be secured if duties are levied in such a way that production-costs may not rise at all or rise to a less extent than the rise in prices.

The rise in prices is temporary or permanent according as the effect of a protective duty is wholesome or otherwise. It may happen that the imposition of the duty will lead to the investment of larger capital in the industry, the adoption of improved methods of production, and the establishment of new factories. In such a case, the increase in the size of the enterprise, securing economies in natural resources, labour, and capital, and making organisation more efficient, will reduce production-costs, and the growth of local competition will ultimately bring down prices. On the other hand, it is possible that the protected manufacturers will remain satisfied with the gain secured to them by the duty, instead of exerting themselves to improve the industry. The rise in the price will then tend to become permanent.

When, as the result of the policy of protection, foreign competition is eliminated, the price of the article in question will be determined by competition among domestic producers. It is not improbable that, under such circumstances, the protected manufacturers will combine in order to maintain a quasi-monopoly price. The State will then find it necessary to take prompt action. And one or all of the following courses will be open to it. Protection may be withdrawn as soon as such an undesirable effect manifests itself, or some legislative measure may be enacted to declare such combination illegal, or a special tax may be levied on the excess profits of the enterprise. The legitimate object of protection is to foster industries, and not to put large profits into the pockets of manufacturers. Under no circumstances, would the State be justified in taxing the poor to benefit the rich.

A tariff is often described in Europe and America as the 'mother of trusts,' and in so far as this description is correct, it must be regarded as an evil. But combinations, in themselves, are not undesirable. They often lead to the maximum efficiency of machinery, capital, labour, and administration. But when they become monopolies, and their real object is found to be, not the perfecting of organisation, but the regulation of output and prices so as to earn unconscionably high profits, they must be discouraged.[1]

Speaking in a general way, it may be said that protective duties will tend to add to the cost of living. Such disadvantage is likely, however, to be counterbalanced, in part, if not wholly, by an increase in the income of at least some classes of the population, provided the right commodities are selected for protection. The establishment of new industries will increase the demand for labour, and, consequently, wages will rise. This rise in the wages of industrial labourers will affect the wages of agricultural labourers, for there is no hard and fast line of division between these two classes of wage-earners. The middle classes will gain in so far as the managers, supervisors, and clerks will be drawn from these strata of society. The

[1] The Committee on Commercial and Industrial Policy point out that the attempts made in different countries to establish State control of monopolies have been directed towards (1) judicial and administrative regulation and limitation, and (2) the securing of publicity.

remuneration of capital is likely also to increase. Whether or not the increase in the incomes of the different classes of the community will compensate them for the loss suffered by them in the shape of the addition to the cost of living is a matter which time alone will show. But it is probable that capitalists and wage-earners will be benefited by the new policy to a greater extent than the men belonging to the clean-handed or the learned professions.

It is more than probable that the adoption of a protective policy by India will induce foreign firms to establish themselves in the country in order to get the benefit of the protective tariff. The authors of the Report on Constitutional Reforms expressed the belief that the protected industries would be "largely financed by foreign capital attracted by the tariff." Mr. T. N. Ainscough, Senior Trade Commissioner for England in India and Ceylon, suggests in several parts of his two interesting Reports that British manufacturers should start branch factories in India. And when British firms establish themselves here, other foreign firms will soon follow suit. It would certainly be wrong to object to such establishment on the mere ground that the owners of these concerns are persons of foreign extraction. A feeling of antipathy towards foreigners ought to be strongly deprecated. But the treatment which Indians have in the past received at the hands of foreign capitalists cannot but make them apprehensive in regard to the future. It has always been the policy of the Government of India not only to maintain an open door in this respect, but to attract foreign capital to the country by various inducements. As a result of this policy the profits of industry have left the country to swell the riches of foreign nations. And the only benefit which the people have so far derived from the prosperous foreign undertakings has been, to use the words of a British official, that a certain number have earned wages "in subordinate positions, or by doing coolie work."[1]

Exploitation has, indeed, been the watchword of foreign capitalists. And in this work they have always received the fullest measure of support from the Government. Not only has no stimulus been afforded to indigenous enterprise, but foreigners have been favoured as against the children of the soil. No attempt has been made to conserve the mineral resources of the country, and the well-being of the labourers has,

[1] Sir A. Chatterton, *Notes on Industrial Work in India*, 1905.

until recently, been sadly neglected. But there is nothing in this to cause surprise. Discussing the different aspects of the question of the export and import of capital in an admirable work, a well-known writer observes: "History shows that capital may be used for purposes of *exploitation* in the worst sense of the word. European relations with India in earlier times, and in more recent years with parts of Africa and South America, are particularly flagrant examples. Capital has been employed in numerous instances to drain countries of their resources, to weaken them economically, and to degrade them morally."[1]

It was the fear of further exploitation which led ardent patriots like Dadabhai Naoroji and Gopal Krishna Gokhale to hesitate to ask for a protective policy for India. They apprehended that the benefits of protection would be reaped by foreign capitalists, while the poor people of India would be saddled with taxes.[2] But even

[1] C. K. Hobson, *Export of Capital*, p. xiv.

[2] Dadabhai Naoroji wrote many years ago: "India sorely needs the aid of English capital; but it is English capital she needs, and not the English invasion to come also, and eat up both capital and produce." *Poverty and Un-British Rule in India*, p. 229.

Mr. G. K. Gokhale said in 1911: "There are two kinds of protection, the right kind and the wrong kind. . . . Influential interests, influential combinations, influential parties in England, who can have ready access to the Secretary of State, to whom we have no access, will not fail to take the fullest advantage of the

more serious than economic exploitation is the danger of political influence[1]. It is unfortunately true that the influence of the European mercantile community of India is often exercised in opposition to the political rights and aspirations of the people. One cannot fail in this connection to recall the various acts of oppression committed by the indigo-planters about the middle of the last century in Bengal, and in more recent years in Champaran.[2]

Some incidental disadvantages of foreign capital are also worth noting. Any considerable importation of foreign capital will lead to an increase of what are called the Home Charges, the amount of which is already large. Besides, as such capital will be imported in the shape of

situation, and this huge engine of protection, which is a vast power, will be employed, not in the interests of the people of India, but in the interests of those parties." And again: "The factories which will receive the protection are those run on European lines, and it is no use disguising the fact that most of these factories are in European hands, and the profits go to Englishmen." Mr. Bhupendra Nath Basu also expressed similar sentiments. *Vide* Debate in the Indian Legislative Council, March, 9, 1921.

[1] With regard to the political danger arising from foreign capital, C. K. Hobson says, "In cases where the borrowing country is weak, lenders may consider that their interests are best served by encroaching upon the political independence of the borrower, and the government policy of the lending State may be formed accordingly." *Export of Capital*, p. xxi.

[2] For detailed accounts of the indigo troubles in Bengal, see Buckland, *Bengul under Lieutenant-Governors* and Mitra, *Indigo Disturbances* Sir Sankaran Nair's Note of Dissent to the Despatches of the Government of India, 1919, gives a short but accurate account of the distress in Champaran.

goods, the large influx of foreign goods will prove harmful to indigenous industries. Lastly, the organisers of foreign concerns will, more often than not, import the stores necessary for their use from their own countries, thus retarding the industrial development of India.

Adequate safeguards are, therefore, needed to prevent the evils which usually accompany foreign capital. It is necessary in this connexion to remember the distinction between loan capital and entrepreneurs' capital. In the former case, only the interest goes out of the country; in the latter, the profit as well. The history of other countries tells us that it is only in the earlier stages of industrial development that foreign entrepreneurs' capital is considered necessary. As a country progresses in industrialization, every effort is made to replace entrepreneurs' capital by loan capital, which, to use the words of a well-known economist, "leaves in the possession of the debtor country the excess of its earnings above interest, thus operating to enrich the latter more rapidly and at the same time eliminating the unavoidable personal influence of the foreign capitalist on the domestic economic policy"[1]. If the want of capital be found to

[1] Grunzel, *Economic Protectionism* p. 254.

prove a real hindrance to industrial development by indigenous agency, the Government may borrow in Europe or America, and lend to Indian industrialists. The loan market is now becoming more and more international, and as the credit of the Indian Government is good, there ought to be no difficulty in obtaining the necessary amount of loan capital.

Of course, no one will grudge to pay the legitimate rate of interest for the use of capital, such as is paid by borrowers in other countries. What in India is really objected to is not so much foreign capital, as control of industrial enterprises by foreigners. At present, a substantial proportion of the capital invested in concerns managed by Europeans is owned by Indians, but there are extremely few Indians on their Directorate Boards or in any positions of real responsibility and influence. One remedy for the present state of things is to encourage mixed enterprises which offer equal opportunities to Indian and European capital, skill, and organising ability. The promoters of prospective foreign ventures may be compelled to open their shares to Indians as well to Europeans. To facilitate the attainment of this object, all flotations should be in rupee currency. Further, the law relating to the formation of Companies may be so amended as to provide for the adoption of a system of proportional representation for the election of the Directors of every Company or to make the appointment of at least one-half of the Directorate Indian in personnel. Similarly, the existing foreign concerns may be partly nationalised. If the foreigners obstinately refuse to come to reasonable terms, a penalty in the shape of an excise duty or sales tax may have to be thought of.

It would be very desirable to avoid all racial questions in matters connected with trade and industry. But this would be possible only when the foreign entrepreneurs who derive so much benefit from their connexion with India agree to accord fair and equal treatment to Indians. Of course, if foreigners set up their skill in the country and impart it to the people, all cause for dissatisfaction will disappear[1]. But if they continue their present policy of domination and exclusion, things are sure to go from bad to worse.

[1] It is interesting in this connexion to note that Count Okuma advocated the admission of foreign capital into Japan; but he wrote, "In such an event, however, foreign capitalists intending to invest in Japanese industries should recognise the advisability of teaching the working of such industries to the Japanese, for if they insist upon employing officers, engineers and workmen of their own nationalities, it is likely that they will find their undertakings to be failures, or, at the best, to yield only small profits". *Fifty Years of New Japan*, Vol. I, p. 642.

Now that India is self-conscious, it is not likely that she will allow her children to remain any longer in the position of hewers of wood and drawers of water, even in fields industrial.

We come now to excise duties. Such duties as are imposed on alcoholic liquors and other intoxicants call for no comment. But countervailing excise duties are of a different character. The theoretical justification for the imposition of such duties is to uphold free trade principles. These duties were originally levied in India to neutralise the protective character of the cotton import duties. The injustice of the measure was so great that it called forth remonstrances from all fair-minded persons, including some high British officials.[1] If a policy of protection is now adopted, there will be no room for excise duties. These duties tend to discourage local production. Besides, their assessment and collection involve a searching enquiry into production and the use of an expensive and cumbersome machinery.

Prof. Pigou is of opinion that a somewhat

[1] Mr. C. C. Stevens said in 1894: "It certainly appears at first sight to be driving the doctrine of free trade rather hard to invite the legislature of a country to impose a somewhat troublesome and unproductive tax, in order that its own manufactures may be free from the suspicion of advantage, however slight, over imported goods". Proceedings, Imperial Legislative Council, 27th December, 1894.

greater advantage would be obtained by a taxing country if a given revenue were collected by a protective import duty, instead of by a customs *plus* excise duty. There is, however, reason to expect that the latter method of raising revenue would, in general, have a smaller effect in raising the price of the taxed article, and, therefore, in injuring consumers. But he holds that, on the other hand, a part of the injury to consumers inflicted by protective duties is compensated by a gain to producers within the country, whereas no part of the injury inflicted by a customs *plus* excise duty is thus compensated.[1]

It is true that the burden of a countervailing excise duty tends to fall on the producer, rather than on the consumer. But the greater part of the cotton excise duty is not countervailing, for the Indian cotton goods which compete with foreign manufactures are only a small fraction of the total of goods on which the duty is levied. In respect of the bulk of cotton goods, therefore, the duty falls on the consumer. The only ground on which an excise duty can reasonably be supported in India is the small measure of protection which it affords

[1] Protective and Preferential Duties, Ch. 1.

to the hand-loom industry. It would be going beyond the scope of this subject to discuss whether the financial exigencies of the Government would justify the imposition of a tax in itself so objectionable[1].

Export duties stand on a footing entirely different from that of import duties. The burden of an export duty falls on the domestic producer, unless the article happens to belong to the category of a monopoly in which case it is borne by the foreign consumer. Ordinarily, therefore, an export duty places domestic produce at a disadvantage as compared with foreign goods in the foreign market, and thus tends to discourage home production. Such a duty should, therefore, be imposed only if there are special reasons for its imposition. At present, revenue considerations dominate the policy underlying export duties. But here also, a policy of protection, if applied with due care and forethought, may prove useful for purposes of industrial development. Sometimes, it may be desirable to levy export duties on raw materials

[1] In 1911, Mr. M. B. Dadabhoy moved a resolution in the Imperial Legislative Council, urging the abolition of the cotton excise duty. It was supported by the leading Indian members and also by Sir Sassoon David representing an important section of the European mercantile community. But it was opposed by the Government on the ground of loss of revenue and also of possible injury to the hand-loom industry. *Vide* Proceedings, 9th March, 1911.

in order to encourage their manufacture within the country. A duty on hides and skins is a case in point. Unfortunately, however, the present duty of 15 per cent. is coupled with a rebate of 10 per cent., for which there is no justification whatsoever. A strong case can also be made out for an export duty on oil seeds. There is bound to be a continuous demand for this commodity in the home as well as the foreign market, and the local manufacture of the raw material is desirable from many points of view. A home market is more certain and steady than a foreign market, and the conditions in the former are better known than in the latter. A small export duty may, on similar though not equally strong grounds, be suggested on cotton. The retention in the country of bones and other kinds of manure may be secured by means of an export duty, and this expedient would also be justifiable for conserving the mineral resources of the country.

But it would not be advisable to extend this policy too far. A high duty may drive the buyers to look for substitutes for the protected articles. And our unfortunate experience in the past ought to make us careful as to the future. The saltpetre industry was practically killed by the high duty imposed on it. Indigo also suffered to some extent from the burden of the export duty. An addition to the export duty on jute is sometimes advocated in some quarters. Whatever may be said in favour of an increased duty on raw jute, it would be very unwise to increase the burden on the manufactured article. In this regard, the discussion as to whether jute is an absolute, or only a conditional, monopoly appears to be of merely academic importance. From the practical stand-point, it would be safe to regard jute as a temporary monopoly. Efforts are being made in Germany to find substitutes for jute, and if the price of the article is artificially raised, the industry is sure to be in great danger. There is one feature with regard to jute which introduces a special difficulty into the question. Jute is grown only in one province of India. The other provinces are not concerned in the production, but they are all interested in the revenue which is derived from this source. The temptation is thus strong to raise a large income by taxing this article. But unless the temptation is resisted, they may, though unwittingly, kill the goose that lays golden eggs.

The question of an export duty on food-stuffs is beset with difficulties. It is open to doubt whether there is, in a normal year, any exportable surplus of food-grains in the country. Some persons, whose opinions are entitled to weight, hold that the total production of food in India is not sufficient for her own consumption, and if everybody were to be adequately fed, she would be a food importing, not exporting, country. The matter demands a full investigation. As the question stands at present there is something to be said on either side of it. The export of food grains causes a rise in their prices. Now, every person in the country is a consumer of food. The rise in the prices thus affects the whole community. From one point of view, therefore, the levy of an export duty, which restricts the exportation of food, may be regarded as beneficial to the community. But, on the other hand, it is argued that agriculturists, who are mostly poor, and who constitute the bulk of the population, are benefited by the high prices of food-grains under a system of free export, and the well-to-do classes can easily afford to bear a slightly higher burden. In this connexion, it is necessary to enquire whether the increase in the prices due to foreign demand actually reaches the cultivator, or is intercepted by middlemen. If the cultivator gets the benefit, the case for free export becomes strong. But if the enhanced price goes to enrich the *mahajans* or the enterprising foreign firms, many economists would support a restriction of export by means of an export duty.

Another argument against restrictions is that a fall in value, artificially created, may lead to the substitution of non-food crops for food-stuffs. It must be admitted that there is great deal of force in this argument. But, of course, none of these arguments would apply to periods of famine or scarcity. In such circumstances, not only an export duty, but even absolute prohibition, would be justifiable. But control of exportation would hardly be desirable even in such cases, for interference by Government officers with the course of trade has come to be associated in the public mind with dishonesty and favouritism.

Import duties in India are partly specific, and partly *ad valorem*. The chief merit of specific duties lies in the ease with which they are administered. But they are inequitable in incidence, inasmuch as they fall more heavily on cheaper varieties of goods. They are thus opposed to the doctrine of ability in taxation. On the other hand, *ad valorem* duties are difficult to administer; but they are more equitable. For the levy of duties *ad valorem* in India, sometimes the invoice values are considered; in other cases, conventional values are fixed for definite periods. On the other hand, in countries like the United States, the goods are taxed according to their value in the local market at the time of assessment. From the administrative standpoint, the Indian system is preferable to the American, but it is less responsive to variations in prices. As a means of affording protection to industry, the latter method is more effective. But it makes so great a demand on the efficiency and honesty of officials that it would be hardly desirable to urge its introduction into the Indian financial system at the present moment.

We come now to the question. What effect will a policy of protection have on the foreign trade of India? This question is not so easy to answer as appears at first sight. One thing, however, is certain, namely, that there will be a change in the character of the trade. India will no longer remain an exporter of raw materials and an importer of finished goods; but these two classes of goods will figure more or less equally on the import and export sides of her transactions. Whether or not there will be a diminution in the total volume of the foreign trade is more than can be prophesied at present. But even if there be some diminution in volume, it would not be injurious to the best interests of the country. The present trade position of India is wholly abnormal. As has been observed by a well-known writer, the annual statistics of the external commerce of India are not, as in the case of other countries, a barometer of the progress and prosperity of the nation[1]. On the other hand, as has been explained in a previous chapter, her foreign trade has grown at the expense of her indigenous industries and her internal trade. The trade returns of India are thus an index of her economic weakness rather than strength. In no country are the interests of foreign trade and local production always and necessarily identical, and in India they have been, and at the present moment are, almost diametrically opposed to each other.[2]

[1] J. W. Root, *Trade Relations of the British Empire*, Ch. V.

[2] L. S. Amery says, "The volume of trade, more specially, the volume of foreign trade, bears no relation whatever to the total national production or to the national well-being dependent upon it. The national interest in foreign trade lies not in the volume of that trade, but wholly in its character as providing sustenance for industry or opportunity of employment." *Fundamental Fallacies of Free Trade*, p. 98. So also, H. Hirst writes: "If trade is to be profitable to any country in proportion to its volume, it is essential that it should busy itself only with the import of such commodities as the land is incapable of growing or producing, and with the largest export of such commodities as

The future well-being of the country will thus depend not upon the growth of its foreign trade but upon its internal development. A wise policy of protection will lead to industrial expansion, which will far outweigh any possible disadvantage arising from the contraction of its external commerce. It need not, however, be apprehended that the possible decrease in the volume of India's foreign trade will be so great as to affect in any appreciable degree her balance of trade. Moreover, such diminution is likely to be only temporary. The increasing industrialisation of the country will continually add to the purchasing power of the people. Besides, as industrial expansion proceeds, India will produce more and more for foreign markets, instead of remaining satisfied with the home market. And in proportion as her exports increase, she will be in a position to buy more goods from abroad.

So far we have confined our attention to large-scale industries and small organised industries.

the land can and does pxoduce". *Some Business Aspects of Tariff Reform*, p. 3.

This view receives support from J. Grunzel, who says: "When an amount equal to or exceeding that which is gained in foreign trade is lost through the restriction of home production, then there is no gain, but eventually a loss is suffered. Importation and exportation do not stand in relation of direct communication, but are separated from each other by production and consumption, and hence a continually favourable inner economic balance may be able to offset an unfavourable outward economic balance." *Economic Protectionism*, p. 131.

But it would not be wise to neglect cottage industries altogether. Apart from their moral value,—and Economics being intimately related to Ethics, moral considerations cannot be wholly ignored,—the economic importance of cottage industries is very great. Every encouragement should, therefore, be afforded to them. Very little can, however, be done in this direction by means of the tariff. But bounties or subsidies may, in carefully selected cases, be of considerable assistance. The hand industries of weaving and spinning are now in a decadent condition, but they still offer employment to large numbers of people. Their greatest usefulness is that they keep agriculturists employed during the off season, when otherwise they would have remained idle. During these months of the year, the labour of the cultivators and of the members of their families has practically no exchange-value, and the earnings derived from weaving and spinning, though small, help to supplement their income from agricultural work. Hand spinning also offers employment to widows and other persons who are incapable of doing out-door work. The finer fabrics produced by hand have a beauty and excellence which have enabled them to withstand, to some extent at least, the competition of mill-made cloths. But the coarser kinds of cotton goods have always tended to disappear as soon as they have come into rivalry with the produce of the mills.

Weaving and spinning are industries in which the interests of the producers are nearly co-extensive with the interests of the consumers, and it is extremely desirable to save them from ruin. A great deal can be done by introducing improved appliances, securing for the hand workers better credit facilities, and teaching them better methods of marketing. But the main solution of the problem is to be found in co-operation. The $3\frac{1}{2}$ per cent. excise duty on the produce of the mills is some advantage to the hand-weavers. But this small measure of protection will be of little use to the industry unless more effective methods are adopted for its resuscitation.

The investigation of various questions, both scientific and administrative, connected with the tariff, will require the establishment of a permanent organisation. Of course, the final decision of questions of fiscal policy will rest, not with this body, but with the Indian Legislature. It may, however, contribute towards intelligent discussion by supplying the necessary information. The Tariff Board will collect all available data on the tariff laws of different countries and the economic and other conditions under which foreign industries work as compared with the industries of India. It will constantly scrutinise the returns of the internal as well as the external trade of India, and carry out large schemes of investigation from time to time. It will enquire into the operation of the customs system of the country including questions relating to railway rates and shipping freights. The Tariff Board will be in close touch with the Industrial Departments of the Government of India and the Provincial Governments, and will keep a watchful eye on the progress of the various industries, specially those which are protected by the tariff. Lastly, it will be the duty of the Board to investigate the claims of particular industries for State assistance and to suggest changes in the customs laws of the country.

The functions of the Tariff Board should be of a purely advisory character, and it should not be invested with either legislative or administrative powers. No attempt should be made to take tariff questions out of the hands of the Indian Legislature. As Prof. Taussig, President of the first Tariff Commission of the United States, says, "No body, however expert, can settle, still less dictate, the position which the country shall take on controverted political and industrial questions."

The constitution of such a Board must be devised with great care. The President of the Board should be a judicial officer of high standing or an eminent lawyer, and he should be assisted by a whole-time expert as Secretary. There should be two other members of the Board, both of whom should be non-officials elected by the Legislative Assmbly. The Legislature should elect only such persons as have no private interests of their own to serve, and are able to consider questions relating to the tariff with a sole regard to the welfare of the country. Economists and public men possessing a full and detailed knowledge of the industrial conditions of the country but not connected, either directly or indirectly, with any industrial or commercial concerns, will be fit persons to serve on the Board. On particular occasions, when matters relating to particular industries are under consideration, representatives of such industries and also of the general public may be appointed as co-opted members or assessors, with power to take part in the deliberations, but not to vote. Sinister influence is the chief danger of a protective system, and must be avoided at all costs. No pains should be spared to secure and maintain the honesty, efficiency, and independence of the Tariff Board.

The conclusion arrived at as a result of a detailed discussion of the tariff question is that a protective policy, wisely applied, will be helpful to the economic reconstruction of India, and will give her a place among the advanced nations of the world. Protective duties will, very probably, add to the cost of living. But a price has to be paid for everything that is worth having. Future gain can only be secured by present sacrifice. The development of productive power is of the utmost importance to the welfare of the country and, in order to secure this object, the people will surely agree to bear the burden of protective duties. Ultimately, the loss is likely to be more than counterbalanced by the gain. The way in which a protective tax is expected to affect the dormant economic forces of a country like India cannot be better described than in the words of Prof. Marshall: "A protective tax", he says, "which helps a young industry to develop its latent strength, may be in the interest of an undeveloped country; even though the tax must inevitably do some hurt to those few industries, which are manufacturing for exportation. For the energy developed in a few high-class progressive industries may spread over a great part of the industrial system of the country ; just as when an iron screen concentrates the whole draught of the chimney on a small part of a nascent fire, it may generate an intense local heat, which spreads and pioneers the way for a broad, strong fire"[1].

But tariff protection alone will not solve the problem of the industrial regeneration of India. Those who expect that a tariff will work wonders are sure to be disappointed in the end. Protection will prove useful if, simultaneously with its adoption, there is a growth of individual enterprise. The State also must adopt various measures to encourage industries. Pioneering and demonstration may often be found extremely useful. Subsidies and bounties may be granted in suitable cases, and dividends may sometimes be guaranteed to Indian Companies so that they may be encouraged to start new industries. At present, foreign imports receive indirect bounties in the shape of preferential rates in transportation both by sea and land. The present policy of the Railway Administrations in India

[1] *After-War Problems*, p. 333.

is to favour foreign goods at the expense of indigenous products. This position ought to be reversed. Internal traffic should, wherever possible, be given greater facilities than traffic with the ports. Freight-rate concessions should be granted to nascent industries, particularly for the carriage of raw materials. In Germany and Belgium, the railways have been used as an instrument for the development of indigenous industries with the most wonderful results[1]. An effort should be made to build an Indian mercantile marine. At present, the whole of the external trade of India is conveyed on foreign vessels, and, naturally, it is directed in the interests of foreigners. If India can develop a shipping industry of her own, it will greatly benefit the economic development of the country[2]. Proper banking facilities should be afforded to indigenous manufactures. A comprehensive scheme of technical instruction should also be devised. But even more important than technical education in schools and colleges is the training of apprentices in factories. It should

[1] *Vide* the opinion of Mr. Lloyd George, quoted in Mr. S. C. Ghose's pamphlet, *State Management of Indian Railways*.

[2] Fisk says, "As a general principle of economics, if we can justify protection to manufactures and agriculture, we certainly cannot deny the right of navigation to an equal consideration." *International Commercial Policies*, p. 247.

be made obligatory on all foreign concerns in India that they should train a number of Indian apprentices[1], and the High Commissioner for India in England should make it a condition of the purchase of stores from British firms that they should admit Indians to apprenticeship.

But the most effective way in which the State will be able to assist Indian industries will be by the local purchase of stores required for the use of the various departments of the State including the railways. The Industrial Commission of 1916-18 reported that the manufacturing capacity of the country had in the past been far from sufficiently utilised by the Government, and this opinion was endorsed by the Stores Purchase Committee, who recommended "the acceptance by the Government of India, as a definite policy, of the principle that all articles required for the public service should be obtained in India, whenever they are procurable in the local market of suitable quality and reasonable price, as well as that preference should be given in all cases to indigenous articles or to those of

[1]On the question of the employment of Indians on the Railway of India, the Indian Railway Committee observed: "The 7,000 (Europeans) were like a thin film of oil on the top of a glass of water resting upon but hardly mixing with the 700,000 below. None of the highest posts are occupied by Indians; very few even of the higher." Report, p. 58. The Committee strongly urged the training of Indians in all the branches of railway activity.

local manufacture, except where it is manifestly disadvantageous to do so." In the matter of industrial development, the Government of India should adopt the enlightened policy pursued by the United States, Germany, and Japan.[1]

Now, supposing India has a protective tariff, the question will be, what use to make of it? It is suggested in some quarters that the Indian tariff should be used as an instrument for bargaining with other countries. It is true that most of the advanced countries adopt this method to further their industrial and commercial policies. But it is open to doubt if India would be wise in following the practice of those countries in this respect. A tariff is at best a dangerous weapon, and if clumsily handled, it is likely to do more harm to the user than to his adversary. Moreover, as has been rightly observed, tariffs are like armaments; when one country increases them, others do the same. India's fiscal policy should, therefore, be one of defence and not of offence. A tariff war is a costly business, and

[1] Count Okuma gives a full account of the various measures adopted by the State to promote industrial development in Japan. Vide *Fifty Years of New Japan*, Vol. 1. Mr. T. M. Ainscough says, "The foreign policy of Japan is primarily a forward and active commercial policy. This cohesion and co-operation of all interests for the general welfare is carried to a degree which is not experienced in the case of any other nation." Report 1919, p. 15.

the prospects of success are not always certain.[1] Besides, regenerated India must try to live up to a higher ideal than that of national selfishness and jealousy. A tariff war should, therefore, be the last thing to be thought of by a patriotic Indian as a policy conducive to the welfare of his country.

It remains now to consider the effect of a tariff on the income of the State. There is an intimate connection between the industry of the people and the finances of the Government. Other things being equal, when the one prospers, the other prospers also. If, therefore, as is expected, a protective tariff proves a success, it will lead to an augmentation of the resources of the State. Until recently, revenue was the sole purpose for which customs duties were imposed in India. But, in future, protection, as well as revenue, will be the object of the Indian tariff. Within reasonable limits, the tariff may be able to serve both these purposes; but if pushed to either extreme, the two ends will

[1] The Committee on Industrial and Commercial Policy after the War observe: "There is a tendency to exaggerate the utility of a tariff to any one country in obtaining a reduction of the tariffs of other countries. It is common experience that both sides to an approaching negotiation start by raising their tariff rates to levels higher than are actually held to be requisite for their respective economic interests, so as to leave ample margin for negotiations, and it is rare that the discussions have ended in the reduction by either side of rates below those previously in force, unless such reduction had in fact been decided from the first". *Vide* Report, p. 49.

perhaps become inconsistent with each other. A moderate tariff will thus be the best from the financial stand-point.

As a tariff implies indirect taxation, we are confronted with the question, namely, whether direct or indirect taxation is the more eligible form. A tax is unpopular all the world over; but a direct tax is more so than an indirect one. The very reason, however, which accounts for the disagreeableness of a direct tax makes it preferable. The tax-payer knows exactly how much he contributes to the revenue of the State, and he makes it his business to enquire how the amount is spent. Another great merit of a direct tax is that, if properly graduated, its burden tends to fall more heavily on those who are able to bear it with comparative ease than on the less fortunate classes of society. Again, the incidence of a direct tax is easier to determine than that of an indirect tax. On the other hand, a direct tax is somewhat inquisitorial in its nature, which an indirect tax is not. It is also an advantage on the side of an indirect tax that the payment is made in a manner and at a time likely to be convenient to the tax-payer.[1] But the tendency towards regression

[1] *Vide* Mill, *Principles of Political Economy.*

or inverse graduation is the great defect of an indirect tax.[1] In comparatively backward countries, and specially in countries governed autocratically, indirect taxation is always preferred to direct taxation. But as a community progresses, it tends more and more to rely upon direct taxes as the chief source of revenue for the State.

In India, the Government, until comparatively recent times, shrank from any recourse to direct taxation, lest it might give rise to discontent. Non-official opinion, particularly among the richer classes, both European and Indian, has also been in favour of avoiding direct taxation as much as possible.[2] But now that some form of popular government is about to be established in the country, it will be desirable to combine direct and indirect taxes in such a

[1] Prof. Marshall says : "Many such (indirect) taxes press with heaviest weight on the poorest classes, and with no appreciable weight on the rich ; while those which fall chiefly on the consumption of the rich, have never been made to yield a large revenue." *After-war Problems*, p. 319. But J. A. Hobson seems to go too far when he says : "Of all the forms of taxation, tariff duties are the most injurious in their numerous, widespread and incalculable shiftings, in their delays and incidental injustice of their incidence, in the uncertainty of their yield, the costliness of their collection, and the business and political corruption which they breed." *Taxation in the New State*, p. 136.

[2] Even Mr. Gokhale who looked to the interests of the poor more than any other Indian statesman, said on one occasion, "We can raise much larger revenue than we do at present from customs without its proving burdensome to any section of the community."

way that the burden of taxation may be distributed equitably over the whole surface of society. In such a scheme of judicious combination, no section of the community will be overtaxed, and it will be possible to properly safeguard the interests of the poorer sections of the community.

There is, however, one difficulty which suggests itself in this connexion. The resources of the Government of India have now been separated from those of the Provincial Governments. The latter are in charge of departments of administrative activity which are intimately connected with national welfare. But their sources of income are very few, and even these are inelastic. On the other hand, indirect taxation is completely in the hands of the Government of India, and so also are two of the most important direct taxes, namely, income-tax and super-tax. The Provincial Governments must have more resources at their disposal if they are to properly discharge the duties that have been assigned to them. And if they find it necessary to resort to fresh taxation, such taxation will necessarily be direct. Under such circumstances, it would be desirable for the Central Government not to encroach further upon the field of direct taxation, which should be left as far as possible in the hands of the Provincial Governments.

A word may be said here about the effect of the tariff policy of India on her international relations. It is sometimes said that free trade is the better policy from the international standpoint, for it produces international amity and concord. But this is an erroneous view. As a matter of fact, it can produce as much bitterness, suffering and hostility as protection. If we appeal to experience, we find that the application of the principles of free trade has resulted in the economic degradation and political subjugation of weak nations. On the other hand, protection may enable the weaker communities to defend themselves against the stronger nations, both economically and politically. Solidarity among the peoples of the world is certainly a most desirable object, but it can be attained only by the adoption of the principle of non-interference and the recognition of the right of each people to its maximum economic development. Of course, this is possible under both systems,—protection and free trade. But so long as national frailties remain what they are, protection seems to be the easier method of achieving the object than free trade[1].

[1] J. S. Hecht expresses a similar opinion in his *Real Wealth of Nations*. Grunzel describes the effect of protection on international relations thus: "In the place of the international division of labour between agriculture and manufactures, assumed by classical

Englishmen often express surprise at the fact that the watchword among Indian politicians, industrialists and business men to-day is protection. This is true, but the reason is not far to seek. If Indians are protectionists almost to a man, thanks are due to the policy which has been so far pursued by the Indian Government in regard to the industries of the country. Indians object not to the principles of free trade but to the way in which these principles are sought to be applied in India. The people of the country are not so thick-headed as to be unable to appreciate the benefits of real free trade, but they may be pardoned if they take the professions of interested supporters of the doctrine with the proverbial grain of salt. Sincere advocates of free trade, however, need not despair. As soon as the country becomes once more self-governed, and she regains her normal economic position, many a free-trader will be found in the ranks of her economists and statesmen. Meanwhile, India must be left free to settle her fiscal policy in the way she finds it best suited to her own needs and conditions.

economics, a division of labour within the sphere of manufacturing appears. If now the development of the productive capacity of a country leads to industrialization, and if industrialization increases the participation of the country in world-economic dealings, it follows that the protective policy, as an important aid to industrialization, must under proper manipulation lead to an extension of world-economic relations". *Economic Protectionism*, p. 342.

# CHAPTER VII

## INDIA AND IMPERIAL PREFERENCE

The history of the British Empire reveals many changes in the attitude of Great Britain towards the other parts of the Empire. An eminent writer points out that, in the seventeenth and eighteenth centuries, colonies were treated as compulsory markets for the industrial products of England; all attempts at an independent industrial development were suppressed, and both importation and exportation were monopolised for the benefit of the ruling part of the Empire. But the revolt and separation of the United States demonstrated how dangerous such measures of compulsion might become. After that event the effort was to actively encourage the development of colonial production along lines in which competition with the ruling power did not arise. This policy met with the greatest success in the tropical colonies and the great dependency of India, where the encouragement of the production of high-value raw materials, such as cotton, jute, coffee, and tobacco, not merely brought profits to the colonies and dependencies, but also facilitated and secured the supply of raw materials for the industries of England. In many parts of the Empire, some restrictions are still in force. But the Self-Governing Dominions now frame their tariff laws in accordance with their own fiscal requirements and are not debarred even from protecting themselves against the mother country[1].

The latest change to be brought into use is the system of preferential trade. It was recommended in the English Colonial Conferences which have been meeting since 1887, and the first step was taken by Canada, when in 1898 she granted a duty reduction of twenty-five per cent., which was increased in 1900 to thirty-three and one-third per cent., on the goods imported from the United Kingdom. This was followed by similar measures adopted by the South African Union, New Zealand and Australia. For many years, however, there was no response from the side of Great Britain, although Imperial Preference formed one of the chief planks of the political platform of the

[1] Grunzel, *Economic Protectionism*, pp. 45 and 46.

Conservative Party in the country. The Liberals were opposed to such a policy, and during the period of their ascendancy the question was practically shelved.

The late war, however, brought the question of Imperial Preference again into prominence. The reason was two-fold. In the first place, public attention was directed to the extent to which the United Kingdom was economically dependent upon foreign countries, particularly for the supply of raw materials. On April 26, 1917, the Imperial War Cabinet passed a resolution, which was afterwards approved by the Imperial War Conference to this effect: "The time has arrived when all possible encouragement should be given to the development of Imperial resources, and specially to making the Empire independent of other countries in respect of food supplies, raw materials, and essential industries. With these objects in view, this Conference expresses itself in favour of the principle that each part of the Empire having due regard to the interests of our Allies should give favourable treatment and facilities to the produce and manufactures of other parts of the Empire."[1]

[1] Quoted in Greogry, *Tariffs*, p. 271.

Of the questions referred to the Committee on Commercial and Industrial Policy After the War, the two most important were : (i) "to what extent and by what means the resources of the Empire should and can be developed", and (ii) "to what extent and by what means the resources of supply within the Empire can be prevented from falling under foreign control". In order to gain these objects, the Committee recommended the readjustment and development of the economic relations of the Dominions and Colonies and of India with the United Kingdom.

The second reason was the growth of the idea of Imperial unity. The whole-hearted and ungrudging assistance rendered by the Dominions, Colonies and Dependencies to the mother country in the greatest crisis with which she had ever been faced considerably strengthened the feeling of solidarity within the Empire. The desire now became common to confirm the bond of sentiment by 'the consolidating force of material interests.' Years ago, Mr. Chamberlain had declared : "The establishment of commercial union throughout the Empire would not only be the first step, but the main step, the decisive step, towards the realization of the most inspiring idea that has ever entered into the minds of British statesmen." The advocates of Imperial unity think that the time is now ripe for giving practical shape to this sentiment.

It is generally believed that Imperial Preference will not only place the relations between Great Britain and the 'sister nations' on a firmer footing than at present, but would apply a stimulus to British industry. On the other hand, it is also claimed that such a policy will prove immensely beneficial to the Dominions. As between Great Britain and the Dominions, therefore, preferential trade is a matter of mutual benefit.

In all discussions about Imperial Preference, India is mentioned only incidentally. In 1903, Lord George Hamilton, Secretary of State for India, drew the attention of the Government of India to a Resolution which had been passed in 1902 at the Conference of Colonial Premiers in favour of preferential tariffs as between different members of the British Empire, and intimated his desire to receive from them any observations and suggestions which they might wish to make from the point of view of Indian interests.

The Government of India sent a despatch in reply to this letter in which they discussed at some length the various economic aspects of the question. They observed at the outset that the recommendation was of an extremely general and indefinite character, and was hedged round with many qualifications and provisos. After examining the figures of the import and export trade of India, they pointed out that about three-fourths of the total imports of India came from the British Empire, and that of the remaining one-fourth a substantial part consisted of articles such as petroleum, beet-sugar, wines, silk manufactures and the like, which the British Empire either did not produce or was not in a favourable position to supply. They pointed out, further, that the imports of India from the British Empire exceeded the exports thereto by 7½ millions sterling; while her exports to foreign countries exceeded her imports from them by about 38 millions sterling and the total exports of India exceeded her total imports by upwards of 30 millions sterling. In this connection they remarked that inasmuch as India was a debtor country, she was dependent on her trade with foreign countries for the discharge of her international obligations.[1]

With regard to exports, the Government of India observed that the situation was somewhat

[1] Letter, dated 22nd October, 1903, Cd. 1931.

different. The value of raw materials, they said, approximated to 50 per cent. of the total value of India's exports. The articles which formed this group were required by the importing countries for their manufacturing industries, and it was to their interest to admit them on the easiest possible terms. Thus, seeds were admitted free everywhere except in Germany, Italy, Austria-Hungary, Russia, and the United States, and in the three latter countries duties were levied only on one or two classes only. Raw cotton from India was free except in Italy and Russia. Raw jute was dutiable only in Russia. Raw hides and skins were free except in the United States and with some slight exceptions in France and Japan. Similar remarks would apply to numerous other articles of this group. Even when duties were imposed they were, as a general rule, of moderate amount. In the three other classes of goods, however, the privilege did not obtain except in the United Kingdom and Holland, and in the former country tea, coffee, tobacco and unrefined sugar were subject to very high duties. Excluding these four articles, India's exports to the United Kingdom in the three classes of food-stuffs, manufactures, and other articles, obtained free entry.

Raw materials also enjoyed the same advantage.

The net result, observed the Government of India, was that Indian exports approximating to one-half of the entire volume of her export trade were admitted free of duty into the consuming markets, while of the remainder a considerable proportion was either subject to relatively moderate duties, or, as in the United Kingdom, to duties imposed for purely revenue purposes and with no attempt to differentiate against her.

The Government of India then went on to discuss in what way the then existing condition of things was likely to be affected by the inclusion of India in any scheme of inter-Imperial preferential tariffs. Two possible alternatives presented themselves to the Government. In the first alternative, India might join the scheme on exactly the same footing as any of the Self-governing Dominions, and would, if there were a need, impose duties of a protective character, against imports from the United Kingdom and other parts of the British Empire, subject to the condition that so far as her circumstances permitted she would give substantial preferential treatment to the products and manufactures of the United Kingdom. This alternative, however, the Government of India did not consider to be within the sphere of practical politics, for all past experience indicated that, in the decision of any fiscal question concerning India, powerful sections of the community in Great Britain would continue to demand that their interests, and not those of India alone, should be allowed consideration.

In the second alternative, India would maintain her import duties on British and Colonial goods, at such low general rates, equal to or somewhat less than that in force at the time as might be required for revenue purposes, and would impose a slightly higher rate on foreign goods, sufficient to give the former class a preference of 25 per cent. or thereabouts. The result of this alternative might be of appreciable advantage to the United Kingdom. But so far as India was concerned, the balance of advantage was distinctly adverse; because, in the first place, the Government of India might be forced to shape their policy not in accordance with their own needs, but according to the interests and demands of other constituents of the Empire; and, secondly, they would lose a portion of the revenue which they received at the time from British and colonial imports, and it would be extremely difficult to make up the deficit by enhanced duties on foreign goods. The Government also pointed out that the last and greatest source of injury to India would be retaliation by foreign countries. And in this connection they emphasised the fact that India was a debtor country, and the only means consistent with national solvency of discharging this obligation lay in the preservation of a substantial excess of exports over imports.

The Government of India summarised their conclusions as to the question of the participation by India in a policy of preferential tariffs within the Empire, thus:

"Firstly, that without any such system, India already enjoys a large, and probably an exceptionally large, measure of the advantages of the free exchange of imports and exports.

Secondly, that if the matter is regarded exclusively from an economic stand-point, India has something, but not perhaps very much, to offer to the Empire; that she has very little to gain in return; and that she has a great deal to lose or to risk.

Thirdly, that in a financial aspect, the danger to India of reprisals by foreign nations, even if eventually unsuccessful, is so serious and their results would be so disastrous, that we should not be justified in embarking on any new policy of the kind unless assured of benefits greater and more certain than any which have, so far, presented themselves to our mind."[1]

No step was taken by the Government of India in the direction of preferential trade until 1919, when a Bill was passed imposing a duty on hides and skins coupled with a rebate in favour of Great Britain, the Dominions and other British Possessions. This was suspected by the public to be a measure involving a principle of more than fleeting interest, but the Government of India denied that it was proposed as part of a scheme of Imperial Preference.

Nearly two decades have elapsed since the Government of India expressed their views on the question. In the meanwhile, there have been a great increase in the volume and extent of the foreign trade of India and a considerable change in its direction. The character of India's commerce has, however, remained substantially unaltered. An examination of the present situation confirms this opinion. But here we are confronted with a difficulty. The abnormal conditions created by the war still subsist to some extent, and it will be some time before they give place to normal conditions. The

[1] Letter, dated 22nd October, 1903, Cd. 1931.

annual statistics relating to Indian trade, therefore, have to be used, for purposes both of comparison and forecast, with a certain amount of reserve and circumspection.

The approximate total value of the annual foreign trade of India may be taken as Rs. 650 crores of which exports are worth about Rs. 350 crores; and imports Rs. 300 crores.[1] Nearly 61 per cent. of the imports comes from the United Kingdom, 5 per cent. from the rest of the British Empire, and 34 per cent. from foreign countries. As for exports, nearly 22 per cent. goes to the United Kingdom, about the same percentage to the other countries of the Empire, and 56 per cent. to foreign countries. India does not import goods in considerable quantities from any of the Self-Governing Dominions, while Australia is the only Dominion to which Indian commodities are exported in any appreciable amounts. It is worthy of note that, as compared with the figures of 1903, while there has been a steady and continuous increase in the amount of imports from the United Kingdom, there has been

[1] In 1920-21, the total value of the foreign trade was Rs. 674 crores, of which exports were worth 292¼ crores, and imports, 381¾. These figures were, however, wholly abnormal. The figures for 1919-20 may be said to have approached more closely to the normal, being Rs. 300 crores for [illegible]orts and Rs. 346½ crores for exports *Vide Review of the Trade of In[illegible]*, 1920-21.

a decrease in the proportionate share of that country in the import trade of India. The same remark also applies to the rest of the Empire. As for exports, there has been a growth in the volume of the trade with the United Kingdom, but a decline in percentages, while the other countries of the Empire, taken together, have increased their total as well as their proportionate share.

Coming to the character of the foreign trade, we find that the bulk of India's imports from the United Kingdom consists of manufactured goods, while much the greater part of her exports to that country consists of either articles of food or raw materials for industries. This is true also, to a greater or less extent, of the trade with the Self-Governing Dominions, jute manufactures being almost the only exception. The goods supplied to India by the United Kingdom and the Self-Governing Dominions generally compete with the products of foreign countries; but commodities exported from India to the United Kingdom and the Dominions compete only in a few cases with commodities from other countries. For instance, in the rice trade with the United Kingdom, India holds her own; in tea, Ceylon comes next to India; in coffee, there is successful competition; in wool, India lags far behind the Dominions; in jute, India has a world's monopoly; in seeds generally, she has the bulk of the market, although in cotton seed India and Egypt are in close competition, and in linseed, Argentine is a keen rival; in hides, India holds her own. Canada imports from India jute manufactures, tea, lac and shellac, and exports to her motor-cars and some miscellaneous articles. South Africa's purchases from India consist of rice, cotton piece-goods and tea, while her exports to her are negligible. Australia takes from India jute manufactures, rice, vegetable oils, tea and coffee, and sends horses, railway plant, and oilman's stores. New Zealand purchases from India jute manufactures and sells her a few miscellaneous articles. The trade of India with the other British possessions is more important than with the Dominions. Ceylon imports from India rice and other food grains, seeds and jute manufactures, and exports to her metals and spices. The imports of the Straits Settlements from India consist of rice and other food grains, cotton yarns and manufactures, jute manufactures, seeds, and tobacco; while the chief exports to India are mineral oils, spices, and dyeing and tanning substances. Sugar is the principal article of import from Mauritius, while food-grains and jute manufactures are the chief exports to that colony[1].

Let us now see whether, as things stand at present, Great Britain has anything to offer to India under a scheme of Imperial Preference. In order that India may derive any benefit from such a policy, preferences must be given in Great Britain to goods which are purchased by her from India in considerable quantities. Such commodities are raw cotton, hides and skins, jute (raw and manufactured), lac, rice, raw rubber, seeds, tea, wheat, raw wool and minerals. Of these, rice, wheat and tea are articles of food, and any preferences in respect of them would mean the levy of duties or increase in the rates of duty on imports of these articles from countries other than India. This would result in a rise of the cost of living, which is hardly likely to be tolerated by the people of a democratic country like England. There is at present a small preference granted to India in respect of tea.[2] All the other articles mentioned above are raw materials for industries. As prices of manufactured goods depend largely upon the prices of raw materials, preferential duties levied on

[1] Vide *Review of the Trade of India*, 1920-21.

[2] The rate of duty on tea was reduced a few months ago.

them would lead to an increase of production-costs. As an eminent colonial statesman puts it, "a great manufacturing country such as Great Britain would be mad to impose a tax on raw materials from which she manufactured her goods for export."[1] Such a possibility was definitely brushed aside by the late Mr. Joseph Chamberlain, the greatest advocate of Imperial Preference, who said on one occasion, "I repeat in the most explicit terms that I do not propose a tax on raw materials".

The only manufactured product imported by England from India is jute. But in this respect the only rival is Dundee. No preference is thus possible in regard to this article. The other imports from India are of comparative insignificance. India's trade with the Self-governing Dominions is, as we have already seen, small, and the preferences now given by them are not of any appreciable use to her. Nor is an extended scheme likely to bring her much profit. The other British Possessions may be ignored for our purpose. They are subject countries,

[1] J. A. Hobson says, "It will be impossible to advocate any new import duties upon either foods or raw materials, in view of the world shortage likely to exist for years to come. With this admission virtually disappears the substance of Imperial Preference." *Taxation in the New State*, p. 140.

The extract is from a speech of Sir William Lyne quoted in Currey's *British Colonial Policy*, p. 245.

and their trade activities are directed not in their own interests, but in the interests of other nations.

Great Britain and the Dominions have thus very little to offer to India under a scheme of Imperial Preference. Let us now consider whether India can offer any advantages to those countries. The most important classes of goods imported by India from England are: cotton manufactures, chemicals, building materials, leather manufactures, hardware, scientific instruments, iron and steel manufactures, alcoholic liquors, motor-cars, railway plant, machinery, rubber manufactures, soap and toilet requisites, stationery articles, woollen manufactures, and cigarettes. Some of these classes of goods compete with goods of local manufacture, and, with the industrial progress of the country, many more classes will also begin so to compete. No advantages can, of course, be given to Great Britain in respect of them. India is now about to adopt a system of protection, and it is necessary to consider how far it is possible to reconcile such a system with preferential trade. As a recent writer puts it, "a policy of protection for producers in any case involves some check to the flow of competing imports, whilst the grant of preference will quicken this flow."[1] No step should, therefore, be taken which may even in the slightest measure neutralise the effect of the protective policy of India.

There are other classes of manufactured goods imported from Great Britain which compete, not with the indigenous manufactures, but with the commodities of such countries as the United States, Germany and Japan. If preferences are to be granted in respect of these, they will take one of the two following forms. Either the duties on goods imported from England may be lowered, while retaining the duties on goods from other countries at the existing rates; or a surtax may be levied on goods from foreign countries in addition to the existing duties, while keeping the duties on British goods unaltered. In both these cases, however, the result will be a loss to India. In the former, there will be a sacrifice of revenue; in the latter, a rise in prices. Similarly, in the matter of exports, a policy of preference is likely to be detrimental to Indian interests. If a higher rate of duty is levied on exports to foreign countries than on exports to Great Britain, India will run the risk of losing some of her markets. On the other

[1] Gregory, *Tariffs*, p. 295.

hand, if a rebate is granted to exports to Great Britain without changing the rate of the export duty payable by foreign countries, the Indian exchequer will suffer.

Great Britain, of course, will derive much benefit from preferential relations between herself and India. Such relations will not only afford a stimulus to British industry, but will quicken the entrepôt trade of Great Britain which is of immense value to her. If substantial preferences are granted in India to imports from Great Britain, the people of the latter country, taking advantage of such duties, will act as middlemen in respect of goods not produced within her borders. So also, in the matter of exports, they will act as intermediaries between Indian producers and foreign purchasers. Her experience in regard to the preferential duty on hides and skins cannot but serve as an object-lesson to India. The grant of the rebate of ten per cent. places leather manufacturers in foreign countries in an unfavourable position as compared with British manufacturers, and the former are thus driven to purchase their raw materials elsewhere. It is also believed that a considerable part of the raw hides and skins exported to Great Britain finds its way to other countries, to whom it is more profitable to buy such goods through Great Britain than direct from India. It seems a bit unreasonable to compel India to incur loss in order that she may give middlemen's profits to the people of Great Britain.

Another question to be considered in this connexion is the possibility of retaliation by foreign countries whose interests may be adversely affected by inter-Imperial preferential trade. It is true that these countries are interested in obtaining India's raw produce. But some of India's raw products compete with similar products of other countries, and differential duties may, in other cases, drive purchasers to seek substitutes. It is sometimes suggested that, in case of retaliation, India may hit back again by levying heavy duties on the manufactured goods imported from the retaliating countries. But it is not improbable that India will hurt herself in trying to inflict harm on others. Besides, such a policy may land her in a complex and long-drawn series of tariff wars the end of which it would be difficult to foresee. Retaliation, therefore, is a real and serious danger, which should be kept in view in considering the question of Imperial Preference.

India can only be asked, with some show of

reason, to adopt a policy of Imperial Preference if a gain can be assured to her to counterbalance the probable loss resulting from such a policy. But, as we have already seen, Great Britain has very little to offer to India, and the risk of retaliation is great. Would it not, therefore, be too much to expect the people of India to "allow themselves to be hurried blindfold to the goal at which the prize will be distributed to their inevitable disadvantage ?"[1]

As a business proposition, therefore, Imperial Preference cannot be supported from the Indian point of view, however desirable it may be from the standpoint of Great Britain. India's trade with the Dominions is exceedingly small, and may be left out of account. As a matter of fact, the advocates of Imperial Preference always look at the question from the British and Colonial, and not the Indian, standpoint. Even persons who ought to feel grateful to India for what they owe her have the same narrow vision. Sir Roper Lethbridge, for instance, said not very long ago: "In any reasonable scheme for the commercial federation of the British Empire, India must occupy the chief place after the mother country. At this moment, among the constituent States

[1] Lord Crewe's speech, 1914.

of the Empire, she is at once the largest producer of food and raw material, and one of the largest consumers of manufactured products. And potentially, with her 300,000,000 of thrifty, industrious, and progressive workers, she is a commercial unit of greater importance in the world, whether for exports or for imports, than almost any other."[1] Evidently, the importance of India is not for her own sake, but for the sake of the Empire. And she is destined for ever to remain a producer of food and raw materials and a buyer of manufactured products. It is thus clear that in spite of all his professed friendliness to India, it is the interests of England that he has really at heart.

Sir Montagu Webb, one of the most successful European merchants in India, after describing the necessity for intelligently controlling the resources of India for Imperial ends, says in the concluding chapter of his interesting brochure: "This being so, our duty in India is plain. We must join our voices to those of Canada, Australia, New Zealand and South Africa in pressing upon the people of the United Kingdom the expediency of modifying their present tariff so as to utilise effectively the many

[1] *India and Imperial Preference.*

opportunities which the Empire now offers of strengthening the position not only of Great Britain itself, but of the British Dominions throughout the world."[1]

This brings us to the political aspect of the question. Indians are often asked to consider preferential trade from the Imperial, rather than the local, stand-point. Sacrifice, say the advocates of such a policy, is the price of Empire. But whose Empire ? Within the British Empire five different varieties of political status are distinguishable. In the first category stands Great Britain, who not only governs herself, but rules the greater part of the Empire. Then come the Self-Governing Dominions, which are practically independent of outside authority, so far as their internal affairs are concerned. The other Colonies come next, which, though subject to Great Britain, possess representative institutions. In the fourth class stand the dependencies and possessions, which are in a state of complete subjection, and are autocratically governed. India stands as a class by herself. She s still a dependent country but has been promised full self-government.

In addition to differences in political

[1] *India and the Empire*, p. 163.

status, there are differences of race and colour, which introduce further complexities into the situation. An Imperial angle of vision may come natural and easy to the people of Great Britain and the white inhabitants of the Dominions and Colonies, who feel pride in belonging to an Empire over which the sun never sets. But the subject races cannot feel anything but humilitation in thinking of an Empire which has deprived them of their freedom and exploited their resources for purposes other than their own. The British Empire is sometimes described as a Commonwealth of Nations. But it looks a misnomer to describe an aggregation of countries as a Commonwealth, three-fourths of which are treated merely as "Estates". However striking the idea of an Imperial Zollverein may be to the imagination, it must remain an absurdity so long as the different countries remain separated, not merely by long distances, but by feelings and prejudices based on race, colour, and political status.

So far as India is concerned, Imperial Preference is not a practical proposition at the present moment. The question rests largely on sentiment. But to appeal to Indian sentiment in the existing state of things in the country is to misread human nature. Some may even regard such an appeal as an attempt to add insult to injury. When the advocates of Imperial Preference point to the attitude of the Dominions, they forget the essential difference between those countries and India. Preferential trade between Great Britain and the Dominions is an 'arrangement between friends', a 'negotiation between kinsmen' by which both sides are to gain and neither to lose.[1] But it is quite different with India. Economically, India is still a field for exploitation by foreigners, and politically, her status is still that of a dependency, while the Dominions enjoy full self-government both in the political and the economic sphere. The Dominions first began to think of giving preferences to Great Britain long after they had been conceded the right of full responsible government. Nobody dares now to question their right to grant, withdraw, or vary of their own will and at their own pleasure, any preferences they like. It is true that fiscal autonomy has in theory been granted to India. But fiscal autonomy can only be real when it is associated with political freedom.

[1] *Vide* Currey, *British Colonial Policy*, p. 251

The essence of a sacrifice is that it should be made in a willing manner. In order that a policy of Imperial Preference may lead to greater solidarity among the component parts of the Empier, preferences should be given by each country of her own free will. But so long as India remains a subject country, any gifts made by her will be open to the suspicion that they are 'forced gifts' like the 'benevolences' granted to English Kings in the Middle Ages. And such suspicion is likely to intensify the discontent of which there is already far too much in the country. Besides, Imperial Preference forced on the people under present circumstances is likely to make them regard it as another expedient devised for the further exploitation of the country. It would, indeed, be extremely unwise to take a step which is calculated to embitter feelings and strengthen prejudices, and which may easily lead to disastrous consequences.

The main principle which knits together the different parts of the Empire, said a British statesman the other day, is freedom. If this principle is applied to India, the result will be the same here as it has been in the Dominions. As soon as India attains full self-government, a community of interests will grow up between her and the other units of the federation, and there is no doubt that she will signify her attachment to the Commonwealth of Nations by agreeing to a policy of preferential trade relations.

The question has now been discussed from the Indian and Imperial points of view. But a word must be said about its international aspect. Preferential trade within the Empire would be beneficial to all parties so far as it would help to develop the resources of its component parts to the fullest extent and enable them to defend themselves against their enemies. But there is no reason why the British Empire should attempt to be absolutely self-sufficient. Mutual dependence of all countries upon one another ought to be the goal. Whether in economics or in politics, the essential unity and the common good of mankind must be kept steadily in view. It is only as a partial league of nations that a large aggregation can be supported. The Britannic Commonwealth of Free Nations, if properly constituted, may be a step towards the federation of the world. But a self-sufficient Empire, conscious of its excess of economic strength and guided by selfish and narrow ideals, would be a danger to the freedom of weak nations and a menace to the peace of the world.

# APPENDIX

# APPENDIX A

## RATES OF DUTY LEVIED IN GREAT BRITAIN ON THE IMPORTATION OF GOODS FROM INDIA

### 27 GEO. 3, C. 13—(CONSOLIDATION)

| Description of manufactures | | Duties levied on manufactures of British India | | |
|---|---|---|---|---|
| | | £ | s. | d. |
| Dimity | per yard | 0 | 1 | 6 |
| and besides | per £100 value | 16 | 10 | 0 |
| Calicoes, plain white | per piece | 0 | 5 | 3 |
| and besides | for £100 value | 16 | 10 | 0 |
| Cotton Yarn | per lb. | 0 | 0 | 3½ |
| Cotton Manufactures not enumerated per £100 value | | 50 | 0 | 0 |
| Muslins, plain; Nanqüin Cloths, Muslins or white Calicoes, flowered or stitched per £100 value | | 18 | 0 | 0 |

The following additional Duties on the above Rates were imposed by the undermentioned Acts.

| | |
|---|---|
| 37 Geo. 3, c. 15 | £5 p. c. |
| 37 Geo. 3, c. 110 | £5 p. c. |
| 38 Geo. 3, c. 76 | £7 per 100 lbs. on Cotton Yarn<br>£3 p. c. on other goods |

### 39 GEO. 3, C. 59

Repeals existing Duties on Goods, the Produce and Manufactures of the East Indies, except the Additional Duty imposed per 38 Geo. 3, C 76, and levies.

### On Warehousing

| | £ | s. | d | |
|---|---|---|---|---|
| Muslins, plain ; Nanquin cloths, Muslins, white Calicoes, flowered or stitched, per £100 value | 7 | 10 | 0 | £ 3 p. c. additional by 38 Geo. 3, C. 76, above-mentioned. |
| Plain white Calicoes and plain white Dimity, ditto | 2 | 10 | 0 | |
| Cotton Manufactures not enumerated ditto | 2 | 0 | 0 | |

### For Home Consumption

| | | £ | s. | d. |
|---|---|---|---|---|
| Calicoes, plain white | the piece | 0 | 6 | 8 |
| and besides | per £100 value | 20 | 19 | 1 |
| Cotton Manufactures not enumerated | do. | 122 | 4 | 5 |
| Dimity, plain white | the yard | 0 | 2 | 0 |
| and besides | per £100 value | 22 | 3 | 6 |
| Muslins, plain ; Nanquin cloths, Muslins, white calicoes, flowered or stitched per £100 value | | 19 | 13 | 9 |

No distinctive rate for goods of British from Foreign India.

## 43 GEO. 3, C. 68 (CONSOLIDATION)

Repeals existing Duties and levies on warehousing East India Goods.

| | £ | s. | d. |
|---|---|---|---|
| Muslins, plain ; Nanquin cloths, Muslins and white Calicoes, flowered or stitched per £100 value | 7 | 10 | 0 |
| Plain white Calicoes and plain white Dimity do. | 2 | 10 | 0 |
| Cotton Manufactures not enumerated do. | 2 | 0 | 0 |

### For Home Consumption

| | £. | s. | d. |
|---|---|---|---|
| Calicoes, plain white per 5,100 value | 50 | 0 | 0 |
| Cotton Manufactures not enumerated do. | 52 | 0 | 0 |
| Dimity, plain white do. | 50 | 0 | 0 |
| Muslins, plain ; Nanquin cloths, muslins and white calicoes, flowered or stitched per £100 value | 20 | 0 | 0 |
| Cotton thread do. | 52 | 0 | 0 |
| Cotton Yarn per lb. | 0 | 0 | 5 |

By 43 Geo. 3, C. 70, 126, 10s. p. c. or one-eighth in addition to the above rates of duties was imposed.

## 49 GEO. 3, C. 98 (CONSOLIDATION)

Repeals 43 Geo. 3, C. 58, and 70 levies on Warehousing East India Goods.

| | £ | s. | d. |
|---|---|---|---|
| Muslins, plain, Nanquin cloths, muslins and white Calicoes flowered or stitched per £100 value | 7 | 10 | 0 |
| Plain white Calicoes and plain white Dimity do. | 2 | 10 | 0 |
| Cotton Manufactures not enumerated do. | 2 | 0 | 0 |

For Home Consumption

| | | Manufactures of British India | | |
|---|---|---|---|---|
| | | £ | s. | d. |
| Calicoes, plain white per £100 value | | 51 | 5 | 0 |
| Caps of Cotton | do. | 54 | 0 | 0 |
| Cotton Manufactures not enumerated | do. | 54 | 0 | 0 |
| Dimity plain white | do. | 51 | 5 | 0 |
| Muslins plain ; Nanquin cloth, muslins and white calicoes flowered or stitched per £100 | value | 20 | 10 | 0 |
| Cotton Stockings | do. | 54 | 0 | 0 |
| Cotton Thread | do. | 54 | 0 | 0 |
| Cotton Yarn | per lb. | 0 | 0 | 6 |

In addition to the above permanent duties, a war duty of £83 6s. 8d. p.c. on one-third of their amounts, is levied in the same Act.

This war duty continued per 55 Geo. 3, C. 53 and made perpetual per 56 Geo. 3, C. 29.

## 59 GEO. 3, C. 52 (CONSOLIDATION)

Repeals all existing Customs Import Duties, and Levies.

### For Home Consumption

| | | Manufactures of British India | | |
|---|---|---|---|---|
| | | £ | s. | d. |
| Calicoes, plain white | per £100 value | 67 | 10 | 0 |
| Calicoes, white, flowered or stitched | do. | 37 | 10 | 0 |
| Caps of Cotton | do. | 67 | 10 | 0 |
| Articles Manufactured of Cotton | do. | 67 | 10 | 0 |
| Dimity, plain white | do. | 67 | 10 | 0 |
| Muslins, plain, or if flowered or stitched | do. | 37 | 10 | 0 |
| Nanquin Cloths | do. | 37 | 10 | 0 |
| Shawls of Cotton | | 67 | 10 | 0 |
| Stockings of Cotton | | 67 | 10 | 0 |
| Thread of Cotton | | 67 | 10 | 0 |
| Yarn of Cotton | per lb. | 0 | 1 | 3 |

# APPENDIX B

## RATES OF DUTY LEVIED IN BRITISH INDIA ON THE IMPORTATION OF BRITISH AND FOREIGN COTTON GOODS FROM THE EARLIEST PERIODS

### PRESIDENCY OF BENGAL

| From | British Bottoms | Foreign Bottoms |
|---|---|---|
| 1773 | 6½ p. c. | |
| 1778 | 7 p. c. | |
| 1795 | 2½ p. c. | |
| 1797 | 3½ p. c. | |
| 1810 | 7½ p. c. | |
| 1811 | 7½ p. c. | 15 p. c. |
| 1815 | | |
| UNITED KINGDOM | 2½ p. c. | 5 p. c. |
| Foreign | 5 p. c. | 10 p. c. |
| 1817 | | |
| United Kingdom | 2½ p. c. | 5 p. c. |
| Foreign Europe | 5 p. c. | 10 p. c. |
| Other Goods | 7½ p. c. | 15 p. c. |
| 1825 | | |
| United Kingdom or other British Possessions | 2½ p. c. | 5 p. c. |
| Foreign Europe | 5 p. c. | 10 p. c. |
| Other Foreign | 7½ p. c. | 15 p. c. |
| 1836 | | |
| United Kingdom or other British Possessions | 3½ p. c. | 7 p. c. |
| Foreign | 7 p. c. | 14 p. c. |
| 1845 | | |
| United Kingdom or other British Possessions | 5 p. c. | 10 p. c. |
| Foreign | 10 p. c. | 20 p. c. |

## PRESIDENCY OF FORT ST. GEORGE

| From | British Bottoms | Foreign Bottoms |
|---|---|---|
| 1803 - - | 6 p. c. | 8 p. c. |
| 1812 - - | 8 p. c. | |
| Do. - - | | 16 p. c. |
| **1816** | | |
| UNITED KINGDOM - - | 2½ p. c. | 5 p. c. |
| Foreign Europe - - | 5 p. c. | 10 p. c. |
| **1819** | | |
| United Kingdom - . | 2½ p. c. | 5 p. c. |
| Foreign Europe - - | 5 p. c. | 10 p. c. |
| Other Foreign Goods - | 8 p. c. | 16 p. c. |
| **1844** | | |
| United Kingdom or other British Possessions - | 3½ p. c. | 7 p. c. |
| Other places - - | 7 p. c. | 14 p. c. |
| **1845** | | |
| United Kingdom or other British Possessions - | 5 p. c. | 10 p. c. |
| Other places - - | 10 p. c. | 20 p. c. |

## PRESIDENCY OF BOMBAY

| | | |
|---|---|---|
| **1799** | | |
| In force since 1795 - - | $2\frac{1}{2}$ p. c. on manifest with exceptions | $2\frac{1}{2}$ p. c. on an advance of 60 p.c. on manifest |
| 1805 - - | $3\frac{1}{2}$ p. c. | $3\frac{1}{2}$ p. c., do. |
| 1813 - - | | $4\frac{1}{2}$ p. c., do. |
| **1815** | | |
| United Kingdom - - | $2\frac{1}{2}$ p. c. | $4\frac{1}{2}$ p. c., do. |
| Foreign Europe - | 5 p. c. | |
| **1817** | | |
| United Kingdom - - | $2\frac{1}{2}$ p. c. | $4\frac{1}{2}$ p. c., do. |
| Foreign Europe - - | $3\frac{1}{2}$ p. c. | |
| **1838** | | |
| United Kingdom or other British Possessions - | $3\frac{1}{2}$ p. c. | 7 p. c. |
| Other places - - | 7 p. c. | 14 p. c. |
| **1875** | | |
| United Kingdom or other British Possessions - | 5 p. c. | 10 p. c. |
| Other places | 10 p. c. | 20 p. c. |

# TEACHER EDUCATION
## Today and Tomorrow

MOHIT CHAKRABARTI

PUBLICATIONS

KALPAZ PUBLICATIONS

DELHI-110052

Teacher Education : Today and Tomorrow

Rs. 450



ISBN: 81-7835-668-6



Published in 2008 in India by
Kalpaz Publications
C-30, Satyawati Nagar,
Delhi-110052
E-mail: kalpaz@hotmail.com
Phone : 9212729499

*Lasser Type Setting by*: Rudra Computer Graphics, Delhi
*Printed at* : Singal Print Media, Delhi

*Dedicated to*
*Professor Surabhi Banerjee*
*Vice Chancellor*
*Netaji Subhas Open University*
*Kolkata*

*Professor M. A. Khader*
*Member Secretary*
*Head, Curriculum Group*
*National Council of Educational Research*
*and Training*
*New Delhi*

# Contents

# Preface

Education today is under countless constraints and challenges. It calls forth setting and settling diverse issues of human resources and probes into some of the crucial problems of humane enlightenment. Teacher education is perhaps more confronted with how to negotiate and significantly address the world of teaching-learning than mere doling with duties and responsibilities and dealing with classroom assignments. It is now at the crossroads of fullness of vision in a mesmerised world of immediate gain in every endeavour and worries and frustrations in fruitless teaching sans joy sans freedom and creative adventure. As a consequence, the challenges of teacher education today for addressing tougher ones of tomorrow remain a far more thrilling adventure to be more worthily undertaken. "Challenges in Teacher Education: Today and Tomorrow" is an ardent quest for that end-in-view.

Technology in every walk of education in general and teacher education in particular is enjoying unparalleled popularity, thanks to education for workaholic marvels. Teacher education, too, is under the same spell. What is appalling is that there is a rapidly growing tendency in setting aside aesthetics bereft of which the role of the teacher in exercising and sensitising learners with finer visions of life comes a cropper.

"Teacher Education: Aesthetics in Technology" is an in-depth study in this dimension.

"Teacher Education for the Schools of Tomorrow" is a critical analysis of the role of teacher education for furtherance of today's vision.

"Teacher Education for Value-Cultivation" is an intensive study on the importance of teacher education for setting and actualising diverse and different agenda for cultivation of values.

"Resurging a New Era in Teacher Education" and "Quality in Teacher Education: Tagorean Aesthetics" may arrest the vibrant attention of anyone devoted to acceleration of quality and excellence in teacher education right now and for days ahead.

Education for peace is never so prominently felt urgent and compulsory as it is at present. Bewildered in continual and aggravating ukase writ large in violence, hatred, malice, misunderstanding and so on, education for peace becomes all the more necessary than anything else. Teachers, too, are often at a loss in arresting undesirable forces in the altars of teaching-learning. "Teacher Education for Peace" may be considered a useful study in exploring new frontiers of teaching for restoration and cultivation of peace education.

Education for spiritual excellence is an unending quest for excellence in inwardness. Self-consciousness in synergy with the Infinite is the essential end-in-view of education. That teacher education today needs to be re-shuffled in the better interest of the learner's world of spiritual development is critically discussed in "Teacher Education and Education for Spiritual Excellence".

"Teacher Education and Pupil Guidance" may contribute to newer thoughts and experiments on how teacher education can improve pupil guidance from diverse dimensions.

# *Preface*

The role of the teacher in the twenty-first century is legion. Challenges and experimentations are continually being encountered and undertaken so that teaching becomes living and pulsating, penetrating and promising. "The Twenty-First Century Teacher" is an intensive quest which might welcome invaluable suggestions.

I gratefully recall my indebtedness to Professor M. A. Khader, Member Secretary, Head, Curriculum Group, NCERT, New Delhi and to Professor Surabhi Banerjee, Vice Chancellor, Netaji Subhas Open University, Kolkata for their inspiring and illuminating suggestions on vibrant teacher education. I humbly dedicate this book to them as a token of my gratitude and reverence.

Sobdo Chakrabarti, my son, has taken all care in computer processing of the book. I express and convey my loving thanks to him.

If the book contributes a little to the advancement of teacher education, I would pray in the words of Rabindranath Tagore: "Let only that little be left of me whereby I may never hide thee." (*Gitanjali*)

**Mohit Chakrabarti**

# 1

# Challenges in Teacher Education

Education is a challenging activity. Teacher education is a more challenging one because the foundation of education including its triumphs and failures is almost entirely dependent on how teachers react and revamp their activities in undertaking multidimensional strategies of teaching. At the same time, quality and innovative approaches in teaching are not only desirable but also mandatory. Gone are the days when chalk and talk were the be all and end all in teaching. With rapid changes and priorities in the arena of education, teachers today cannot but judiciously address the diverse problems and constraints in teaching-learning where both the teachers and the learners of any educational institution—rural, urban or otherwise—make a conjoint and communicated endeavour which consolidates and strengthens both knowledge and experience in terms of creativity and critical efficiency in theory and practice. The recent large-scale failure in English in the Higher Secondary Examination definitely points to the fact that justice in teaching was terribly denied to the students who, for no fault of their own, have become victims to poor and sub-standard teaching, thanks to unscientific and undesirable lack of relevance and farsightedness in between Secondary and Higher Secondary patterns of the syllabi. Who denies that many unqualified teachers in English are the hapless end-products of poverty and paralysed teaching?

Admittedly, content mastery is the need of the hour. If teachers suffer from poverty in content mastery, how can the students learn in classrooms from their teachers and how can they fare satisfactorily in examinations? Leaving aside the fact that preparations for effective teaching are in most cases ignored and averted in utter absence of seriousness, how can students attend to their lessons? If teaching turns out to be cheating in diverse forms of irrelevance, killing precious class hours and destroying the learners' mind-sets for inquisitive learning as one very often encounters in passive, dull, mechanical and lifeless teaching, can pupil-performance be ever satisfactory?

Delving deep into the immediate problems of teaching necessitates a thorough and pinpointed observation of and remedial measures for a series of problems on priority basis:

First, identification of the vulnerable areas of teaching and teachers in the light of orientation programmes for better teaching should be introduced on war footing.

Second, exchange of experienced, expert and trained teachers well chalked out and carefully directed towards pupil motivation and quality assurance should be launched with renewed zeal.

Third, bridge and sandwiched courses for negotiating appalling deficiencies in teaching should be introduced in right earnest.

Fourth, integrated teacher enrichment programmes should be developed with a special approach to eliminating the major deficiencies in teaching including poor knowledge in contents and methodologies in teaching.

One must be always aware of the fact that there is neither any shortcut nor vain mesmerism in teaching. The real teacher is an eternal and endless learner. What he or she knows is only a pointer to further knowledge and enrichment. The adventure in teaching always beckons, and he or she cannot but rise up 'to strive, to seek, to find, and not to yield'.

Innovations in teaching and, for that matter, teacher preparation are challenges that can hardly be averted. Undeniably, with astounding advancement in knowledge explosion, teachers today are in dire need of updating their own knowledge from apposite perspectives. Newer avenues and strategies of teaching by applying latest gadgets and aids call forth earnestness and dedication, seriousness and perfection. Passivity in teaching should obviously be replaced by dynamic and vibrant teaching. Otherwise, our learners would be terrible losers in learning how to learn and utilising the learning outcome in a scientific and purposeful manner. Moreover, if teaching cares for creativity which is one of the most significant ends-in-view of teaching-learning, the pupils enjoy freedom to innovate and love for learning. When the world of joy in learning is appropriately exposed to the learners by the teacher, half the battle for teaching is really won in worthwhile education.

The essential skills of teaching like exposition, questioning, writing on the blackboard and receiving appropriate answers from pupils should be sincerely and diligently practised through simulated teaching assignments. For this purpose, micro-teaching and mini-teaching programmes should be introduced in a phased manner. Care should be taken to see that the plus points of teaching thus practised or exercised are given adequate boosters, while the minus ones are outright eliminated. In the final analysis, a good deal of coordination between micro and macro teaching programmes is to be cordially and cautiously maintained by honouring creativity and critical alertness at any cost. That teaching is a thrilling and joyous activity should be given the highest priority. Then, and then only, teaching contributes to living education that cares for advancement and excellence.

A major departure from dull and mechanical teaching calls forth a definite and important paradigm shift in the process of teaching. It is often said that a good teacher talks less and allows every learner to be seriously and actively involved in the lesson. In fact, in modern teaching, it is the duty of the teacher to motivate all learners by applying interesting strategies for their better involvement and relegate himself/herself to the background. If the qualities like curiosity, presence of mind, logical and independent attitude towards learning are nurtured by pupils, the teacher's job is well done. As the Delors Commission characteristically observes:

> In the past, pupils were generally obliged to accept whatever was offered by the school, in terms of language instruction, content and organisation. Today, communities increasingly expect to have a say in decisions concerning the organisation of schooling. Such decisions have direct influence on teachers' working conditions and the demands made on them, and are responsible for another contradiction inherent in modern teaching: on the one hand, for children to learn properly, teachers must use the knowledge children bring to school with them as the starting-point: this applies not only to the language of instruction but also to science, mathematics or history: on the other hand, if children are to acquire the qualities of independence, creativity and inquisitiveness that must complement their acquisition of knowledge, teachers must at all costs maintain a certain distance between school and social environment, so as to give children and young people the opportunity to exercise their critical judgement.
>
> —*Learning: The Treasure Within,* UNESCO, pp. 143-4.

Undeniably, the greatest challenge in teacher education is how to make teachers most useful, purposeful, meaningful and respectful to the learners so that teaching and learning enjoy the best possible ambience of education for sympathy and co-operation, excellence and promotion. Reflection of an honest evaluation of pupil-performance is the key to success in teaching. For this, teachers ought to undergo training and practice in how to motivate learners in creative and critical thinking right from the beginning. The essential strategies are:

First, it is the duty of the teachers to help their students to believe in themselves. In fact, no learning can take place unless the learner is equipped with self-belief.

Second, pupil-accomplishments should be given due recognition by their teachers. This not only strengthens pupils' thought-processes but also encourages reshuffling of ideas and experiences in terms of appropriate suggestions, cues or hints received from their teachers or from peers or others associated directly or indirectly with teaching-learning.

Third, appreciation of pupil-performance is one of the vital components of successful teaching. But care should be taken to see that any undue appreciation by teachers does not take place anyhow or anytime.

Fourth, teachers ought to be sincere enough to teach students how to think about and exercise on realistic ideas with realistic goals. This enables pupils to be restrained in being unusually emotional, sentimental and imaginative. "Teach them how to live", as Dickens prominently proclaims in *Hard Times,* is the eternal guideline to teaching.

- Fifth, apposite feedback by teachers should be provided for pupils who would be able to improve and enrich their own ideas from time to time.

The present system of ability or homogeneous grouping of students should as far as practicable be avoided. In fact, no true teaching is possible in such grouping. Besides, this type of grouping makes pupil passive and disinterested in learning. It also hinders teachers from appropriately guiding and challenging pupils' thinking and learning, bereft of which a genuine exercise of teaching and learning becomes a myth. If our young learners fail to use their incomparable and unparalleled power of intelligence to solve real-world problems, what is the value of teaching?

There are other limitations of pupil-grouping as above in teaching. These may be identified as follows:

(a) Group consciousness breeds selfishness and inferiority or superiority complexes.

(b) Grouping is against the principle and practice of democracy in teaching.

(c) The tendency of imposing authoritarianism by the teacher becomes very positive and prominent.

(d) Discipline in teaching is more often than not shattered.

(e) Punctuality is most often punched to be extinct.

(f) Poor performance in teaching is neither arrested nor eliminated because of the absence of feedback by a large number of students of heterogeneous identities.

(g) Motivation becomes almost a myth.

(h) Teaching-learning items often remain untaught and unlearnt for misuse of time and ill-planning of teaching-learning.

(i) Administration and supervision in teaching-learning enjoy uninterrupted ukase.

(j) The joy and freedom in teaching-learning are not very often allowed to be

Teachers ought to know about the loss of the exercise of pupil-ability and talent in a heterogeneous grouping of classification of pupils, where it is very difficult for the former to pay appropriate attention to the really deserving learners. Sometimes it so happens that the very congenial classroom climate for learning is utterly lost in the melee of undesirable indiscipline. The ideal strategy of a teacher under such constraints is to individualise instruction as best as possible so that the gifted ones are not neglected at any cost. Tutoring beyond classroom periods to make up the loss whatsoever is what a sincere teacher never forgets to discharge.

Use of media for better teaching-learning can hardly be overestimated. In fact, good educational institutions for teaching pay serious attention and involvements in introducing appropriate gadgets for enrichment in teaching. It is undeniable that if teachers can skilfully introduce and encourage reading on screen side by side with traditional form of reading, advancement of knowledge is ensured and proficiency in teaching is well relected. It is now universally agreed that contextual learning is consolidated by digital media including formats, hypertext and multimedia. As Shih and Weekly strongly advocate:

> Having both high-quality content and efficient dissemination of that content is important in any educational programme. While freely available websites like Google and Wikipedia have their merits, students may learn best when using software and content developed for their respective age groups.
>
> Computer-based reading can offer automated evaluation and progress-tracking of reading comprehension, better accommodation for the diverse starting points and paces of different learners, and rapid, consistent feedback. Moreover,

> younger people may more readily and comfortably read on screens than adults who may have been trained to read books.
>
> With digital media, it is possible to include images, diagrams, sound and even video alongside text; but there may be some disadvantages to doing so. Audio and visual elements require much more digital storage space than text; adding such elements to such text increases download times and can limit the number of works that can be put on a CD. A single photograph can consume as much a digital storage as a book!
>
> In most cases, however, adding a small number of graphics or sounds is not only acceptable, but desirable, as images and sounds can quickly explain difficult concepts and make material more appealing to students. But between the added complexity of editing documents with graphics and the increased cost of distributing 'media-rich' files, we recommend that graphics and sound be used in moderation and only where they significantly enhance the understanding and appearance of the text they accompany.
>
> —Clara Chung-wai Shih & David E. Weekly: *Using New Media,* UNESCO, 2005, pp. 13-14.

Suggestively, teachers can introduce and discuss the content of a lesson before starting for activation and assurance of prior knowledge of pupils. This very often eliminates and guards against learners' false beliefs, if any, and helps better identification of queer misconceptions, ambiguities and doubts. Teachers can also launch some genuinely interesting programmes which allow the learners to make a healthy and sound cohesion between what they know and what they are actually learning. Understanding the world and understanding others are the touchstones of success in teaching where the learners, indeed, are the key players, and teachers are the most significant partners to ascent and excellence in education for social and global advancement. As the Report to UNESCO of the International Commission on Education for the Twenty-first Century categorically suggests:

> Teachers must adapt their relationship with learners, switching roles from 'soloist' to 'accompanist', and shifting the emphasis from dispensing information to helping learners to seek, organise and manage knowledge guiding them rather than moulding them.
>
> —*Ibid,* p.144.

Effective teachers are always concerned about passive learners. It is really a very arduous and challenging task for every teacher to inspire learners to have active involvements in lessons. Frankly, it is a sad state of affairs in classrooms where learners are hardly encouraged in actively participating in lively discussions and other similar activities and highlight their own comments, however insignificant it might appear. How can they learn to have their worth of knowledge unless they reflect?

The role of teacher educators for effective teacher preparation in the backdrop of the above is legion. In training institutes for teachers, intensive programmes for teachers' training and orientation courses should incorporate some essential strategies for vibrant and dynamic teaching that pay the learners with permanent dividends like keenness of mind, creativity in approach and economy in expression and elucidation. Every teacher should be so oriented in teaching strategies that he/ she can easily and unobtrusively assure the learners with the best learning environment inside the classroom. Bearing in mind developmental and individual differences, he/she should honour, uphold and encourage learners' freedom and joy in learning in a living and cordial atmosphere, where he/she also actively participates as and when necessary. In this connection, the recommendations put forward by Vosniadou deserve every teacher's attention:

* Learn how to assess children's knowledge, strategies and modes of learning adequately.
* Introduce children to a wide range of materials, activities and learning tasks that include language, mathematics, natural sciences, social sciences, art, music, movement, social understanding, etc.
* Identify students' areas of strength, paying particular attention to the interest, persistence and confidence they demonstrate in different kinds of activities.
* Support students' areas of strength and utilize these areas to improve overall academic performance.
* Guide and challenge students' thinking and learning.
* Ask children thought-provoking questions and give them problems to solve. Urge children to test hypotheses in a variety of ways.
* Create connections to the real world by introducing problems and materials drawn from everyday situations.
* Show children how they can use their unique profiles of intelligence to solve real-world problems.
* Create circumstances for students to interact with people in the community, and particularly with adults who are knowledgeable and enthusiastic about the kinds of things that are of interest to the students.

—Stella Vosniadou: *How Children Learn*, UNESCO, pp. 25-26.

Setting a newer and more dynamic agenda for advancement in teacher education is nevertheless an uphill task. As it is a national concern, care should be taken to see that it sincerely addresses the most crucial problems of teachers working in remote areas especially in the north-eastern parts of our country. It is no wonder that in spite of severe teaching-learning constraints in these vulnerable areas, there are lots of dedicated teachers in almost inaccessible areas in this region, who never care for their personal promotions in service and share their assignments with colleagues in inspiring zeal. When teaching climate is critically jeopardised due to reasons beyond their control, they try their best to maintain discipline and decorum in educational institutions even under trying circumstances. Honour and recognition of these selfless teachers necessitate immediate attention for national development.

The quest for excellence in teaching demands a concerted and disciplined endeavour anew and afresh. Research avenues with regard to teaching and teacher education should be more intensive and disseminating, more adventurous and probing. Are we ready?

# 2

# Quality in Teacher Education: Tagorean Aesthetics

Teacher education in India today is undergoing rapid changes. With overhauling of curriculum and evaluation in particular, the parameters of teacher education for quality assurance and quality acceleration are being continually reshuffled so that the learners and the teachers are well directed in course of newer and more challenging avenues of advancement in learning and teaching. Naturally, the task of the teacher educator is so vast and multi-dimensional that she/he has no way out but to ardently devote to identifying, exploring, analysing, introducing and evaluating the plus and the minus points of strategies for teaching-learning best suited to the attitudes, aptitudes, skills, interests, understandings and appreciations of teachers and learners under different teaching-learning situations. Hence, better teaching for better quality assurance and quality maintenance, and *vice versa* is undeniable.

How to be assured of better teaching for better quality and its maintenance, advancement and efflorescence notwithstanding? How to conduct the programmes of teacher education where quality is primarily and solely characterised by the promises of the ascent and catholicity of knowledge in the poignancy of wisdom? That bare knowledge and information that are indiscriminately and, more often than not, inanely doled out in the camouflaging show of advancement in teaching-learning, whatsoever or howsoever, terribly betray development and dissemination of finer sensibilities and softer visions of life is yet to be taken into serious and urgent consideration. Whither teacher education for quality concern? Whither experimentations for quality for knowledge turned wisdom for identity of the individual as a global citizen?

Unlike any other visionary in education, Rabindranath Tagore has always education as a continual quest for joy and freedom. It is an eternal challenge for making an unending adventure in finding out the sky of the mind—*chidakas*—that alone has the indomitable power to be both subjective and altruistic and the invariable thread that weaves the wonders of man is the aesthetics of truth, beauty and goodness in particular. Apart from the fact that Tagore is more conscious and interested in quality than anything else in education in general and teacher education especially, what prompts him to ponder over and experiment in aesthetic education as an indispensable and inseparable component of being justified to quality. It eliminates dullness and drabness in teaching that kills the lifeblood of the innovative mind. When quality in teaching is pressurised by mechanical, system-schizophrenic, imitating, routine-bound, monotonous and imprisoned world of knowledge with petty objectives like passports to living somehow or living in passivity and indifference, it terribly betrays true education of the mind and the heart. What a demotion of man from the promises of poignancies in aesthetic exercises!

Admittedly, teacher education for advancement of quality in and through nursling of aesthetic sensibilities demands immediate attention. Being disgusted with education that pays more attention to work-based education that has of late being characterised in workaholic super-fast dimensions and ignores the creative, critical and aesthetic visions of either the teacher or the learner, Tagore wants to introduce the aesthetic education of the mind and the heart that cares and boosts the education of how to revive and restore the harmony of humane joy and freedom. Like a 'torn out line of a verse', he himself has experienced the trauma of schooling that kills the joy of learning as the educational institutions almost everywhere are simply prison houses with learners caged and cornered, stuffed and silenced in the name of learning discipline by letters and never in spirit. As a matter of fact, his bitter experiences in the pursuit of studies in not less than four schools in Calcutta have presented him with at least five dubious and dangerous prizes: the horrible scene of corporal punishment, cruel regimentation, lifeless teaching outcome, absolute elimination of joy and freedom of both the teacher and the learner and utter matter-of-fact and mechanical teaching-learning climate. The results are obvious. In the name of teaching, the teacher enjoys uninterrupted holidays in an atmosphere of aggravating chaos. He/ she neither involves himself/herself in education for development of aesthetic efflorescence nor is he/she interested in how to teach children to be spontaneously and thrillingly motivated in learning and practising the finer components of aesthetics like truth, beauty, goodness, grace, etc. What, then, do we normally receive as the inevitable outcome of teaching? The less said the better because quality in teaching is identified and assessed in terms of the so-called proficiency in intellectual performance by means of cramming and hardly by assimilation and effulgence of aesthetic vision that refines intellect with relentless crystallisation of emotion. One recalls in this connection how Tagore has marvellously exposed the appalling outcome of an overdose of intellectual education that turns humans into numbers like 47-A or 69-E as one comes across in

*Red Olienders (Raktakarabi).* Unless aesthetics is fine-tuned with intellect in education in general and teacher education in particular, quality concern cannot but be a myth.

The aims and objectives of quality enhancement in teacher education for development of aesthetic sense and sensibilities as Tagore has thought and experimented, may be spelt out as follows:

(i) To enable the teacher to explore and utilise the very incubation period of the learners' aesthetic curiosity.

(ii) To stimulate the teacher to be a dynamic and living partner to every student probing deep into the world of aesthetics in course of studies or/and allied affairs.

(iii) To inspire the teacher to find out newer avenues of efflorescence of the learners' aesthetic thoughts and experiments through creative contributions in diverse forms like fine arts, histrionics, music, debates, discussions, symposia etc. and participation in the same along with the students in an atmosphere of spontaneous joy and freedom.

(iv) To instil in the mind of the teacher the inherent values of the culture of aesthetic sensibilities that stand the test of time as an ever abiding and inspiring stamp of quality for ascent and excellence.

(v) To encourage every teacher to be justified and alert in identifying, analysing and executing the different components of aesthetics in accordance with the interest, attitude and aptitude of each learner under varying teaching-learning atmosphere for better and more sensitised quality in aesthetic education.

(vi) To allow freedom of the teacher to cultivate his/her creative and critical thinking in the transparency strategies of quality in aesthetic education, and, in doing so, provide ample opportunities for probing into the finer and more delicate components of aesthetics that highlight a broader canvas of catholicity of vision and grace of perfection in quality education.

The beauty in quality education that Tagore proposes and translates in teacher education is primarily concerned with the aesthetics of ceaseless refinement. Unless the teacher is aware of refinement, the joy of teaching evaporates and, instead, is filled in stuff and nonsense in the camouflaging name of quality. This is all the more viable in literature where quality assurance in the teaching of poetry is essentially concerned with not apparently what to teach, and how, but the more refined 'how' that makes freedom of exercise in appreciation in close consonance with typical imagery-patterns.

A close study of aesthetic education as one of the most essential means of accelerating quality refinement in teacher education, as Tagore is concerned with the role of teachers in this direction, reveals the fact that the teacher must be natural with Nature and responsive to exercise of aesthetic sensibilities. This is a spontaneous exercise where aesthetics in education welcomes external as well as internal components of aesthetics. While the teacher encourages the learner to catch the subtler components of aesthetic education by means of decoration of classrooms with flowers, foliage and leaves, application of incense, sandal paste, flower bangles and ornaments with natural objects that might appear insignificant, the inherent exercise of aesthetic sensibilities can very well be cultivated in sincerely adhering to how abstract ideas like goodness, truth, beauty, benevolence, compassion and so on which enrich and enlighten aesthetic visions in every walk of life.

The more thrilling strategies of quality refinement in aesthetic education which the teacher ought to adopt in course of teaching is introducing aesthetics through histrionics and other creative and aesthetic activities like literary functions, fine arts and music, dance and educational tours are all encapsulated in Tagore's experiments in education where the teacher is a living and active partner to the learners in unfolding newer horizons of aesthetic education.

That Tagore was a continual propagator of aesthetics in the world of creation is a veritable pointer to the fact that he always wants every teacher's nearness to the learner, her/his closest association and involvements in the learner's quest for serenity and joy in the world of aesthetic exercises. He has, in fact, warned that as the teacher is never a pre-historic huge animal but a loving, affectionate and sympathetic partner to the learner, she/he should never dissociate herself/himself from the latter. Otherwise, quality education in aesthetics would never be translated into a thriving reality.

The hunger for self-expression and self-identity in tune with Nature, the great aesthetic teacher never needs any substitution as it is rampantly thrust by the teacher in the same way as the hydraulic pressure. And this is the key to the aesthetics of education for the excellence and advancement of man. This is Tagore's vision of education for which the teacher ought to be spontaneously prepared. As he pronounces in his seventieth birthday address:

> What I had wished for was to give vent to the human hunger for form, for self-expression. I had looked for a forest retreat, *tapovan,* as its proper ambiance. Not in the midst of sordid city-built houses, but under the blue canopy, form morn to eve I had longed to be a playmate of these boys and girls. To express, growing out of this shared life, beauty's happy and blessed form, that was my one and only concern. I have had, naturally, to introduce other utilitarian activities as well. But you will not find me in these. I am where life is trying to express itself. The classes that I have started or taught here are secondary. My real work has been to awaken, in Nature's vast playground, the tender grace of

> childhood, its budding effort, the first rays of knowledge falling across its horizon. Otherwise I would have been swamped by the trivia of routine, statute and syllabus. My happiness, my fulfilment has been in trying to rouse the young ones to the Delight of the unseen Player, to set them in tune with the Dance of Life itself. It is not in me to be more serious than that. The Master of Games has mercifully released me from the fetters of the mature and the elder. Those who try to set me on a pedestal I tell them that I was born with my seat below, on the lap of the Earth. In these trees and forests, the dust, earth and grass, have I poured out my life. Those who are close to the spirit of the Earth, those who are made and shaped by her, and who will find their final rest in her, of them all I am the friend.
>
> —Sisirkumar Ghose: *Rabindranath Tagore,* Sahitya Akademi, New Delhi, 1986, pp. 123-124.

Every teacher, to be truly justified to teaching, cannot but be a poet in the cultivation of truth, beauty and goodness as essential components of aesthetics. For this, the art of teaching as Tagore has always advocated should always be unique. Here success in teaching is not evaluated in terms of rules and regulations, so-called success in pen-paper-pencil tests or any utilitarian approach to teaching-learning. The teacher ought to come out of commonality in teaching. Not a single method but a diversity of methods so that in the aesthetics of teaching allows the learners learn more than a single way of learning and ponder over the invaluable possibilities of finding out newr avenues of learning through his own method.

Admittedly, Tagore's aesthetics of teaching is an endless pointer of progress in enriched and pupil-loving activity. The teacher knows that his aesthetics of teaching is not to force the learners to listen but to achieve the goal as a listener to the learner's achievement in learning how to translate listening into creativity and aesthetic fulfilment. From the psychological point of view as well, maintenance of judicious silence adds poignancy to teaching:

> Teachers of difficult and controversial subjects, who know it is essential for themselves and their pupils to keep calm and analyse the matter dispassionately, often adopt a tone of studied tranquillity which is very useful as long as they are audible, but is apt to sink into chattiness, triviality, and ultimate silence. Philosophers are prone to this because they spend their whole lives thinking about subjects of the highest importance and dignity, they know it is useless and dangerous to discuss them with emotional excitement, they have learnt that it is an insult to a good student to assume that he has not seen quite as far into the argument as his teacher, and sometimes they are discouraged by a lifetime of battling with problems which they know they will never solve.
>
> —Gilbert Highet: *The Art of Teaching,* Methuen, London, University Paperbacks, 1963, p. 90.

Quality in teacher education is closely dependent on pupil motivation. The better they are motivated aesthetically, the greater is the success in teaching. Let students be so motivated that the learner enjoys autonomy in learning. This is what differentiates Tagore's philosophy of aesthetic education from others. Let the learner think, feel and act alone. The role of the teacher, as Tagore advocates, is like that of a lamp just to enlighten and then to relegate himself into the background for better aesthetic advancement in education.

To keep multidimensional ends-in-view in cohesion is the great challenge in teacher education today. The students come to the classroom with a wide canvas of knowledge power. It is the ideal role of a teacher, as Tagore believes and translates into action in his own educational institutions at Visva-Bharati, to assure the learner of the fact that sincere and devoted endeavour to unfold the mystery of knowledge and experience is the key to be justified to education for aesthetic excellence. In this connection, the following necessitates every teacher's attention:

> Students bring their own goals into the classroom and want to negotiate with you about how, when, and with whom they want to reach the learning goals. It is important to realize that you impose many goals on your students, including social goals (e.g. 'You have to work individually, without the support o help from your peers': or 'You have to work in small groups and take responsibility for the learning of members of your group'). Peers also impose goals on other students (e.g. 'Ignore the teacher when he asks for volunteers'). When students realise that their own goals are discordant with your goals, they make attempts to align the circular goals with their own goals. For example, Sandra may ask: 'Can I hand in my handwork tomorrow because I did not have enough resource material to make a good job of it?' Similarly, Stefano may request: 'Can I do this task alone, because I have a different opinion than the rest of my group?' If you grant these requests, your students will experience self-determination. The positive cognitions and feelings that are part of that experience will further the learning process. On the contrary, if you deny these requests, they will experience a conflict of goals and may not take responsibility for achieving the curricular goals. Many forms of misbehaviour in class can be interpreted in terms of a goal conflict. You will deal more flexibly with misbehaviour when you view it

> as a signal that a salient goal is being frustrated. For example, Stefano may say: 'How can I work efficiently on a math problem if you want me to help students who always run into problems?' Likewise, Sandra may ask: 'Why can't we do this task together?' It is important to realize that your students want to be treated with respect. They expect you to explain why you turn down their requests.
>
> —Monique Boekaerts: *Motivation to Learn,* International Bureau of Education, UNESCO, 2002, p. 23.

As an incomparable connoisseur of quality in education by means of cultivation of aesthetics, Tagore reminds us of the fact that no genuine education for fullness is possible through dissociation with Nature. At the same time, he also makes us aware of the fact that the education of the child should always be flexible and purposeless in the sense that it should always be allowed to grow and develop its unique personality amidst uninterrupted and unalloyed freedom. To make it aware of mere materialistic success alone is to banish it from the world of beauty and joy, freedom and adventure as the essential aesthetic appreciation to fullness and perfection of life. Tagore's pointers to our erroneous system of education are remarkably elucidated in his straightforward and vibrant observation:

> Our system of education refuses to admit that children are children. Children are punished because they fail to behave like grown-up people and have the impertinence to be noisily childish. Their educators do not know or refuse to acknowledge that this childishness is Nature's own provision and that the child through its restless mind and movements should always come into new facts and stumble upon new information. Thus the child becomes the battle-ground for a flight between

the school master and Mother Nature herself. The school master is of opinion that the best means of educating a child is by concentration of mind, but Mother Nature knows that the best way is dispersion of mind. When we were children, we came to gather facts by such scattering of mental energy through unexpected surprises. The surprise gave us that shock which was needed to make us intensely conscious of the facts of life, of the world. Facts must come fresh to children to startle their minds into full activity.

It is the utter want of purpose in child-life which is important. In adult age, having made our life a bundle of a few definite purposes, we exclude all facts outside their boundaries. Our purpose wants to occupy all the mind's attention for itself, obstructing the full view of most of the things around us; it cuts a narrow bed for our deliberate mind which seeks its end through a restricted passage. The child, because it has no conscious object of life beyond living, can see all things around it, can hear every sound with a perfect freedom of attention, not having to exercise choice in the collection of information. It gives full reign to its restlessness which heads its mind into knocking against knowledge.

I have a deep-rooted conviction that only through freedom man can attain his fullness of growth, and when we restrict that freedom it means that we have some purpose of our own which we impose on our children, and we have not in mind Nature's own purpose of giving the child the fullness of growth.

If we have some purpose expressed through our educational institutions—that children should be

> producing patriots, practical men, soldiers, bankers, then it may be necessary that se have to put them through the mechanical drill of obedience and discipline! But that is not the fullness of life and the fullness of humanity. He who knows that Nature's own purpose is to make the boy a full man when he grows—full in all directions, mentally and mainly spiritually—he who realises this, brings up the child in the atmosphere of freedom.
>
> Rabindranath Tagore: "The School Master," *The Modern Review*, Calcutta, 24 October, 1924.

Enrichment and efflorescence of a child's sub-conscious mind should, according to Tagore, be guiding principle for accelerating quality in teacher education. If the teacher is aware that a child is a child and never an adult, there is the promise of teaching children without interfering with its being natural in thought and action, freedom and joy. This also ensures the latter of unrestricted mental development. Tagore spells out the above in terms of experiences he had to encounter in his own childhood days:

> I had at least acquired a negative experience in course of my school days. I had learnt how not to treat children. What I had particularly suffered in my childhood was to feel that the education that I had received was separated from life. I admit I had a certain special sensibility which others did not share with me in the same degree. Otherwise, I would undoubtedly have more easily resigned myself to my suffering, and would, in the course of those days at school, have succeeded like the others in stifling in me that passionate zest for life, for nature, from which everyday I had to be dragged away as from a mother in order to enter the classroom.

I recall it, the door of the class-room, gaping each morning like a big mouth, its bare walls, its wooden benches, its wooden desk at which the teacher stood giving his lesson like a living phonograph. I still know it by heart, and I can hear it the repetition of the same, which had neither the beauty of melody nor rhythm, which every morning we chanted in chorus on the wooden verandah of the school before entering the class. It spoke of many good things no doubt, that it was necessary to be wise, not to steal, nor borrow. But it was, nevertheless, a bad beginning for the day.

* * * * * *

It was not, however, that I believed that I had any special gift for teaching, but it seemed to me that I had the secret of making them [children] happy.

To tell you the truth, nobody had any faith in me. I had neither a university degree, nor distinction of any kind. I passed for an extremely unpractical hand, who knew nothing except writing verse. It was now a matter of finding blankets and sheets and of procuring food and lodging for the five boys who had been entrusted to my care.

I tried to live their daily life. Education, properly speaking, was a secondary matter. What was of the first importance was that our life was lived in our common comradeship.

For me, indeed, a child up to its twelfth year lives much more in the sub-conscious than in clear consciousness and what is important during these first years is not to burden his memory with knowledge which taxes his mind, but to see that his sub-conscious is saturated with beauty through the contact with living nature.

—Rabindranath Tagore: "A Poet's School," *March of India,* March-April, 1951, Delhi Translated by Sasadhar Sinha from "Les Educateur", No. 12, 11 June, 1921, *Social Thinking of Rabindranath Tagore,* Asia Publishing House, Bombay, 1962, pp. 149-150.

How should a teacher educator assess quality enrichment in teacher education? As one dedicated to advancement of right teaching in right earnest for effulgence of aesthetics in the acme of the promise of perfection, Tagore's poignant words would certainly pay benign dividends:

Day after day, O lord of life, shall I stand before thee face to face. With folded hands, O lord of all worlds, shall I stand before thee face to face.

Under thy great sky in solitude and silence, with humble heart shall I stand before thee face to face.

In this laborious world of thine, tumultuous with toil and with struggle, among hurrying crowds shall I stand before thee face to face.

And when my work shall be done in this world, O King of kings, alone and speechless shall I stand before thee face to face.

—Rabindranath Tagore: *Gitanjali,* Macmillan India Limited, New Delhi, Macmillan Pocket Tagore Edition, 1983, pp. 50-51.

# 3

# Teacher Education for the Schools of Tomorrow

Teacher education today is confronted with a lot of confusions. What should be the appropriate role of the teacher, and, for that end-in-view, that of a teacher educator? What should be the role of the schools of today to prove the assurances of quality and excellence not only now but for tomorrow and tomorrow? What are the positive and meaningful avenues of curriculum framework in tune with individual and group advancement in education? What should be the essential creative and aesthetic parameters of teacher education programmes suited to the needs and possibilities of guaranteeing quality and excellence in school education from time to time? All these and numerous other direct and/or allied queries necessitate objective, scientific, reliable, valid, specific and teacher-pupil friendly solutions for the schools of tomorrow as everyone interested in education ardently aspires.

Keeping sincerely in mind, the role of teacher education for quality and excellence in school education for today and tomorrow, the National Council of Educational Research and

Training (NCERT) has come out with vibrant visions. In the Foreword to the *National Curriculum Framework 2005,* Professor Yash Pal, Chairperson of the National Steering Committee, poignantly observes:

> The document frequently revolves around the question of curriculum load on children. In this regard we have fallen into a pit. We have bartered away understanding for memory-based, short-term information accumulation. This must be reversed particularly now that the mass of what could be memorised has begun to explode. We need to give our children some taste of understanding, following which they would be able to learn and create their own versions of knowledge as they go out to meet the world of bits, images and transactions of life. Such a taste would make the present of our children wholesome, creative and enjoyable; they would not be traumatised by the excessive burden of information that is required merely for a short time before the hurdle race we call examination. The document suggests some ways of getting out of this self-imposed adversity. Achieving some degree of success in this area would also signify that we have learnt to appreciate the capacity of learning and the futility of filling up children's memory banks with information that is best kept as ink marks on paper or bits on a computer disc.
>
> —"Foreword", *National Curriculum Framework 2005,* National Council of Educational Research and Training, New Delhi, 2005, p.iii.

That the schools of today or, for that consequential points of view, those of tomorrow must not under any circumstances be imprisoned in either the world of mere 'ink marks' or computer happiness telling heavily upon 'children's memory banks' necessitates a thorough re-shuffling. The three very important components in teaching-learning yet to be given their appropriate dues are love, freedom and joy in the world of education. Bereft of these components, the education of our children today, the children of tomorrow notwithstanding, cannot but be stuff and nonsense—the parrot's training— in teaching and learning.

Quality education must ensure the education of the heart. It ought to be the education of today that amply and genuinely promises the fullness of the education of tomorrow. The education of the heart indicating and absolutely representing the quality education we strive and seek is the education of love. Is teacher education prepared for imparting the education of love for children in the right direction towards efflorescence of personality right now? One really interested in doing away with dole-dry sub-standard education would say in reply, 'No, certainly not.' The why-s and how-s of our failure in teacher education are so much confused in utopia and abstraction that quality wails in the undiscovered Arcadia of teaching and learning. Meanwhile, the ill and/or half-baked education of apathy is allowed to be nurtured in the camouflaged spree of so-called quality explosion. Nearly a century ago, Rabindranath Tagore poignantly remarked, "Apathy and ignorance are the worst forms of bondage for man." That we are far away from the 'education of sympathy' as one of the most prominent components of quality education for children of today and many more days to come is not beyond anybody's guess.

Quality education also demands teachers who never fail to do justice to freedom in education. The reverse procedure of child-to-teacher in lieu of teacher-to-child under the crystallised and disciplined exercise of freedom works wonders in quality education. Teaching becomes adventurous and pulsating. At the same time, learning becomes an undeterred endeavour in nursling the world of introspection and innovation. Moreover, with freedom so exercised in a conjoint and communicated climate of teaching-learning, quality is prized with a healthy ground of sincerity and togetherness in teacher-learner relationship.

Cultivation and dissemination of joy in quality teacher education can hardly be ignored. Apart from the fact that our schools of today more often than not fail to come out of the traditional web of chalk, talk and stock mentality in teaching-learning, the green learners in schools know the only and perhaps yet to be strongly challenged so-called prize in education: marks. A little bit of student-friendly alternative in the name of grades has also failed to bring forth the lost paradise of joy in education. And marks-free or grade-free education for quality and advancement is beyond our imagination. As a result, neither teacher educators nor teachers nor even the children as invaluable learners have an enviable entry into the diverse parameters of joy that serves as the unparalleled and incomparable elixir of education. If the schools of tomorrow do not serve the purpose of cultivation of joy, why not de-schooling and de-teaching which might open newer avenues of joy and wonder?

It is high time right now or never to make a sanguine blueprint for teacher education for the schools of tomorrow, where teaching methods ought to be varied, inquisitive, pupil-oriented, innovative, freedom-adorned, love-embraced, joy-thrilled and above all, living. In this connection , teacher education for the schools of tomorrow should right now focus on positive thinking where the method of teaching every subject needs more flexibility and quality-assured and the role of the teacher and teaching is given a finer and more sensitized assignment of promise translated and action in perfect symphony with the learner's unique world. As the National Focus Group on Teacher Education for Curriculum Renewal categorically suggests:

> There is no one 'method' that is effective in causing all learners to learn in similar ways. Each teacher has to find one's own 'style' of learning through perceptive practice but recognise the fact that *all learners learn in their own ways*. 'Teaching method' therefore, has two aspects for assessing its effectiveness or appropriateness. One pertains to teacher's style with which she uses method or methods. It relates to one's own rationale. The second is the learner's (school student's) way of learning. The participation in unique ways speaks of the role of teacher and learner in the pursuit of knowing or learning. While both teacher and learner participate in learning situation, they are beneficiaries. Acquisition of learning on the part of the student has been a major concern in educational situations. In this sense, technically, thy both are learners.
>
> —*Position Paper: National Focus Group On Teacher Education for Curriculum Renewal,* National Council of Educational Research and Training, New Delhi, 2006, p. 20.

Admittedly, pupil motivation in the apposite perspective of advancement and excellence is one of the greatest challenges in teacher education, and. For that particular end-in-view, the multidimensional motivation maps in education for quality acceleration ought to be prioritised in right perspectives. As students learn by effectively exercising the fourfold flexible strategy of understanding, reasoning, recalling and solving different problems in upholding individuality as justified to creative and critical thinking, a major shift from teacher cues and suggestions to curiosity-caressed pupil thinking with subtlety and serenity would obviously enrich teaching-learning.

What, then, should teachers do in the classroom? Here is a very positive suggestion:

> Teachers must recognise the importance of students knowing and using a variety of strategies. The teaching of strategies can be done directly or indirectly. In the latter case, the teacher can give students a task and provide a model of the inquiry process or ask key questions. For example, in reading, teachers can explicitly show students how to outline the important points in a text and how to summarise them. Alternatively, they can ask a group of students to discuss a text and summarise it. They can help in this process by participating in the discussion and by asking critical questions. In science, teachers can show students how to conduct experiments: how to form hypotheses, how to keep a systematic record of their findings, and how to evaluate them.
>
> It is important to ensure that students learn these strategies on their own and do not always rely on teachers to provide the necessary support. Teachers need to gradually fade their assistance and allow students to take greater responsibility for their learning.
>
> —Stella Vosniadou: *How Children Learn,* International Bureau of Education, UNESCO, 2001, pp.14-15.

Undeniably, self-supporting and self-assisted learning by learners as an approach to quality teaching is beyond any parallel or equivalent or even minimum viable substitute. As such, if students are self-motivated, the assignments of the teacher become more challenging because henceforth finer nuances and softer sensibilities look forward to marking an altogether newer habitation and climate of quality-culture where the symphony of success endlessly beckons.

As quality teacher education meant for the schools of tomorrow cannot but honour individual differences. The psychology of teaching should guarantee a fool-proof shift from generalised strategies to specific human intelligence oriented ones where developmental psychology is allowed to have its skill-justified role in teaching learning. How to accelerate such kind of education in and for teaching? How to crystallise the potentiality inherent in every learner? Here are some significant suggestions:

* Learn how to assess children's knowledge, strategies and modes of learning adequately.
* Introduce children to a wide range of materials, activities and learning tasks that include language, mathematics, natural sciences, social sciences, art, music, movement, social understanding, etc.
* Identify students' areas of strength, paying particular attention to the interest, persistence and confidence they demonstrate in different kinds of activities.
* Support students' areas of strength and utilize these areas to improve overall academic performance.
* Guide and challenge students' thinking and learning.
* Ask children thought-provoking questions and give them problems to solve. Urge children to test hypotheses in a variety of ways.
* Create connections to the real world by introducing problems and materials drawn from everyday situations.
* Show children how they can use their unique profiles of intelligence to solve real-world problems.

* Create circumstances for students to interact with people in the community, and particularly with adults who are knowledgeable and enthusiastic about the kinds of things that are of interest to the students.

—*Ibid.*, pp. 25-26.

Are the teachers at present enjoying favourable conditions that guarantee effective and quality teaching? The less said in reply, the better. And so, the schools of today are still in a quandary as how teaching and learning are serenely clubbed for a tumultuous progress in teacher education for the schools of tomorrow. The contents of teacher education well attuned to methodologies ought to set radical and revolutionary agenda. The challenges are yet to be identified on priority basis where every area of rationale is to be blended with reasoning and reflection, poignancy and dedication. As the Report to UNESCO on the International Commission on Education for the Twenty-first Century concludes:

> Clearly, there are no easy answers to the different problems inherent in improving the quality of teachers, the teaching process and teaching content. Teachers deservedly claim recognition for their endeavours, in terms of their working conditions and status. They must be given the tools to carry out their roles as well as possible. In return, their pupils and society as a whole are entitled to expect them to discharge their duties with dedication and a strong sense of their responsibilities.
>
> —*Learning: The Treasure Within,* UNESCO, 1996, p. 152.

Meanwhile, let us also make a more positive paradigm-shift in teacher education for the schools of today and tomorrow at the behest of a new economy where technology enjoys a strong platform in consolidating quality in diverse strategies of teaching and learning. Education for the new economy should, therefore, be technology-friendly. As it is aptly suggested:

> There is no better legacy, no greater hope we can leave for our children than the possibility of a good education. Education is the greater equaliser in life. And, when paired with the internet, good education becomes a global possibility; and more equally distributed prosperity takes one more step towards reality.
>
> When faced with fundamental yet strategic difficulties, nations that have addressed them successfully have become leaders and set the pace for economic growth. The same will be the case with 21st century education. The sky is not falling; this is not a doomsday prediction. It's merely a simple math equation. A solid education system added to a supportive government plus strong broadband infrastructure equals sustainable advantage that leads to a strong economy. Subtract the solid education system, and the equation won't just add up.
>
> —John Chambers: "Education for the New Economy", *The Economic Times,* New Delhi, 21 June 2006.

Teacher education for the schools of tomorrow should have a bright heritage with that of the schools of today that promise and perform accordingly with the happy unison of the intuitive mind and rational intelligence. This is an assignment whereon the legacy of success of teacher education depends and where precious little activities would definitely show excellence and ascent in education as the life-blood of humans. Intuitive education is the need of the hour. The schools of today and tomorrow should emphasise on development of the power of insight through better individualisation of instruction for greater and more worthy socialisation of every learner at every stage of school education. In the words of Sri Aurobindo:

> ...the action of the intuitive mind must complete the action of the rational intelligence and it may even wholly replace it and do more powerfully the peculiar and proper work of the intellect itself; it may explain more intimately to us the secret of the form, the strands of the process, the inner cause, essence, mechanism of the defects and limitations of the work as well as of its qualities. For the intuitive intelligence when it has been sufficiently trained and developed, can take up always the work of the intellect and do it with a power and light and insight greater and surer than the power and light of the intellectual judgment in its widest scope. There is an intuitive discrimination which is more keen and precise in its sight than the reasoning intelligence.
>
> —Sri Aurobindo: *Education of the Future,* Sri Aurobindo Society, Pondicherry, 1974, pp. 12-13.

How to be justified to the learner as best as possible? How to be error proof in the methodology of teaching? How to come nearer to the learner in imparting instructions? The skill of questioning well applied wins half the battle against inadequacy with respect to each of the items of teaching. Here is a very practical suggestion to the teachers:

> One of the sharpest worries of the conscientious teacher is his own inadequacy. He has not made this vital point clear. Did they [the learners] really understand his sketch of that theory, and his refutation of it? Should he have given more time to the first half of the programme? These worries can be removed, or at least mitigated, by three or four hours saved at the end of the term for revising the

course, filling in the gaps, and re-emphasising the important points. It is tempting sometimes to end a lecture course with a rousing peroration on the final topic, but its impression soon fades, whereas a steady, cool, clear review of the entire ground will, in a comparatively short time and with comparatively little effort, make a far deeper and more lasting mark on these flexible minds.

As the class retraces its journey, it will have a fine opportunity to ask *questions,* and you to prompt them and answer them. Never underestimate the power of a well-put question to illuminate the darkness. Students who have been passively absorbing information and allowing it to trickle out almost as fast as it was poured in will often come to life and take an active interest in their work when questions start flying. But the real value of the question-period at the end is for the conscientious students. It is worth while to read through a lecture-notebook kept by a student of good intelligence and industry. The gaps and misunderstandings in it will astound you. Often these youngsters are afraid to ask you to fill in the gaps, because they do not want to give themselves away. They think you will snub them, or answer perfunctorily. If you do, you are committing a crime. Instead, you should make it easy for them to ask for corrections, full names, the exact figures, the complete references. Don't simply wait for them to demand help. Offer it. You have not often always spoken clearly. Foreign names and complex formulas are difficult to write down quickly. A cough will cover up half a vital sentence; and, in many cities nowadays, at least five minutes of every hour's teaching is made inaudible by the

> roar of transport aircraft apparently flying just above the roofs. The last few meetings of the class are your opportunity to wash away all that mud, and reveal your own lost pearls.
>
> —Gilbert Highet: *The Art of Teaching*, University Paperbacks, Methuen, London, 1963, pp. 148-149.

Nearness to the learner with all sincerity and cautious assistance in quest of learning are the two strong pillars of success for a teacher. Sometimes the class goes on in the dreams of the quality teacher who also encourages his learners to dream for better and more promising learning.

Acceptability, dependability, quality and excellence in education in general and teacher education in particular are never-ending challenges. The more we are involved in these as teachers, learner assistants, comrades and partners in the purity and essence in teaching by learning and vice versa, the more are the worthy dividends.

Meanwhile, let us pray for the Light Eternal as the lasting force for a brighter tomorrow in every altar of learning:

> Light, oh where is the light! Kindle it with the burning fire of desire! It thunders and the wind rushes screaming through the void. The night is black as a black stone. Let not the hours pass in the dark. Kindle the lamp of love with thy life.
>
> —*Gitanjali,* Macmillan India Ltd., New Delhi, Macmillan Pocket Tagore Edition, 1983, p.16.

# 4

# Teacher Education and Value-Cultivation

Education today is undergoing unprecedented stress and strain. This is all the more alarming in rapid and rampant deterioration of the minimum essentials of values in day-to-day life. Parents and relatives close or distant are perplexed. Educational institutions fail to maintain apposite teaching-learning climate under severe pressure of value crisis. The community climate is hardly favourable for decent and quality living. Even administration for preservation and supervision of moral and aesthetic values are continually negotiating violence and ukase. One cannot but recall the unfortunate and terrible mental and physical pressure which engulfed almost the whole academic scenario in a neighbouring State in particular where political investments were prioritized in education through learner-abduction. Complex and compromise have engulfed the serene arena of values in education so much so that a stern and strict administrator in education has been shunted out from his assignment in maintenance of discipline in a public examination as recently reported in the news media. Under the circumstances, teacher education necessitates an earnest overhauling in value cultivation.

Admittedly, education is a challenging task, and teacher education is more challenging because it is concerned with teachers who are dedicated to the task of teaching and moulding the minds of young learners in inspiring them in value-cultivation in diverse and enlightened directions. The contents and methods of teaching values await a simple, heartening and easily accessible atmosphere of teaching-learning where values are exercised in a natural atmosphere of freedom and joy. Even the skills for communication at every step ought to be so crystallised and disseminated as to leave a permanent stamp of grace and lucidity, goodness and beauty. Values as mere values in theories or definitions rarely make any appeal either to be taught or to be learnt. In fact, no lesson on values becomes effective unless there is a living response for direct cultivation in an ambience of stimulating interest and accrediting appreciation. Values in terms of multi-dimensional components extensively spelt out with newer strategies of pupil-appreciation enjoy avenues of efflorescence in education for fullness.

The nursling of subjectivity in values is one of the best means of how to cultivate values. Sadly enough, this has been ruthlessly given an unusual backseat in education today. While the burden of education is astoundingly increasing, thanks to computer-crazy education in the jet-joyous twenty-first century, the Arden of education appallingly suffers from crisis in values. In upholding beauty, for instance, as an invaluable component in value education, what most of the teachers formulate and elucidate in course of teaching may fall in deaf ears to a learner because, contrary to the generally accepted and normal concept of beauty as a value component, he/she has his/her own world of beauty where the so-called antithetical concepts of beauty like ugliness, unfairness, abnormality and strangeness under diverse but more arresting circumstances become more appropriate, telling and down-to-earth in perfect tune with humane sense and sensibilities.

Apart from the fact that personalised values are severely neglected and relegated to the background in the whole arena of education, teacher education is yet to make assured inroads to equip teachers in teaching how to translate values in teaching into vibrant and worthwhile reality. It is also a challenge in teacher education to preparing teachers for a broader canvas of value integration where isolated values with assimilation and precision become more meaningful and significant, purposeful and convergent with challenging needs and priorities of life. Simultaneously, value-uniqueness should have its characteristic exposures in and through activities. A certain pattern of well-embracing inner discipline and decency always looks forward to being happily wedded to the harmony of conceptual clarity and vibrant vision.

In teacher education, the world of values has a specific and urgent appeal because teachers are the direct disseminators of values to their learners who have the proneness to take up and brand all values as abstraction and inconsistent to set-patterns of life bruised and battered under artificiality and demoralisation. The rebuilding of the ached and stunted structures and imagery-patterns of every external value concept presupposes orientation in the right avenues of performance and perfection. At the same time, a thorough study of the essentials of value-orientation prior to launching programmes thereon well advances identification of the plus and the minus points of implementation and evaluation of the work-schedule of value education.

The ends-in-view of teacher education for cultivation of values should be directed towards the following parameters:

(i) To enable the teacher to better identify values best suited to the learner at different stages of school education in particular.

(ii) To stimulate the teacher to make continual and careful explorations as the values so identified with adroit analysis and interpretations under desirable and/or changing situations.

(iii) To make a convenient platform in quest of the essentials of values for exercise in real life situations quite vulnerable for young learners.

(iv) To locate and penetrate into the delicate issues and constraints of value-cultivation with a view to bringing about a favourable climate of application and exercise without allowance of advance in any form of stigma or syndrome, delicacy or deficiency.

(v) To manipulate teachers' own approaches and strategies of values side by side with a comparative and judicious approach to pupils' attitudes, aptitudes, interests and appreciations for finer enhancement and manifestation of the world of values.

(vi) To allow teachers to exercise a decisive and definite pattern of value-cultivation which would enable the learner to be precise and distinct, categorical and pin-pointed in value-conceptualisation and value-exercise with all appropriateness and clarity of vision.

(vii) To foster a liberal approach to teaching of values especially needed for the beginners in schools who would certainly enjoy and appreciate values in terms of freedom to grow, think and learn in a flexible and adoring exercise of interesting value components related to their tastes and temperaments.

(viii) To expand and elicit different value-stylistics among teachers who delve deep into value education for creative and reflective thinking.

(ix) To inspire teachers to be oriented in value education for development of aesthetic sensibilities.

(x) To provide teachers with opportunities for expanding the horizons of value education for kindred responses to the ethos and moorings pertaining to national and trans-national heritage and culture.

(xi) To stimulate teachers in preparation and experiments on cross-cultural synergies amongst rural and urban pupils with value-diversities.

(xii) To encourage teachers to plan and execute programmes of activities related to education for development of essential values by means of relevant co-curricular activities including exhibitions, workshops, debates, discussions, symposia, educational tours, social and cultural activities etc. that ensure worthwhile fusion of values in decent living.

It is high time for teacher orientation in value education with specific strategies in school education. Teachers serve as live models for values to be *caught* by young learners in particular. A slight deviation from this readily invites devaluation of values with utter ugliness and assassination, as it were, of refinements in all aspects of life. Unless there is a missionary zeal for consolidation of mind and character on the part of a teacher, values are destined to be replaced by mischief and crime with deadly arms of violence of the worst patterns. Therefore, orientation of teachers calls forth five strategies:

1. Care for pupil-interest and appreciation to different value-concepts should be prioritised.
2. Involvements in enrichment of pupils' value-concepts and experiments should be greatly encouraged.
3. Setting agenda for pupils for value-analysis in terms of comparative significance should be sincerely chalked out and judiciously introduced.
4. Arrangements of adequate platforms for value cultivation and exposure should be thoroughly made.

5. Crystallising the outcome of pupils' unique presentation of value-exercises should be a major teaching assignment.

The strategic avenues for cultivation of values in the middle and the senior stages of school education obviously presuppose success in this direction at the early stage. Indeed, if the groundwork for cultivation of values fails to ensure a sound platform, it is very difficult for the teacher to introduce newer strategies of teaching for values. This is why orientation programmes for teachers on value education require a third horizon in anticipation that a special programme in the form of a refresher course on values already introduced and exercised may enlighten the right road to negotiate abstraction and irrelevance, limitations and constraints for desirable advancement.

The two stages of school education referred to as above are complementary to each other in respect of pursuit of values. The teachers concerned ought to be more alert in the strategic roles preferred and selected by pupils themselves for cultivation of values. The more each of the pupils' work-schedules are self-supported and self-enriched, the better is the outcome of value education. Teachers, therefore, ought to undergo training and orientation on when and how to appositely relegate themselves into the background on the issue of value-involvement and success signals on the teaching of values.

As regards socio-cultural and socio-aesthetic parameters of value education, orientation of teachers necessitates a catholic backdrop of humane sensibilities and altruistic submission to indigenous needs and priorities. It is prime time that value education is caught in topmost sincerity of purpose and devotion and never taught in a stereotyped, moralistic, sermonized and schizophrenic manner by following a few bogus and slovenly written text-books that are enough for the burial of value education.

Parental care in education for values is gradually turning into a myth. Frankly, children hardly receive the warmth of security and affection, involvement and guidance from parents and guardians with regard to value-exercise. With several entertainment gadgets cheap and abundantly available and rampantly used without care and caution, they become easy and forceful victims to obscenities in audio-visuals. Who cares? Family imbalance and disturbances as reflected in broken homes, separation, loneliness, addiction and evasiveness, to mention a few, have amply provided a fertile ground for value-crisis and value- moratoria. Let there be conjoint and communicated programmes for parent-teacher orientation of values. Unless the 'education of sympathy' so poignantly stressed by Rabindranath Tagore is synchronized in the cultivation of values, the cathedrals of education would be compelled to produce 47-As or 69-Es so gravely characterised in *Raktakarabi* ("The Red Oleanders") in the name of future citizens.

Teacher education for cultivation of self-reliance and self-activity as essential values in life necessitates more emphasis than ever. Gone are the days of the role of the teacher as a mere transmitter of knowledge and information. Instead, it is time to prepare teachers who are well-trained in the task of infusing the spirit of individual responsibility in foreseeing and solving diverse issues related to value cultivation. Thus a major shift in training for teachers in pupils' value exercise as suggested below is necessary:

> The teacher's work is not confined simply to transmitting information or even knowledge; it also entails presenting that knowledge in the form of a statement of problems within a certain context and putting the problems into perspective, so that the learner can link their solution to broader issues. The teacher-pupil relationship aims at the full

> development of the pupil's personality, with emphasis on self-reliance; from this point of view the authority vested in teachers is always paradoxical, since it is not based on the assertion of their power but on the free recognition of the legacy of knowledge. This function of the teacher as a figure of authority will probably evolve, yet it remains essential as a source of the answers to questions raised by the pupil about the world and as a key prerequisite for the full success of the learning process. Besides, it is becoming increasingly necessary in modern societies for teaching to help form individual judgement and a sense of individual responsibility, so as to enable pupils to develop the ability to foresee changes and to adjust to them, in other words to continue learning throughout their lives. It is through working under, and through dialogue with, the teacher that a pupil's critical faculty is helped to develop.
>
> Teachers' great strength lies in the example they set, of curiosity, open-mindedness, willingness to put their assumptions to the test and to acknowledge mistakes; most of all, they must transmit a love of learning.
>
> —*Learning: The Treasure Within,* UNESCO, 1996, pp. 145-146.

A great deal of responsibility on the part of every teacher is to inspire every learner in cultivating values and, for this end-in-view, overhauling teacher education for teacher preparation is undeniable. The curriculum for teacher education should accommodate all viable strategies for training and orientation of teachers who ought to be aware of the basic values and their significance in translating the vision of the fullness of man. A paradigm-shift in teacher education for value cultivation cannot but be an evolving procedure where the teachers are well concerned and adequately equipped in tracing, locating, diagnosing, suggesting and encouraging innovative, individualistic, value conscious, probing and continuing programmes of learning. In fact, the curriculum for teacher education should be so oriented as to abundantly accommodate teacher assignments in value cultivation from different dimensions of school education. Therefore, the curriculum for teacher education for value cultivation should be aware of the following:

> The curriculum must enable children to find their voices, nurture their curiosity—to do things, to ask questions and to pursue investigations, sharing and integrating their experiences with school knowledge—rather than their ability to reproduce textual knowledge. Reorienting the curriculum to this end must be among our highest priorities, informing the preparation of teachers, the annual plan of schools, the design of textbooks, learning materials and teaching plans, and evaluation and examination patterns.
>
> Children will learn only in an atmosphere where they feel they are valued. Our schools still do not convey this to *all* children. The association of learning with fear, discipline and stress, rather than enjoyment and satisfaction, is detrimental to learning. Our children need to feel that each one of them, their homes, communities, languages and cultures, are valuable as resources for experience to be analysed and enquired into at school; that their diverse capabilities are accepted; that all of them have the ability and the right to learn and to access knowledge and skills; and that adult society regards

> them as capable of the best. We are becoming more aware of the importance of thee needs as our schools expand and increasingly include children from all sections of society. The midday meal and the provisioning of infrastructural support and pedagogic concern for inclusive education are among the most significant developments in recent times. A strong stand must be taken against all forms of corporal punishment. The boundaries of the school need to become more porous to the community. At the same time, the problems of curriculum load and examination-related stress require urgent attention in all their dimensions. Physical and emotional security is the cornerstone for all learning, right from the primary to the secondary school years, and even afterwards.
>
> —*National Curriculum Framework, 2005*, National Council of Educational Research and Training, New Delhi, 2005, pp. 13-14.

While concern for quality in teacher education can hardly be ignored, the programmes of teacher education making sufficient room for training and orientation of teachers in inclusive education for value exchange leading to value enrichment will definitely act as a scanner in identifying the plus and the minus points of endeavour in teaching values. Inclusive education widens the vision of value cultivation and also eliminates controlled planning and administration for selected students under a specific category. This type of categorisation in education for teaching goes against cultivation of values. A major step to curb this deficiency would be to be generous in introducing inclusive education which would certainly allow cultivation of diverse values in a panorama of heterogeneous value outcome. The advantages in welcoming inclusive education as a platform of education for values through training and orientation for in-service and student teachers or fresher students may be stated as follows:

(a) The value of co-operation is best caught in a heterogeneous set up of pupils.

(b) The problem of maintaining discipline, itself a value component, is easily negotiated. The teaching strategies of the teacher are more conveniently introduced as discipline becomes a natural and spontaneous affair, and it is more interesting for both the teacher and the learner because more emphasis is given to its spirit than to its letters. Thus teachers in the operational strategies for teaching the value of discipline encounter no taxing constraint.

(c) Inter and intra-relational value components become more explicit for the teacher to encourage learners to learn and practice without any hindrance whatsoever and also without sacrificing creativity and critical thinking. When values are evaluated in terms of creativity and the teacher becomes sincerely involved in pupils' value identification, analysis, interpretation and evaluation, teaching for values take an enviable role for excellence inviting greater excellence. Therein lies the pride of a teacher.

(d) It is always to be particularly and sincerely observed that the teacher never fails to unfold and enrich extinction of personality in dealing with values. This acts as a set-pattern to be emulated and given individualistic aroma of effulgence in contemplation and action on any value component under scanner.

(e) Uploading values with precautions against verging more on narrowness and self-interest than on altruism and self-negation is a challenging task of teacher education for value culture and value dissemination.

The vision for orientation of teachers in value-cultivation is always to be nurtured in transparencies of promise and poignancy, perfumes of elegance and decency. The task is tough and challenging, no doubt. But who else than teachers can accept and negotiate that challenge best as pioneers?

Are we prepared to address a cross-evaluative knowledge society in the value-bruised twenty-first century?

# 5

# Resurging a New Era in Teacher Education

Education is a crucial and complex activity. Teacher education is perhaps more crucial and complex because it calls forth a series of promises to be fulfilled and poignancy to be translated in action well planned in and through contemplation. What one, indeed, expects from teacher education at the very outset is: Is it prepared from diverse and different perspectives of training and education of pre-service and in-service teachers? At the same time, is it equipped with really qualified and devoted teacher educators who are in a very sound position of discharging their duties and responsibilities in boosting teacher preparation and teacher competency in order to be justified to the great vision of presenting the nation and the world at large with the best citizens for national and global all round prosperity?

Admittedly, as are the teachers so are the institutions. An institution may have a very adequate and enviable infra-structure: buildings, class-rooms, laboratories, libraries, playgrounds, hostels and other facilities; but if there is an absence of minimum number of efficient, qualified, hard-working, devoted and sincere teachers, the whole purpose of education and teaching is terribly defeated. As there are lots of individual differences as well as similarities amongst learners in an academic institution from the psychological points of view, a good teacher knows how to deal with this heterogeneous class-room climate. Necessarily, he/she is expected to stick to the golden principle of individualizing the instruction and teaching in judicious concurrence with and devotion to socializing the learners as best as possible. The greatest challenge of teacher education today is how to orient and train our teachers so that they may be justified to teaching for a grand unison of individualization and socialization without sacrificing quality and excellence in teaching learning under any circumstances whatsoever.

The revelation of the perfect child in order to create the right atmosphere of joy, freedom and creativity is the primary and mandatory need of the hour. Thinking, feeling, involving, having and loving are the five genuine and penetrating pointers of advancement in quality teaching. A radical paradigm-shift in teacher education keeping in view spontaneity, happiness, introspection and adventure in quest of the unknown and untraced, unearthed and undiscovered, very transparent in vibrant, conjoint and communicated teaching-learning can no longer be stifled and relegated to the background by stuffing the learner with lifeless information and sub-standard drudgeries of details.

At the same time, teacher education is now at the critical juncture of eliminating excessive dependence on memory-banks and crude craziness with computer fall-outs. Let passivity in learning be eliminated and substantially replaced by fine tunings in teacher education that cares for sense and sensibilities, aesthetics and in-depth queries. As Professor Yash Pal categorically asserts:

> Education is not a physical thing that can be delivered through post or a teacher. Fertile and robust education is always created, rooted on physical and cultural soil of the child and nourished through interaction with parents, teachers, fellow-students and community. The role and dignity of teachers in this function must be strengthened and underlined. There is mutuality in genuine construction of knowledge. In this transaction the teacher also learns if the child is not forced to remain passive. Since children really perceive and observe more than grown-ups, their potential role as knowledge creators needs to be appreciated.
>
> —"Foreword", *National Curriculum Framework 2005,* National Council of Educational Research and Training, New Delhi, p.i.

Undeniably, teacher education in the twenty-first century looks forward to revamping in sevenfold direction:

(i) Mapping the vulnerable areas of quality in teaching.

(ii) Re-structuring the curriculum for school education.

(iii) Revising and improving text-books and teaching learning materials.

(iv) Individualising instruction for all-round efflorescence of pupil-personality.

(v) Sensitizing the apposite approach to strengthening and mobilising social and aesthetic values.

(vi) Caressing and igniting pupils' creative and critical thinking.

(vii) Exploring and fine-tuning the heartland of little learners with apposite and challenging strategies of teaching from time to time even under trying and unfavourable circumstances.

Let there be an eternal farewell to apathy and ignorance. Let teacher education be all the time spearheaded by the education of nearness, cordiality and sympathy for the learners under countless constraints in particular.

Pre-service teacher education holds a very prominent place in the arena of education in general and teacher education in particular. That all education is pre-service education gets a very wrong signal in teacher education. It averts and, to a great extent, negates the very aims and objectives of teaching as a profession because it allows stagnation for the whole period of unemployment or the absence of recruitment and involvement in the profession of teaching. The reasons why pre-service teacher-trainees, of their greater interest and sincerity, better involvement and all-round performance notwithstanding, fail to do justice to the challenging task of teaching may be spelt out as follows:

(i) With staggering problems of unemployment and very tough and unhealthy competitions everywhere, pre-service teachers take a very casual and careless interest in teacher education under excessive stress of uncertainty and loss of faith.

(ii) The pre-service teacher students study the course of teacher education and follow the different programmes of activities in a disinterested manner because most of them are very busy in preparations of one or more than one of the following:

  (a) Higher studies in the allied or different disciplines.
  (b) Competitive examinations.
  (c) UGC/ State Level Qualifying Examinations.
  (d) Other courses unrelated to teacher education.

(iii) The pre-service teacher-trainees very often become victims to complexes and delicacies of different patterns in association with the in-service teachers in particular. Teacher-educators, too, are sometimes at a loss how to overcome these constraints and fail to arrive at a judicious consensus.

(iv) Absence of a separate curriculum framework for pre-service teacher-trainees very often creates a dismal and disturbing class-room situation.

(v) Teacher educators often fail to do justice to any or both pre-service or in-service groups of teacher-trainees in a compound or mixed class-room climate.

(vi) Very often teacher educators suffer from content poverty or deficiencies in content mastery in dealing with the pre-service teacher-trainees in particular.

(vii) Orientation courses for pre-service teacher-trainees exclusively are still now not seriously and adequately taken into consideration in teacher education.

(viii) Research and innovation in teacher education fail to attract pre-service teacher-trainees as these turn out to be irrelevant and redundant due to rejection of discipline-validity or multi-disciplinary approach in an antithetical climate of uncertainty in judicious and worthwhile engagement and blurred vision of employment in future.

(ix) Narrowness of vision in pre-service education for teacher trainees in sandwiching academic and administrative proficiencies cripples progress in teacher education.

(x) Freedom of exercising innovative strategies of teaching by talented pre-service teacher-trainees is dwarfed under heavy pressure of traditional contents and methods of teaching.

(xi) Any endeavour at contribution to preparation followed by addition, alteration and enrichment of text-books by pre-service teacher-trainees is in most cases discouraged or disallowed as undue encroachment either implicitly or explicitly.

(xii) The joy of learning how to be a successful teacher in future is lost in the melee of sub-standard or commercial assignments covered under the pretext of the curriculum of teacher education, where teacher educators and others involved in curriculum reconstruction or renewal remain passive and silent spectators.

(xiii) The dream of a pre-service teacher-trainee to make newer adventures in the world of teaching and learning fades away in sordid and painful absence of individualised, dynamic and stimulating instruction by teacher educators.

(xiv) The role of teacher-trainees in the pre-service period is unduly and utterly relegated to the background in the lame excuse that they are not of immediate necessity as they are not directly connected with any school as regular appointed teachers.

(xv) The pre-service teacher-trainees as invaluable knowledge workers hardly get ample support in undertaking challenging plans, programmes and projects in teaching for development of insight and innovation under a more or less passive and/or indifferent social environment.

To ensure an enlightened and humane advancement in pre-service teacher education, the curriculum cannot but address the following:

(i) Highlighting pre-service teacher education as a potent force for accelerating and widening newer horizons of an enviable knowledge society.

(ii) Allowing ample scope for efflorescence of creative, aesthetic and critical thinking of pre-service teacher educators.

(iii) Boosting individual plans and programmes of teaching under diverse constraints and crises.

(iv) Stimulating healthy, conjoint and communicated teaching assignments.

(v) Maintaining discipline in dealing with day-to-day programmes of activities.

(vi) Looking into special needs and priorities of pre-school teacher-trainees especially in contribution to and transaction of radical and evolving teaching.

(vii) Upholding quality in teaching the pre-service teachers.

(viii) Arranging and sticking to appropriate selection procedures for pre-school teacher-trainees strictly on the basis of merit.

(ix) Introducing special programmes for pre-service teachers in the teaching of values and culture-synthesis and culture-dissemination.

(x) Launching comprehensive programmes for pre-service teachers to be efficient transmitters of the best Indian ethos and moorings and sensitizers of finer sensibilities and softer visions of life.

Teacher education for in-service teachers at the different stages of school education necessitates a fresh and thorough overhauling. For this purpose, the following points may be considered:

(i) Elimination of poverty in content mastery and appropriate exercise thereof.

(ii) Regular and systematic orientation in methods of teaching.

(iii) Exchange programmes for teachers with a view to ensuring quality and excellence in vulnerable institutions.

(iv) Special programmes for proficiency in teaching for aesthetic and creative efflorescence.

(v) Package programmes for teachers dealing with crucial and priority-based issues and ideas on national and social solidarity.

(vi) Involvement of teachers in scissoring heavy loads of learning and teaching.

(vii) Departure and dissociation from the existing pattern of training of pre-service and in-service teachers together as it calls forth constraints in desirable maintenance of quality and balance in teaching besides inviting unavoidable complex and delicacies.

(viii) Fostering the spirit of improving the quality of teaching through igniting the importance of life-long learning by appropriately manipulating the skills well formulated in terms of self-study and self-experiments. (ix)Steering the teachers' attention towards right ideas, right concepts, right interpretations, right comprehension and right strategies whatsoever insignificant or marginal these might appear.

(x) The pedagogic deliberations ought to be in perfect tune with learners' abilities, proneness and contextual appeal in addition to the teachers' own models of imparting instructions well-scanned under training schedule of activities in diverse socio-cultural climate.

The vision of in-service teacher education for all the stages in school education as above is to make a perfect fusion between thought and action, resolution and accomplishment, promise and fulfilment in a continually and tellingly newer and more arresting avenues of advancement of knowledge and wisdom, erudition and precision, serenity and simplicity, catholicity and crystallisation, and, above all, transparency and transcendence in the solemn and arduous task of teaching-learning.

For a very dependable and sound programme of professional enrichment of teachers, the first and foremost target area is to be well trained in how to learn the motivational maps and spurts of students and decide introducing teaching strategies accordingly. The end-in-view, therefore, is to launch vigorous and sustained teacher education programmes for committed and proficient teachers with all-encompassing evidence of enlivening competency and assured ascent of progress in different dimensions.

Moreover, with increasing demands for re-education and supplementary teaching learning inputs, in-service teacher education is also concerned with the following:

(i) To enable in-service teachers to deal with the most apposite strategies in pupils' teaching by learning how to teach with a view to bringing the latter up in quest of making incomparable and unparalleled inroads to excellence by themselves.

(ii) To inspire and accelerate newer strategies for adventures into the world of pupils' learning progress through learning by introducing education for joy and freedom, creativity and critical awareness.

(iii) To stimulate them to explore, analyse, compare and synthesise the typical individual learner's approach to finer aesthetic sensibilities and nobler visions of life, and allow them to effectively ponder over each item of knowledge and experience as they encounter in course of interaction.

(iv) To highlight preparations for in-service teacher education in alert tune with the changing needs and priorities of individual learner's reaction to learning in a heterogeneous class-room atmosphere.

(v) To encourage in-service teachers to be well informed and trained in management education in association with organisation, supervision, guidance, evaluation, research and upgrading of quality and assessments towards desirable and profitable excellence.

Teacher education for in-service teachers poses an uphill task of evolutionary, diversifying and extending living visions of education for the enlightened all. Care should be taken to maintain a healthy climate of coordination among the different stakeholders of training and research in teacher education viz. missionary and private institutions, open universities and university departments of education including advanced study centres in education and colleges under universities. A paradigm shift in quality assurance in in-service teacher education looks forward to reshuffling of work-schedule in right earnest without inviting unnecessary ukase.

With increasing demand for value-added education, education in general and in-service teacher education in particular, the importance of being adept in disseminating the spirit of knowledge-connectivity through e-education is undeniable. In a fast changing era of knowledge, let our in-service teachers contribute their best possible endeavour towards fulfilment of we-can-do-it mission of education of ever vibrant fullness.

# 6

# Quality in Teacher Education: Tagorean Aesthetics

Teacher education in India today is undergoing rapid changes. With overhauling of curriculum and evaluation in particular, the parameters of teacher education for quality assurance and quality acceleration are being continually reshuffled so that the learners and the teachers are well directed in course of newer and more challenging avenues of advancement in learning and teaching. Naturally, the task of the teacher educator is so vast and multi-dimensional that she/he has no way out but to ardently devote to identifying, exploring, analysing, introducing and evaluating the plus and the minus points of strategies for teaching-learning best suited to the attitudes, aptitudes, skills, interests, understandings and appreciations of teachers and learners under different teaching-learning situations. Hence, better teaching for better quality assurance and quality maintenance, and *vice versa* is undeniable.

How to be assured of better teaching for better quality and its maintenance, advancement and efflorescence notwithstanding? How to conduct the programmes of teacher education where quality is primarily and solely characterised by the promises of the ascent and catholicity of knowledge in the poignancy of wisdom? That bare knowledge and information that are indiscriminately and, more often than not, inanely doled out in the camouflaging show of advancement in teaching-learning, whatsoever or howsoever, terribly betray development and dissemination of finer sensibilities and softer visions of life is yet to be taken into serious and urgent consideration. Whither teacher education for quality concern? Whither experimentations for quality for knowledge turned wisdom for identity of the individual as a global citizen?

Unlike any other visionary in education, Rabindranath Tagore has always education as a continual quest for joy and freedom. It is an eternal challenge for making an unending adventure in finding out the sky of the mind—*chidakas*—that alone has the indomitable power to be both subjective and altruistic and the invariable thread that weaves the wonders of man is the aesthetics of truth, beauty and goodness in particular. Apart from the fact that Tagore is more conscious and interested in quality than anything else in education in general and teacher education especially, what prompts him to ponder over and experiment in aesthetic education as an indispensable and inseparable component of being justified to quality. It eliminates dullness and drabness in teaching that kills the lifeblood of the innovative mind. When quality in teaching is pressurised by mechanical, system-schizophrenic, imitating, routine-bound, monotonous and imprisoned world of knowledge with petty objectives like passports to living somehow or living in passivity and indifference, it terribly betrays true education of the mind and the heart. What a demotion of man from the promises of poignancies in aesthetic exercises!

Admittedly, teacher education for advancement of quality in and through nursling of aesthetic sensibilities demands immediate attention. Being disgusted with education that pays more attention to work-based education that has of late being characterised in workaholic super-fast dimensions and ignores the creative, critical and aesthetic visions of either the teacher or the learner, Tagore wants to introduce the aesthetic education of the mind and the heart that cares and boosts the education of how to revive and restore the harmony of humane joy and freedom. Like a 'torn out line of a verse', he himself has experienced the trauma of schooling that kills the joy of learning as the educational institutions almost everywhere are simply prison houses with learners caged and cornered, stuffed and silenced in the name of learning discipline by letters and never in spirit. As a matter of fact, his bitter experiences in the pursuit of studies in not less than four schools in Calcutta have presented him with at least five dubious and dangerous prizes: the horrible scene of corporal punishment, cruel regimentation, lifeless teaching outcome, absolute elimination of joy and freedom of both the teacher and the learner and utter matter-of-fact and mechanical teaching-learning climate. The results are obvious. In the name of teaching, the teacher enjoys uninterrupted holidays in an atmosphere of aggravating chaos. He/ she neither involves himself/herself in education for development of aesthetic efflorescence nor is he/she interested in how to teach children to be spontaneously and thrillingly motivated in learning and practising the finer components of aesthetics like truth, beauty, goodness, grace, etc. What, then, do we normally receive as the inevitable outcome of teaching? The less said the better because quality in teaching is identified and assessed in terms of the so-called proficiency in intellectual performance by means of cramming and hardly by assimilation and effulgence of aesthetic vision that refines intellect with relentless crystallisation of emotion. One recalls in this connection how Tagore has marvellously exposed the appalling outcome of an overdose of intellectual education that turns humans into numbers like 47-A or 69-E as one comes across in *Red Oliendors (Raktakarabi).* Unless aesthetics is fine-tuned with intellect in education in general and teacher education in particular, quality concern cannot but be a myth.

The aims and objectives of quality enhancement in teacher education for development of aesthetic sense and sensibilities as Tagore has thought and experimented, may be spelt out as follows:

(i) To enable the teacher to explore and utilise the very incubation period of the learners' aesthetic curiosity.

(ii) To stimulate the teacher to be a dynamic and living partner to every student probing deep into the world of aesthetics in course of studies or/and allied affairs.

(iii) To inspire the teacher to find out newer avenues of efflorescence of the learners' aesthetic thoughts and experiments through creative contributions in diverse forms like fine arts, histrionics, music, debates, discussions, symposia etc. and participation in the same along with the students in an atmosphere of spontaneous joy and freedom.

(iv) To instil in the mind of the teacher the inherent values of the culture of aesthetic sensibilities that stand the test of time as an ever abiding and inspiring stamp of quality for ascent and excellence.

(v) To encourage every teacher to be justified and alert in identifying, analysing and executing the different components of aesthetics in accordance with the interest, attitude and aptitude of each learner under varying teaching-learning atmosphere for better and more sensitised quality in aesthetic education.

(vi) To allow freedom of the teacher to cultivate his/her creative and critical thinking in the transparency strategies of quality in aesthetic education, and, in doing so, provide ample opportunities for probing into the finer and more delicate components of aesthetics that highlight a broader canvas of catholicity of vision and grace of perfection in quality education.

The beauty in quality education that Tagore proposes and translates in teacher education is primarily concerned with the aesthetics of ceaseless refinement. Unless the teacher is aware of refinement, the joy of teaching evaporates and, instead, is filled in stuff and nonsense in the camouflaging name of quality. This is all the more viable in literature where quality assurance in the teaching of poetry is essentially concerned with not apparently what to teach, and how, but the more refined 'how' that makes freedom of exercise in appreciation in close consonance with typical imagery-patterns.

A close study of aesthetic education as one of the most essential means of accelerating quality refinement in teacher education, as Tagore is concerned with the role of teachers in this direction, reveals the fact that the teacher must be natural with Nature and responsive to exercise of aesthetic sensibilities. This is a spontaneous exercise where aesthetics in education welcomes external as well as internal components of aesthetics. While the teacher encourages the learner to catch the subtler components of aesthetic education by means of decoration of classrooms with flowers, foliage and leaves, application of incense, sandal paste, flower bangles and ornaments with natural objects that might appear insignificant, the inherent exercise of aesthetic sensibilities can very well be cultivated in sincerely adhering to how abstract ideas like goodness, truth, beauty, benevolence, compassion and so on which enrich and enlighten aesthetic visions in every walk of life.

The more thrilling strategies of quality refinement in aesthetic education which the teacher ought to adopt in course of teaching is introducing aesthetics through histrionics and other creative and aesthetic activities like literary functions, fine arts and music, dance and educational tours are all encapsulated in Tagore's experiments in education where the teacher is a living and active partner to the learners in unfolding newer horizons of aesthetic education.

That Tagore was a continual propagator of aesthetics in the world of creation is a veritable pointer to the fact that he always wants every teacher's nearness to the learner, her/his closest association and involvements in the learner's quest for serenity and joy in the world of aesthetic exercises. He has, in fact, warned that as the teacher is never a pre-historic huge animal but a loving, affectionate and sympathetic partner to the learner, she/he should never dissociate herself/himself from the latter. Otherwise, quality education in aesthetics would never be translated into a thriving reality.

The hunger for self-expression and self-identity in tune with Nature, the great aesthetic teacher never needs any substitution as it is rampantly thrust by the teacher in the same way as the hydraulic pressure. And this is the key to the aesthetics of education for the excellence and advancement of man. This is Tagore's vision of education for which the teacher ought to be spontaneously prepared. As he pronounces in his seventieth birthday address:

> What I had wished for was to give vent to the human hunger for form, for self-expression. I had looked for a forest retreat, *tapovan,* as its proper ambiance. Not in the midst of sordid city-built houses, but under the blue canopy, form morn to eve I had longed to be a playmate of these boys and girls. To express, growing out of this shared life, beauty's happy and blessed form, that was my one and only concern. I have had, naturally, to introduce other utilitarian activities as well. But you will not find me in these. I am where life is trying to express itself. The classes that I have started or taught here are secondary. My real work has been to awaken,

> in Nature's vast playground, the tender grace of childhood, its budding effort, the first rays of knowledge falling across its horizon. Otherwise I would have been swamped by the trivia of routine, statute and syllabus. My happiness, my fulfilment has been in trying to rouse the young ones to the Delight of the unseen Player, to set them in tune with the Dance of Life itself. It is not in me to be more serious than that. The Master of Games has mercifully released me from the fetters of the mature and the elder. Those who try to set me on a pedestal I tell them that I was born with my seat below, on the lap of the Earth. In these trees and forests, the dust, earth and grass, have I poured out my life. Those who are close to the spirit of the Earth, those who are made and shaped by her, and who will find their final rest in her, of them all I am the friend.
>
> —Sisirkumar Ghose: *Rabindranath Tagore,* Sahitya Akademi, New Delhi, 1986, pp. 123-124.

Every teacher, to be truly justified to teaching, cannot but be a poet in the cultivation of truth, beauty and goodness as essential components of aesthetics. For this, the art of teaching as Tagore has always advocated should always be unique. Here success in teaching is not evaluated in terms of rules and regulations, so-called success in pen-paper-pencil tests or any utilitarian approach to teaching-learning. The teacher ought to come out of commonality in teaching. Not a single method but a diversity of methods so that in the aesthetics of teaching allows the learners learn more than a single way of learning and ponder over the invaluable possibilities of finding out newer avenues of learning through his own method.

Admittedly, Tagore's aesthetics of teaching is an endless pointer of progress in enriched and pupil-loving activity. The teacher knows that his aesthetics of teaching is not to force the learners to listen but to achieve the goal as a listener to the learner's achievement in learning how to translate listening into creativity and aesthetic fulfilment. From the psychological point of view as well, maintenance of judicious silence adds poignancy to teaching:

> Teachers of difficult and controversial subjects, who know it is essential for themselves and their pupils to keep calm and analyse the matter dispassionately, often adopt a tone of studied tranquillity which is very useful as long as they are audible, but is apt to sink into chattiness, triviality, and ultimate silence. Philosophers are prone to this because they spend their whole lives thinking about subjects of the highest importance and dignity, they know it is useless and dangerous to discuss them with emotional excitement, they have learnt that it is an insult to a good student to assume that he has not seen quite as far into the argument as his teacher, and sometimes they are discouraged by a lifetime of battling with problems which they know they will never solve.
>
> —Gilbert Highet: *The Art of Teaching,* Methuen, London, University Paperbacks, 1963, p. 90.

Quality in teacher education is closely dependent on pupil motivation. The better they are motivated aesthetically, the greater is the success in teaching. Let students be so motivated that the learner enjoys autonomy in learning. This is what differentiates Tagore's philosophy of aesthetic education from others. Let the learner think, feel and act alone. The role of the teacher, as Tagore advocates, is like that of a lamp just to enlighten and then to relegate himself into the background for better aesthetic advancement in education.

To keep multidimensional ends-in-view in cohesion is the great challenge in teacher education today. The students come to the classroom with a wide canvas of knowledge power. It is the ideal role of a teacher, as Tagore believes and translates into action in his own educational institutions at Visva-Bharati, to assure the learner of the fact that sincere and devoted endeavour to unfold the mystery of knowledge and experience is the key to be justified to education for aesthetic excellence. In this connection, the following necessitates every teacher's attention:

> Students bring their own goals into the classroom and want to negotiate with you about how, when, and with whom they want to reach the learning goals. It is important to realize that you impose many goals on your students, including social goals (e.g. 'You have to work individually, without the support o help from your peers': or 'You have to work in small groups and take responsibility for the learning of members of your group'). Peers also impose goals on other students (e.g. 'Ignore the teacher when he asks for volunteers'). When students realise that their own goals are discordant with your goals, they make attempts to align the circular goals with their own goals. For example, Sandra may ask: 'Can I hand in my handwork tomorrow because I did not have enough resource material to make a good job of it?' Similarly, Stefano may request: 'Can I do this task alone, because I have a different opinion than the rest of my group?' If you grant these requests, your students will experience self-determination. The positive

> cognitions and feelings that are part of that experience will further the learning process. On the contrary, if you deny these requests, they will experience a conflict of goals and may not take responsibility for achieving the curricular goals. Many forms of misbehaviour in class can be interpreted in terms of a goal conflict. You will deal more flexibly with misbehaviour when you view it as a signal that a salient goal is being frustrated. For example, Stefano may say: 'How can I work efficiently on a math problem if you want me to help students who always run into problems?' Likewise, Sandra may ask: 'Why can't we do this task together?' It is important to realize that your students want to be treated with respect. They expect you to explain why you turn down their requests.
>
> —Monique Boekaerts: *Motivation to Learn*, International Bureau of Education, UNESCO, 2002. p. 23.

As an incomparable connoisseur of quality in education by means of cultivation of aesthetics, Tagore reminds us of the fact that no genuine education for fullness is possible through dissociation with Nature. At the same time, he also makes us aware of the fact that the education of the child should always be flexible and purposeless in the sense that it should always be allowed to grow and develop its unique personality amidst uninterrupted and unalloyed freedom. To make it aware of mere materialistic success alone is to banish it from the world of beauty and joy, freedom and adventure as the essential aesthetic appreciation to fullness and perfection of life. Tagore's pointers to our erroneous system of education are remarkably elucidated in his straightforward and vibrant observation:

Our system of education refuses to admit that children are children. Children are punished because they fail to behave like grown-up people and have the impertinence to be noisily childish. Their educators do not know or refuse to acknowledge that this childishness is Nature's own provision and that the child through its restless mind and movements should always come into new facts and stumble upon new information. Thus the child becomes the battle-ground for a flight between the school master and Mother Nature herself. The school master is of opinion that the best means of educating a child is by concentration of mind, but Mother Nature knows that the best way is dispersion of mind. When we were children, we came to gather facts by such scattering of mental energy through unexpected surprises. The surprise gave us that shock which was needed to make us intensely conscious of the facts of life, of the world. Facts must come fresh to children to startle their minds into full activity.

It is the utter want of purpose in child-life which is important. In adult age, having made our life a bundle of a few definite purposes, we exclude all facts outside their boundaries. Our purpose wants to occupy all the mind's attention for itself, obstructing the full view of most of the things around us; it cuts a narrow bed for our deliberate mind which seeks its end through a restricted passage. The child, because it has no conscious object of life beyond living, can see all things around it, can hear every sound with a perfect freedom of attention, not having to exercise choice in the collection of information. It gives full reign to its

> restlessness which heads its mind into knocking against knowledge.
>
> I have a deep-rooted conviction that only through freedom man can attain his fullness of growth, and when we restrict that freedom it means that we have some purpose of our own which we impose on our children, and we have not in mind Nature's own purpose of giving the child the fullness of growth.
>
> If we have some purpose expressed through our educational institutions—that children should be producing patriots, practical men, soldiers, bankers, then it may be necessary that se have to put them through the mechanical drill of obedience and discipline! But that is not the fullness of life and the fullness of humanity. He who knows that Nature's own purpose is to make the boy a full man when he grows—full in all directions, mentally and mainly spiritually—he who realises this, brings up the child in the atmosphere of freedom.
>
> Rabindranath Tagore: "The School Master," *The Modern Review*, Calcutta, 24 October, 1924.

Enrichment and efflorescence of a child's sub-conscious mind should, according to Tagore, be guiding principle for accelerating quality in teacher education. If the teacher is aware that a child is a child and never an adult, there is the promise of teaching children without interfering with its being natural in thought and action, freedom and joy. This also ensures the latter of unrestricted mental development. Tagore spells out the above in terms of experiences he had to encounter in his own childhood days:

> I had at least acquired a negative experience in course of my school days. I had learnt how not to treat children. What I had particularly suffered in my childhood was to feel that the education that I

had received was separated from life. I admit I had a certain special sensibility which others did not share with me in the same degree. Otherwise, I would undoubtedly have more easily resigned myself to my suffering, and would, in the course of those days at school, have succeeded like the others in stifling in me that passionate zest for life, for nature, from which everyday I had to be dragged away as from a mother in order to enter the classroom.

I recall it, the door of the class-room, gaping each morning like a big mouth, its bare walls, its wooden benches, its wooden desk at which the teacher stood giving his lesson like a living phonograph. I still know it by heart, and I can hear it the repetition of the same, which had neither the beauty of melody nor rhythm, which every morning we chanted in chorus on the wooden verandah of the school before entering the class. It spoke of many good things no doubt, that it was necessary to be wise, not to steal, nor borrow. But it was, nevertheless, a bad beginning for the day.

* * * * * *

It was not, however, that I believed that I had any special gift for teaching, but it seemed to me that I had the secret of making them [children] happy.

To tell you the truth, nobody had any faith in me. I had neither a university degree, nor distinction of any kind. I passed for an extremely unpractical hand, who knew nothing except writing verse. It was now a matter of finding blankets and sheets and of procuring food and lodging for the five boys who had been entrusted to my care.

> I tried to live their daily life. Education, properly speaking, was a secondary matter. What was of the first importance was that our life was lived in our common comradeship.
>
> For me, indeed, a child up to its twelfth year lives much more in the sub-conscious than in clear consciousness and what is important during these first years is not to burden his memory with knowledge which taxes his mind, but to see that his sub-conscious is saturated with beauty through the contact with living nature.
>
> —Rabindranath Tagore: "A Poet's School," *March of India,* March-April, 1951, Delhi Translated by Sasadhar Sinha from "Les Educateur", No. 12, 11 June, 1921, *Social Thinking of Rabindranath Tagore,* Asia Publishing House, Bombay, 1962, pp. 149-150.

How should a teacher educator assess quality enrichment in teacher education? As one dedicated to advancement of right teaching in right earnest for effulgence of aesthetics in the came of the promise of perfection, Tagore's poignant words would certainly pay benign dividends:

> Day after day, O lord of life, shall I stand before thee face to face. With folded hands, O lord of all worlds, shall I stand before thee face to face.
>
> Under thy great sky in solitude and silence, with humble heart shall I stand before thee face to face.
>
> In this laborious world of thine, tumultuous with toil and with struggle, among hurrying crowds shall I stand before thee face to face.
>
> And when my work shall be done in this world, O King of kings, alone and speechless shall I stand before thee face to face.
>
> —Rabindranath Tagore: *Gitanjali,* Macmillan India Limited, New Delhi, Macmillan Pocket Tagore Edition, 1983, pp. 50-51.

# 7
# Teacher Education and Education for Peace

Education throughout the world is undergoing unprecedented stress and strain. Conflict and misunderstanding, tension and agitation, disturbance and disintegration have already cast a very deep spell over the whole arena of teaching and learning. Teachers everywhere are really concerned with education for peace. Educational policies and programmes on teacher education, therefore, necessitate a thorough, scientific, objective, pinpointed and reliable overhauling with a view to negotiating crisis in peace education.

With multidimensional tensions from which the twenty-first gravely suffers and which have been identified and spelt out as follows, teacher education cannot but explore and prepare teachers who would solemnly discharge their duties and responsibilities in upholding and strengthening the positive vision of education for peace so that the learners of the global village and, for that end-in-view, the global society appreciate and enrich Oneness of Humans:

· The tension between the global and the local: people need gradually to become world citizens without losing their roots and while continuing to play an active part in the life of their nation and their local community.

· The tension between the universal and the universal: culture is steadily being globalized, but as yet only partially. We cannot ignore the promises of globalization nor its risks, not the least of which is the risk of forgetting the unique character of individual human beings; it is for them to choose their own future and achieve their full potential within the carefully tended wealth of their traditions and their own cultures which, unless we are careful, can be endangered by contemporary developments.

· The tension between tradition and modernity: which is part of the same problem: how is it possible to adapt to change without turning one's back on the past, how can autonomy be acquired in complementarity with the free development of others and how can scientific progress be assimilated? This is the spirit in which the challenges of the new information technologies must be met.

· The tension between long-term and short-term considerations: this has always existed but today it is sustained by the predominance of the ephemeral and the instantaneous, in a world where an over-abundance of transient information and emotions continually keeps the spotlight on immediate problems. Public opinion cries out for quick answers and ready solutions, where many problems call for a patient, concerned, negotiated strategy of reform. This is precisely the case where education policies are concerned.

· The tension between, on the one hand, the need for competition, and on the other, the concern for equality for opportunity: this is a classic issue, which has been facing both economic and social policy-makers and educational policy-makers since the beginning of the century. Solutions have sometimes been proposed but they have never stood the test of time. Today, the Commission ventures to claim that the pressures of the competitions have caused many of those in positions of authority to lose sight of their mission, which is to give each human being the means to take full advantage of every opportunity. This has led us, within the terms of reference of the report, to rethink and update the concept of lifelong education so as to reconcile three forces: competition, which provides incentives; cooperation, which gives strength; and solidarity, which unites.

· The tension between the extraordinary expansion of knowledge and human beings' capacity to assimilate it: the Commission was unable to resist the temptation to add some new subjects for study, such as self-knowledge, ways to ensure physical and psychological well-being or ways to an improved understanding of the natural environment and to preserving it better. Since there is already increasing pressure on curricula, any clear-sighted reform strategy must involve making choices, providing always that the essential features of a basic education that teaches pupils how to improve their lives through knowledge, through experiment and through the development of their own personal cultures are preserved.

· Lastly—another perennial factor—the tension between the spiritual and the material: often without realizing it, the world has a longing, often unexpressed, for an ideal and for values that we shall term 'moral'. It is thus education's noble task to encourage each and every one, acting in accordance with their traditions and convictions and paying full respect to pluralism, to lift their minds and spirits to the plane of the universal and, in some measure, to transcend themselves. It is no exaggeration on the Commission's part to say that the survival of humanity depends thereon.

—*Learning: The Treasure Within,* Report to UNESCO of the International Commission on Education for the Twenty-first Century, UNESCO, 1996, pp. 17-18.

With the above perspective of education as put forward by the International Commission on Education for the Twenty-first Century, the role of the teacher as a peace builder requires re-identification in right earnest. The pedagogical skills and strategies should be so organised and oriented as to bring about a positive result in replacing rudeness and violence committed either by the teacher or by the learner in terms of maintenance of 'discipline' or punishment respectively inside or outside the classroom. The process of integrating curricular and co-curricular activities for which the teacher necessitates training and orientation on some fundamental skills in education for peace for every learner should encapsulate the following thrust areas:

(a) To identify the learners' creative thinking areas and inspiring them to cultivate creativity in a positive and constructive manner. It may be necessary for the teacher to incorporate his own suggestions on how to enrich creativity in organised behavioural exercises under simulated classroom activities.

(b) To arrange participatory programmes with a view to negotiating wrong and destructive information, conflicts and violence where teachers' training and practice in the related matters under abnormal psychology would facilitate restoration and enrichment of education for peace.

(c) To equip teachers to be proficient in directing and instructing he learners to intensively study the immediate environment with multiple cultural, social, economic, religious differences and diversities and independently explore newer avenues of cohesion, solidarity and peace.

(d) To train teachers to organise training camps for learners to undergo practical assignments related to maintenance and enrichment of peace.

(e) To stabilize the role of the teachers in the dissemination of peace education for appropriate teaching and research on the divisive forces and undercurrents that stand in the way of the culture of peace by the learners coming from socially disadvantaged areas in particular.

Bearing in mind the thrust areas as above, teacher education should also pay adequate attention to the following teaching-learning activities which cover a wide spectrum of subjects, as significantly suggested by the National Focus Group on Education for Peace:

**Children may be asked to:**

- Demonstrate the many ways in which one can show respect to elders at home and in school. How do we show respect while asking for things, listening, or talking? (Environmental Studies/Language).
- Express the meaning of the word 'cooperation' in different ways.

- Demonstrate using puppets, how to resolve conflicts peacefully through the usage of proper words and gestures [Environmental Studies (EVS)/Language.
- Imagine a peaceful world and what would it be like (Social Science).
- Describe how anger destroys peace (Social Science/ Language).
- Explain the paradox: everyone wants a peaceful world, but the world is not peaceful. Why is thi so? Analyse the factors that come in the way of peace. (Social Science).
- Identify the changes we need to bring about, if we are to have a peaceful world. These changes include changes in respect of one's feelings and values. (Social Science).
- Identify as many activities as possible, which indicate the good that we can do to others with our hands. (Language).
- Complete an incomplete story in different ways with peace messages. (Language).
- Demonstrate different ways, i.e., emotions/ gestures, to be supportive and caring to a person in a wheel chair. (Language).
- Role-play different objects like trees, a broom, various civic facilities, showing how they benefit us. (EVS/ Language).
- Write a story or poem or come up with a quotation based on the picture displayed on a chart. The story, besides being original, must carry some social/ moral message. (Language).
- Write a story on tolerance, sensitivity to others, etc. collect newspaper clippings, magazines, articles on different themes and create a wall magazine. (Language).

- Improvise the solution to a problem affecting weaker students through team work, utilising available resources. (EVS/ Social Science).
- Show the students an object, for example, a flower, and ask them to write a few lines, a poem, or a song, comparing the qualities of a flower or other object with those of a good human being. (Language).
- Compose various value-words, using a set of letters provided. For example, qualities like honesty and truthfulness, making new associations among them. (Language).
- Compose a poem or a song depicting values like honesty, hard work, etc. (Language).
- Write a letter pertaining to a misunderstanding between two friends, suggesting a way to resolve the problem without either one feeling humiliated. (Language).
- Imagine being the victim of violence, for example, having to pay a bribe, being humiliated, having to live in fear of one's life, being a victim of red tapism, etc. and express what it means to be a victim.
- Collect the works of relatively lesser known people who have contributed to the welfare of others and analyse the qualities. (Social Science).
- Identify problem areas in the community that require creative solution. (Social Science).
- Write a composition on 'A Day in the Life of a Teacher'. (Language).
- Imagine different ways to help a street child. For example, the students could write a letter to the editor of a leading newspaper circulating in the area about how to be more caring to others especially the young and the needy. (Language).

- Organise field visits to local orphanages or old age homes to sensitise students to the loneliness, deprivation, and helplessness of these sections of society.
- Organise programmes, talks, workshops, film shows, etc. to inculcate in the students love and concern for the human family. A case in point is the science and ethics of organ transplants, where unscientific assumptions and anxieties stand in the way of improving the quality of life of thousands.
- Develop projects on ecological changes over the years and their effect on local crops. This exercise is of special significance to rural students. Discuss how environmental degradation affects the poor.
- Provide opportunities for development of social skills through dramatics, plays, community singing, and group work, etc.
- Undertake a survey on how many children below the age of 14 are not attending school in the village, town, or neighbourhood in question, explaining also the reasons why they are out of school.
- Organise discussions on daily news items, current affairs, etc.
- Organise conflict resolution sessions on selected themes.
- Study problems linked with violence. Encourage the students to share their experiences with violence so that others in the class can also learn strategies for coping with fears and anxieties.

—National Curriculum Framework 2005, Position Paper, National Focus Group on *Education for Peace,* National Council of Educational Research and Training, New Delhi, 2006, pp. 11-12.

Training of teachers for consolidation and promotion of education for peace is a very delicate and, at the same time, challenging task. Here the role of the teacher very often depends on that of the teacher educator who ought to be a serious and thrilling partner in enabling the teacher to be confident enough to negotiate different problems of education for peace. His continual innovative suggestions theoretical and practical as well go a long way in sincerely devoting to encounter the challenges of violence, indiscipline, conflicts, superstitions, doubts, misunderstandings and various other socio-cultural ills.

As an enterprise for re-humanising and re-stimulating the nation teacher education for peace education should also set new agenda for the education of sympathy and togetherness. Peace education is, as an alert and sensitive teacher always knows and identifies, never education as such. A few lessons on peace education in the different patterns like stories, poems, plays, songs etc. incorporated in books and introduced as study materials would hardly meet the aims and objectives of promoting education for peace. Mere theoretical activities concerned with learning what constitutes education for peace may sometimes fall in deaf ears to the students. Teachers ought to involve themselves in real life situations where peace has been disturbed and where for maintenance and continuation of peace active participation of teachers in association with students would be much more effective than simply dealing with theories inside the classrooms.

The primary component associated with peace education is self-awareness. Teachers in classrooms ought to inspire students to cultivate peace education in and through self-awareness. It is a matter that can be caught and can hardly be caught. Often it is found that very attractive and interesting classroom climate for learning a lesson of education for peace has been created by the teacher with utmost sincerity and seriousness of purpose and yet it fails to ignite self-awareness of the learners. They simply follow the lesson very mechanically. Even when asked to explain some of the issues related to constraints in peace, they readily give more or less creditable and intelligent answers. But what is more interesting is that a very simple problem of peace education, simpler than any one of the issues raised and discussed earlier, turns out to be very difficult to answer. This proves that there is a vulnerability of being overpowered with a routine work in learning or exercising a lesson on peace education which can hardly avert failures.

In fact, there is always a tendency on the part of the learner to fall an easy prey to commonality in following a lesson on peace. The primary end-in-view of self-awareness is controlled and regimented by rules and regulations where inwardness of vision for understanding and appreciating peace both in contemplation as well as in action is unfortunately relegated to background. Passivity and dullness are the two negative components that very often stand in the way of how to know and translate education for peace into real life situation.

Again, it is also equally true that toying with hypothetical assumptions on peace education as it has nowadays been a fashion in teaching-learning cannot but yield poor and unworthy dividends. Launching several programmes on teacher education for peace education without a disciplined, regular, evaluation-guaranteed programme of action or setting multiple agenda for teacher preparation for imparting peace education without caring for inner advancement is something like putting a cart before the horse in the name of seminars, workshops, symposia, conferences etc. that violence is a pre-lesson, in particular, for peace education and can under special and controlled circumstances be a strong fillip-point or booster dose may be a new dimension of peace education purified and crystallised in an altogether different but marvellous manner.

Teacher education right now awaits a newer programme of action on education for peace in the arduous task of innovating sensitising but at the same time elegant avenues of making a fine fusion between value education and peace education. In reality, these are not different but one and the same with patterns of efflorescence varying under different, positive, people and society friendly conceptual climate. The more we endear transfer and transparency, the better is the opportunity for transcendence and fullness of vision.

The twenty-first century looks forward to creating and consolidating an enlightened platform of teacher education where training and orientation of education for peace encompass a spirit of catholicity and vastness of vision that well accommodates and enriches the culture of silence in teaching-learning. It is time to realise that the teacher is not simply a task master nor is he an analyst and evaluator but a learner as well, more a learner than a teacher in the culture of peace. He is a learner-assistant, cordial partner and appreciator of peace education as it ought to be. His prayer is: let me wholeheartedly unite myself in idealising and upholding peace in close cooperation with my learner-students. Let us be joint pathfinders of the world of peace. Let us sing together the victory of peace even under absolutely challenging situations.

Do we join the prayer?

# 8

# Teacher Education and Education for Spiritual Excellence

Education is a continual and devoted search within for excellence and ascent. Teacher education for spiritual excellence is primarily concerned with how to prepare and train teachers so that the essence of spirituality can be best appreciated and exercised by the learners in every educational institution under their sincere guidance and close observation, positive support and fool proof evaluation. As spiritual education is essentially nursed in subjective vision where self-realisation and self-activity go hand in hand in the igniting teaching strategies under cautious and loving care of teachers in imparting instructions, teacher education is entrusted with launching package programmes with check lists for safeguarding individuality. Moreover, teachers should be so oriented as to naturally and spontaneously become partners to learners' development of spirituality where efflorescence of spiritual excellence becomes a matter of self-awakening rather than merely learning the if-s and but-s of spirituality.

Freedom in education for spiritual excellence is a very important component for which teacher education cannot but make ample avenues of appreciation, understanding and exercise notwithstanding. What is freedom in education? How is it related to spirituality? How does it foster self-consciousness and self-involvement as inseparable components of the exercise of spirituality in and through education? All these and a host of questions otherwise and allied to education for spiritual excellence come under the purview of redesigning teacher education for spiritual development.

Teacher education to equip teachers in finding out the inner excellence of the learner and encourage him for refinement necessitates re-visualising in the exercise of freedom. In this context, the concept of freedom as an essence of spiritual excellence in education becomes distinct and explicit in its true realisation in the invaluable words of Tagore:

> The more man acts and makes actual what was latent in him, the nearer does he bring the distant Yet-to-be. In that actualisation man is ever making himself more and yet more distinct, and seeing himself clearly under newer and newer aspects in the midst of his varied activities, in the state, in society. This vision makes for freedom.
>
> Freedom is not in darkness, nor in vagueness. There is no bondage so fearful as that of obscurity. It is to escape from this obscurity that the seed struggles to sprout, the bud to blossom. It is to rid itself of this envelope of vagueness that the ideas of our mind are constantly seeking opportunities to take an outward form. In the same way, our soul, in order to release itself from the midst of indistinctness and come out into the open, is continually creating for itself fresh fields of action, and is busy contriving new forms of activity, even such as are not needful for the purposes of its earthly life. And why? Because it wants freedom. It wants to see itself, to realise itself.

> When man cuts down the pestilential jungle and makes unto himself a garden, the beauty that he thus sets free from within its enclosure of ugliness is the beauty of his own soul: without giving it this freedom outside, he cannot make it free within. When he implants law and order in the midst of the waywardness of society, the good which he sets free from the obstruction of the bad is the goodness of his own soul; without being thus made free outside it cannot find freedom within. Thus is man continually engaged in setting free in action his powers, his beauty, his goodness, his very soul. And the more he succeeds in so doing, the greater does he see himself to be, the broader becomes the field of his knowledge of self.
>
> —Rabindranath Tagore: "Realisation of the Self", *Sadhana*, Macmillan India Limited, New Delhi, Macmillan
>
> Pocket Tagore Edition, 1983, pp. 102-103.

For regeneration and cultivation with greater awareness for spiritual vision, teacher education necessitates quality assurance in teaching spiritual values. The diverse components of aesthetics that come under the domain of spiritual excellence e. g. truth, love, beauty, goodness, humility, austerity, tolerance, sympathy etc. require urgent and sincere attention for practice and accentuation in teaching-learning. The truth of the universe with its manifold manifestations in Nature is itself a symbol of spiritual effulgence. The sincere teacher in spiritual lesson will draw the attention of the learner not through teaching as such but through self-involvement where the aroma of experience will indicate how far it is poignant in spiritual fusion. Again, appreciation to beauty as a pointer to spiritual excellence often calls forth awe and wonder where the so-called ugliness is looked upon as a spiritual vision of purity inherent and awaiting revelation in perfect symphony of aesthetics and spirituality.

To understand and appreciate serenity and beauty at the same time with all components of uniqueness, it is the teacher who ought to have that spiritual vision to unfold both and enlighten the learners to explore and appreciate spirituality in whatever thought and action he engages himself. Precisely, the teacher ought to feel the pulse of the learner in such a way as to allow him to enter into the heartland of spiritual fulfilment. If the learner is in a position to understand and appreciate the play of everything, every item, every vision he encounters in terms of transmutation, the teacher wins almost three-forth of the desirable battle in the name of teaching for spiritual excellence and the remaining assignment is happily entrusted with the latter who in turn begins a chapter of spiritual ascent anew and afresh.

The education of the heart which a teacher ought to impart as a precious process of dealing with spiritual education of ascent and excellence is a way of putting oneself in perfect tune with the learner's own world of spiritual development. It is more observation than teaching, more penetration into the learner's mind and the heart where exercise of freedom and inquisitiveness, creativity and critical thinking are allowed to enjoy more self-efflorescence than emulation, more self-involvement than guidance and supervision. In fact, a true teacher devoted to enkindle the learner's lamp, as it were, of spiritual excellence never commands. This is why, in education for spiritual excellence the teacher does not know when and how he mingles himself with the learner's world of spiritual exercise. As Sri Aurobindo advocates:

> The best method of suggestion is by personal example, daily converse and the books read from day to day. These books should contain, for the younger student, the lofty examples of the past given, not as moral lessons, but as things of supreme human interest, and, for the elder student, the great

thoughts of great souls, the passages of literature which set fire to the highest emotions, the records of history and biography which exemplify the living of those great thoughts, noble emotions and aspiring ideals. This is a kind of good company, *satsanga,* which can seldom fail to have effect so long as sententious sermonising is avoided, and becomes of the highest effect if the personal life of the teacher is itself moulded by the great things he places before his pupils. It cannot, however, have full force unless the young life is given an opportunity, within its limited sphere, of embodying in action the moral impulses which rise within it. The thirst of knowledge, the self-devotion, the purity, the renunciation of the Brahmin,—the courage, ardour, honour, nobility, chivalry, patriotism of the Kshatriya,—the beneficence, skill, industry, generous enterprise, and large open-handedness of the Vaisya,—the self-effacement and loving service of the Sudra,—these are the qualities of the Aryan. They constitute the moral temper we desire in our young men, in the whole nation. But how can we get them if we do not give opportunities to the young to train themselves in the Aryan tradition, to form by the practice and familiarity of childhood and boyhood the stuff of which their adult lives must be made?

—"Education of the Child", *Education and the Growing Child,* Sri Aurobindo Institute of Research and Social Sciences, Sri Aurobindo Society, Pondicherry, 1996, pp. 8-9.

Admittedly, teacher education for advancement of education for spiritual excellence is always to be strengthened by the spirit of culture that cares more for evolution of consciousness than for mere progress as it is generally aimed at. The teacher ought to exercise the skills of how to best suggest the learner and avert every temptation of sermonising or thrusting some spiritual values with which the child is introduced but not allowed to explore the wonderland of wisdom adorned in the innumerable spurts of spiritual appreciation. To deny the learner to unfold the casket of purity and perfection with which he is incomparably blessed and authenticated in an unparalleled way. In this connection, the 'true teaching' as asserted by Sri Aurobindo directs a teacher how to deal with the inherent strength of the learner as a spontaneous spiritual visionary:

> The first principle of true teaching is that nothing can be taught. The teacher is not an instructor or task-master, he is a helper and guide. His business is to suggest and not to impose. He does not actually train the pupil's mind, he only shows him how to perfect his instruments of knowledge and helps and encourages him in the process. He does not impart knowledge to him, he shows him how to acquire knowledge that is within: he only shows him where it lies and how it can be habituated to rise to the surface. The distinction that reserves this principle for the teaching of adolescent and adult minds and denies its application to the child, is a conservative and unintelligent doctrine. Child or man, boy or girl, there is only one sound principle of good teaching. Difference of age only serves to diminish or increase the amount of help and guidance necessary; it does not change its nature.
>
> —*Sri Aurobindo and the Mother on Education*, Sri Aurobindo International Centre of Education, Pondicherry, 1966, p. 20.

Admittedly, teacher education for advancement of spiritual excellence pays great attention to the teacher's own world of spiritual endeavour. It is this world where subjectivity plays a significant part in how to approach the learner in exercising spiritual values and concepts. If there is a predominance of his own teaching items on spirituality rather than enabling the learner to go ahead with his own approach, the results cannot but come a cropper. As already hinted, it is the learner's world and hardly the teacher's. All stereotyped experimentations and mechanical suggestions should as far as possible be allowed by the teacher to eternally enjoy holidays in teaching. It is the duty of the teacher to differentiate facts from truth. Unless truth triumphs over facts, 'pure joy' which is the invaluable outcome would never effulge in spiritual grandeur. And if knowledge is continually crystallised in the essence of spirituality, realisation of more intense and refined spirituality leading to realisation of 'one great principle of unity' in everyone becomes a serene and luminous reality:

> Facts are many, but the truth is one. The animal intelligence knows facts, the human mind has power to apprehend truth. The apple falls from the tree, the rain descends upon the earth—you can go on burdening your memory with such facts and never come to an end. But once you get hold of the law of gravitation you can dispense with the necessity of collecting facts *ad infinitum*. You have got at one with truth which governs numberless facts. This discovery of a truth is pure joy to man—it is a liberation of his mind. For, a mere fact is like a blind lane, it leads only to itself—it has no beyond. But a truth opens up a whole horizon, it leads us to the infinite. That is the reason why, when a man like Darwin discovers some simple general truth about Biology, it does not stop there, but like a lamp

> shedding its light far beyond the object for which it was lighted, it illumines the whole region of human life and thought, transcending its original purpose. Thus we find that truth, while investing all facts, is not a mere aggregate of facts—it surpasses them on all sides and points to the infinite reality.
>
> As in the region of knowledge, so in that of consciousness, one must clearly realise some central truth which will give him an outlook over the widest possible field. And that is the object which the Upanishad has in view when it says, *Know thy own soul.* Or, in other words, realise the great principle of unity that is there in every man.
>
> —Rabindranath Tagore: "Soul Consciousness", *Sadhana,* Macmillan India Limited, New Delhi, Macmillan Pocket Tagore Edition, 1983, p. 22.

Truly, the lessons for spiritual excellence have a very broad and serene canvas where the role of the teacher is very delicate but at the same time exciting, strenuous but illuminating. The perfume of promise in dealing with spirituality is a sudden splendour of journey to the beyond of knowledge and transcending to the lotus land of purity and poignancy. In order to make an adventure into the world of education for such purity and poignancy through excellence in spirituality, teacher education might consider the following strategies:

### (a) Allowing the learner to discover and rediscover self-knowledge and self-experiments

As one conversant in child psychology, the teacher ought to provide the learner with every possible opportunity for discovery and rediscovery of knowledge and experiments in his own unique ways. Often it may so happen that silence becomes the touchstone of stimulation for the learner's self-knowledge and self-experiments enjoying a favourable climate of development.

Again, the teacher in his observation of the apparently most trivial details of the learner's expression of spiritual endeavour of manifestation might correlate aesthetic stylistics in the form of cues or hints verbal or non-verbal to encourage bringing about newer jolts of spiritual fullness of vision.

(b) **Stimulating the Learner's Spiritual Imageries**

This is a very sophisticated strategy for the teacher for the learner's better efflorescence of spiritual development. As it is a strategy for the learner's excellence and ascent of spirituality, the role of the teacher is primarily to remain as an alert and bias-free observer and note the following:

(i) The nature of the learner's imagery-pattern.

(ii) The source of the learner's imagery-pattern.

(iii) The significant points of departure from the imagery-patterns of other learners as well as from the teacher concerned.

(iv) The climax of the imagery-patterns sought at individually or in association with others essentially at the stage of incubation.

(v) The suggestive measures adopted in inspiring the learner in crystallisation of spiritual exercise.

(c) **Setting Work-Schedules Directly or Indirectly associated with the Learner's world of Spirituality**

This is a very delicate task to which a sincere teacher is always devoted. In this assignment, he ought to be well aware beforehand as forewarning compliments him with forearming against any failure in the strategy he adopts. The fundamental points of enquiry with regard to the concerned teacher's pre-awareness are as follows:

(i) Is the learner in the most apposite mood or position to attend, involve and positively react to the set work-schedules?

(ii) How far are the work-schedules user-friendly for spiritual excellence?

(iii) What is the actual time span and how far is it justified for the learner in his endeavour at spiritual effulgence?

(iv) How are the convergent and the divergent avenues of spirituality negotiated?

(v) What are the expected significant results from the teacher's investment as such, and how long would these thrive as boosters to the learner's own spiritual exercise?

(vi) How is inner discipline safeguarded for the learner's freedom and joy in spirituality?

It is time that teacher education upholds and disseminates teaching for spiritual transmutation in the different strategies as above to ensure higher consciousness where the spiritual end-in-view of education is elevated from the mental plane to the vital plane. Let the learner's realisation of his own spiritual being be honoured. Let us restore and enrich the beyonding of being rather than mere becoming. Then, and then only we are on the right track of spiritual excellence. As Sri Aurobindo characteristically reminds us:

> Life cannot be entirely rational, mind is not the destined archangel of the transformation. As a reaction against such chimerical ideals the mind is then used—as seems to be the case with modern civilisation—as a slave of life and body. The result has been a vital titanism, and it has ended badly as it always must. For a while the pressure of events has forced a nobler ethics and reason as a means for the better ordering of individual national and international life. But this, well enough for a first step, is not the real and final solution.

> For that we have to return to the pursuit of an ancient secret, the ideal of the Kingdom of God. This cannot be done, as past attempts show, either by a divorce between life and spirit or a departure into other worlds or a compromise or by a superimposing of the spiritual life or some of its ideas and motives on the mental, vital and physical life. This is the most that human society has done in the past.
> The secret of information lies in the transference of our centre of living to a higher consciousness and in a change of our main power of being. All that we have done so far is some half successful effort to transfer the will and power to the mental plane. To complete this upward transference we must go further, choose between the domination of the vital part in us and the spontaneous obedience of the spiritualised man to the truth of his own realised being, which will be other and greater than the limited perfection of arrested development we see already accomplished in the working of physical Nature. Hence this perfection cannot come by the mental idea dealing with the Spirit –that was Asia's mistake—as it deals with life. For the mind and the intellect are not the key powers of our existence. Only when this transference and the dynamic transformation that follows it have been completed we shall be on the right road to become ourselves, live in our true, satisfied self-existence in our real being and divine nature.
>
> —Sri Aurobindo: "The Necessity of the Spiritual Transformation", *The Human Cycle,* Sri Aurobindo Pathamandir, Calcutta, 1972, pp. 79-80.

Is teacher education dedicated to the exploration of the 'real being and divine nature' by means of excellence in spiritual education? Does it really welcome the advent of a spiritual age?

# 9

# Teacher Education and Pupil Guidance

Teacher education nowadays is elevated to the position of a torch-bearer of essential and foolproof pupil guidance. Teaching now also looks forward to finding out and experimenting with newer strategies of how to introduce several programmes of action for both the teacher educators and teacher trainees for advancement of pupil guidance.

It has now been admitted by one and all associated with teaching-learning that mere accomplishment of duties in dealing with the prescribed curriculum is not enough for the learner students. Nor is it desirable that the teacher remains in the dark and somewhat ambiguous about the learners in the learning outcome exposed or likely to be exposed as a consequence to classroom exercise. Again, it is also not desirable that the role of the teacher ends with in-school activities where the students sometimes involve themselves with learning mechanically sans reflection sans appreciation. As a result, teaching becomes a routine activity and learning mechanical, drab, dull and lifeless.

That a little bit of pupil guidance works wonders in teaching-learning is hardly denied. Mere talking and talking in the classroom without any depth of vision for applicability and enrichment of pupil progress and self-learning is never an effective way of teaching. The teacher as a live and dynamic tutor ought to feel the pulse of every learner-tutee and devise, meaningful, purposeful, relevant, attractive, interesting and tutee-friendly guidelines. He ought to scientifically edit tutee-directed guidelines useful for the latter. In this connection, the following suggestions put forward by Professor Topping would, to a great extent, ensure success in teaching:

- **Select material.** Have the tutee choose any reading material of high interest to them. Difficulty should be above the tutee's independent readability level, but not above the tutor's.
- **Read together.** Support the tutee by both reading all the words aloud together. Adapt your reading speed to exactly match that of the tutee. The tutee must read every word.
- **Correct errors.** When the tutee reads a word wrong, just tell the tutee the correct way to say the word. (Do not give clues, or the flow of reading will be interrupted.) The tutee must repeat it correctly. Then you continue. Always correct all errors this way, and no other way.
- **Pause.** However, do not jump in and put the word right straight away. Pause and give the tutee four seconds. If they put it right by themselves (self-correct) in this time, there is no need to interfere. (However, with a reader who rushes, you might need to pause for less time, and finger point back to the error word).
- **Agree on a signal for reading alone.** Agree on a way for a tutee to signal to stop 'reading together',

for when the tutee wants to read an easier section without support. This signal could be a knock, a sign or a hand squeeze. The tutor must stop 'reading together' immediately at the signal.

- **Return to reading together.** Sooner or later while 'reading alone' the tutee will make an error, which they cannot self-correct within four seconds. Correct the error (as above) **and** join back on 'reading together'.
- **Continue.** Go on like this, switching from 'reading together' to 'reading alone', to give the tutee just as much help as they need at any moment, but no more. 'Reading together' will still be needed as the tutee moves on to harder and harder books.
- **Praise.** Praise your tutee for good reading of hard words; signalling for 'reading alone'; reading alone correctly for longer; getting all the words in a sentence right; and self-correcting. Try to use a variety of different praise words, **and** look pleased.
- **Review.** Talk about the book. Why is it interesting? Talk about the meanings of difficult words. What were the main ideas of the book? In what order?

—Keith Topping: *Tutoring,* International Bureau of Education, UNESCO, 2000, p. 18.

Admittedly, training the tutors in order to be justified to the tutees necessitates and presupposes a well-planed programme of action followed by appropriate feedback activities. The materials used as teaching aids for guidance should be fool proof and of a very high and sophisticated quality. Otherwise, quality guidance programme for tutee advancement will invite errors and omissions of tutoring. As Professor Topping suggests some important and invaluable steps:

- **Goals of monitoring.** Seek to: detect and solve any problems before they become large; find opportunities to give plentiful praise and show enthusiasm to keep motivation high; ensure the tutoring technique does not show signs of 'drift'; check that pairs are maintaining positive social relationships; be sure that materials are used from an appropriate sequence/level of difficulty; and generally review the complexity and richness of the learning taking place.

- **Self-help guide.** Make a simple self-help guide of common problems of tutoring, with suggestions about how these might be solved. You will keep adding to this. With 'packaged' techniques, clues about likely problems will be found in the literature.
- **Self-referral.** Let tutors and tutees know it is usual for many pairs to encounter some temporary difficulty, so this is not the fault of either helper or helped. They should know who to ask if one or both have any difficulty (with a particular problem, the tutoring technique or each other). They could seek help from other pairs before approaching a teacher.
- **Self- recording.** The pair should record their progress, and a monitoring teacher or tutoring organiser can then check these records or diaries from time to time.
- **Discussion.** Talk with the tutors and tutees about how things are going, perhaps at 'planning' or 'de-briefing' meetings. You might do this individually or in groups, with tutors and tutees together or separate.
- **Direct observation.** Carefully observe tutoring as it happens. (Do not assume that even the most intelligent tutor will be aware if they are going wrong.) a checklist of the elements of the tutoring technique will be helpful to structure these observations consistently. You could also ask 'spare' tutors to monitor sometimes, using the checklist. It is possible to use video or audio recording for monitoring, and this can be useful for feedback to

individual pairs or the group as a whole, as well as being valuable as a training aid for subsequent projects.

- **Further training.** If several pairs are having problems, it is probably worth holding another 'refresher' training session.

—*Ibid.*, pp. 28-29.

Pupil guidance in and through teaching is a very delicate and painstaking activity. In many cases, teachers are confronted with peculiar behavioural problems where very judicious decisions are not only necessary but also obligatory. Adolescence and delinquency often overpowered by smoking, drug and alcohol use are some of the primary constraints where new directions and guidelines come with the parameter of teacher education. Special refresher courses in teacher education, workshops, symposia etc. might encapsulate the following assignments:

Theoretical classes for teachers in learner psychology for an intensive brush-up of each of the following components should be arranged for better pupil guidance:

(a) knowledge
(b) understanding
(c) skill
(d) interest
(e) attitude
(f) aptitude
(g) appreciation.

For practical teaching, regular and disciplined exercises and involvements in the following ensure effective pupil guidance:

(a) preparing cumulative record cards
(b) maintaining diaries
(c) keeping note pads of pupil informatics
(d) dealing with case studies
(e) upholding crucial issues

(f) marginalising peculiar habit patterns in interactions between the teacher and the taught

(g) building better bridges over individual differences amongst pupils

(h) restoring humane values and sensibilities

(i) promoting excellence and ascent in curricular and co-curricular activities.

(j) Assuring the teacher's own creative and critical contributions as models of guidance.

Negotiating with aggressive behaviour of learners is a challenge to every teacher. In teacher education it has now been awarded adequate and sufficient attention through simulated classroom teaching in different skills for doing away with behaviour problems.

The following points in this connection deserve every teacher's attention:

- Identify children who have problems with aggressive behaviour and make specific plans to reduce their aggression. Look for children who harm others by fighting, hitting, bullying, calling names or excluding peers.
- Use effective positive consequences to encourage children to behave co-operatively, follow classroom rules and use non-violent ways of resolving conflicts.
- Communicate clear rules that aggression is not permitted and use effective immediate negative consequences to respond to aggressive behaviour.
- Work with parents so that they learn effective ways of disciplining aggression and encouraging alternative behaviour at home.
- Offer parent-and teacher-training programmes that teach effective ways of working with children to help them develop non-aggressive skills to reduce aggressive behaviour.

—Sharon L. Foster et al.: *Preventing Behaviour Problems: What Works,* International Bureau of Education, UNESCO, 2002, p. 25.

It may so happen that in case of failure in guidance programmes of activities for some incorrigible learners, assistance from health professionals particularly psychiatrists may be sought. What is, however, necessary is effective intervention and appropriate pupil guidance.

Training of teachers in teaching pupils to observe and practice skills that promote interpersonal and academic advancement is very important for positive and effective pupil guidance. Teachers ought to explore newer possibilities and favourable dimensions for intimate and useful co-operation with parents, peers and others directly or somehow associated with the learners. This would definitely enable problem solving and smooth pupil learning. The role of parents and teachers in unison may be strengthened by considering the following for better pupil guidance:

- Teachers and parents should act in ways that show children how to handle problems well. Children imitate the behaviour of those who are important to them.
- Teach young children interpersonal skills for handling conflict non-violently and co-operating with others. Children can also benefit from learning cognitive skills for recognising problem situations, stopping to think rather than responding impulsively, generating ways of solving problems, and evaluating the consequences of different solutions.
- Teach young adolescents specific ways for handling situations in which peers invite or pressure them to use drugs, tobacco, alcohol or to become involved in delinquency activities or risky sexual behaviour.

- Incorporate teaching interpersonal skills into classroom teaching. make sure children have many opportunities to practise the skills they are learning and to receive feedback on how they are doing.
- Train children to use skills that are likely to be effective in real-life situations. Whenever possible, make sure that they receive positive consequences for using their skills. Children are likely to abandon what they have learned if they try a new behaviour and it fails to work for them.
- Children who have problems getting along with others are likely to have more difficulties than others with learning and mastering important interpersonal skills. They may need more practice and feedback than others and more systematic attempts to help them apply what they have learned.

—*Ibid.,* p. 15.

As regards some pre-activity programmes for the benefit of the learners who suffer from indecision, hesitation, anxiety, morbidity and many other intricate problems of behaviour,

Teachers might introduce a network of pupil guidance in accordance with the following strategies:

(a) Creating a variety of opportunities for the learner to cautiously and significantly mix with the seniors in order to bring about desirable academic and behavioural excellence.

(b) Providing the learner to be blessed with the benefit of balanced and crystallised teaching both inside and outside the classroom.

(c) Stimulating the learner in sharing learning experiences with classmates, teachers, parents and interested members of the immediate community.

(d) Helping the learner to take a substantial role in the world of creativity and critical thinking.

(e) Organising different constructive programmes of education for pupil guidance under co-curricular activities and involving the learner to exercise freedom and joy in learning.

(f) Manipulating the obsessions and knowledge constraints under complex and confrontations with worthwhile and impressive strategies of teaching for advancement in exercising alternative visions of accomplishment.

Redesigning teacher education for pupil guidance is a continual challenge. It cannot be altogether addressed nor can it be prescribed instantaneously. Newer situations and startling problems in pupil guidance are always welcome and necessitate natural spurt for operation. Teachers ought to update themselves with the latest trends and tendencies of teacher education. It is to be always remembered that the twenty-first century teacher education is education of a totally different kind where training *is* self-assertion and self-revolution for pupil excellence first and the same ends-in-view last even after every splendid achievement as it would transpire. Therefore, transcendence is more than a target initially undertaken and launched followed by analysis and evaluation in pupil guidance activities. As the Delors Commission characteristically reminds us:

> The world in general is evolving so rapidly today that teachers, like most other professional groups, now must face the fact that their initial training will not see them through the rest of their lives; they need to update and improve their own knowledge and techniques throughout the lifetime. A careful balance has to be struck between competence in the subject taught and competence in teaching. In some countries, the system is

> criticised for neglecting method; in others, overemphasis on method, it is felt, produces teachers who know too little about their subject. Both are needed: neither should be sacrificed to the other in initial or in-service training. Teacher training has additionally to inculcate a view of teaching that transcends the utilitarian and encourages questioning, interaction and the consideration of several alternative hypotheses. One of the main functions of teacher education, both pre-service and in-service, is to equip teachers with the ethical, intellectual and emotional wherewithal to develop the same range of qualities in their pupils, as society demands.
>
> —*Learning:The Treasure Within,* UNESCO, 1996, p. 149.

Do we prepare our programmes of teacher education in tune with the test of time and pupil-savvy programmes of action?

# 10

# The Twenty-First Century Teacher

Education today is a challenge to excellence in every endeavour. Teacher education is a greater and more thrilling challenge because it calls forth more earnestness and better involvement with clarity of vision and transparency of purpose. It is an encouragement within to find out newer avenues of advancement. It is also a peep into the constraints of progress desirable or likely to be desirable in order to crystallize knowledge and experience for the sake of advancement.

The twenty-first century teacher cannot but be well equipped with the latest trends and experiments in education in general and education for children in particular. Newer and more vibrant areas of education have already come under the purview of teaching-learning. Using the new media that make education interesting and thrilling to the teachers as well as the learners in every educational institutions is rapidly becoming very necessary and popular amongst the teaching and the learning communities. Health education and teaching with special areas like sex education, life style education, gender awareness and aesthetics education, education of the otherwise able, publication stylistics education—all these have now attained immense public attention for educational and professional training right from the school level. It is no longer a novel strategy that teachers especially in metropolitan areas instruct children in schools how to be aware of HIV/AIDS. Encouraging learners in the open and frank discussions on so-called confidential and controversial issues promote education and teaching for healthy citizens of tomorrow. As Schenker and Nyirenda adroitly observe:

> Teaching HIV prevention and anti-discrimination presents several challenges for educators. A primary challenge involves the ability to openly discuss controversial issues with students in the classroom. Educators who feel comfortable with their sexuality, who adhere to human rights values, and who respect their students are more successful when discussing important controversial issues relating to HIV/AIDS, such as the disclosure of HIV status, pre-marital sex, homosexuality and drug use.
>
> The 'S' factors—shame, silence and stigma—are among the basic reasons behind continued HIV/AIDS fears leading to denial, blame and discrimination, thereby delaying positive action. Teachers must recognise these factors in the community in order to address them in class. Development of an open and honest atmosphere and a caring relationship between teacher and student is critical to AIDS education.
>
> However, openly discussing sex, drug use and HIV/AIDS in class does **not** mean being vulgar or diminishing one's social beliefs and values. Good communication skills allow AIDS educators to examine various behavioural options in front of their students and to discuss them in a respectful and frank manner.

—Inon I. Schenker and Jenny M. Nyirenda: *Preventing HIV/AIDS in Schools*, International Bureau of Education, UNESCO, 2002, p. 14.

Admittedly, teacher education cannot but provide teachers with ample and fool-proof orientation and training programmes in the different skills for psycho-social developmental needs. Our young learners should never feel isolated or ashamed, introvert or intimidated in dealing with any physical, mental or emotional factor and, in such cases, they should not at any cost be alienated or ignored. The curriculum, therefore, of teacher education necessitates radical and revolutionary change to especially address our adolescent learners from this end-in-view.

Recently, the National Focus Group on Health and Physical Education, recommending very strongly on curriculum reform for the importance of the above, 'that the curricular area must guide the scope and determine the appropriateness of the design, materials and pedagogy that are prescribed by health programmes as interventions in the school curriculum', categorically highlights:

> Adolescence is a critical period for development of self- identity. The process of acquiring a sense of self is linked to the physiological changes and also learning to negotiate the social and psychological demands of being young adults. Responsible handling of issues like independence, intimacy, and peer group dependence are concerns that need to be recognised and appropriate support be given to cope with them. The physical space of the outside world, one's access to it and free movement influence construction of the self. This is of special significance in the case of girls who are often constrained by social conventions to stay indoors. These very conventions promote the opposite

> stereotype for boys, which associate them with outdoor and physical process. These stereotypes get especially heightened as a result of biological maturational changes during adolescence. These physiological changes have ramifications in the psychological and social aspects of an adolescent's life. There is a growing realisation that the health needs of the adolescents, particularly their reproductive and sexual health needs require to be addressed. Since these needs predominantly relate to sex and sexuality that is culturally a very sensitive area, they are deprived of opportunities to get the appropriate information. As such, their understanding of reproductive and sexual health and their behaviour in this regard are guided predominantly by myths and misconceptions, making them vulnerable to risky situations, such as drug/substance use and HIV/AIDS transmission. Age-appropriate context-specific interventions focussed on adolescent reproductive and sexual health concerns including HIV/AIDS and drug/substance abuse, therefore, are needed to provide children opportunities to construct knowledge and acquire life skills so that they can cope with these concerns that are related to their process of growing up.
>
> —"Position Paper: National Focus Group on Health and Physical Education", *National Curriculum Framework 2005*, National Council of Educational Research and Training, New Delhi, 2006, pp. 9-10.

In monitoring and evaluation of pupil progress in the education as above, the teacher should prepare an appropriate and pupil-friendly check-list. This check list should deal with the following and add or delete any one or more of them, if necessary for successful teaching-learning:

(i) The functional knowledge of the learner
(ii) The time frame for imparting instruction
(iii) The attitude of the learner
(iv) Appropriate teaching-learning climate
(v) Individual involvement of the learner
(vi) Group involvement of the learner
(vii) Curriculum viability and appropriateness
(viii) The aesthetic effectiveness
(ix) The currency of the content matter followed by pre-assurance of its validity and reliability
(x) Operational stylistics.

In dealing with the above-mentioned check-list, the teacher must be well conversant with the techniques of monitoring and evaluation. In this connection, the following suggestions to teachers deserve sincere attention:

- Plan to include monitoring and evaluation components as an integral part of your intervention programme. Write notes on how you plan to teach, on comments and questions you receive from colleagues and students, on special events that happen in the classroom, on the number of classes on HIV/AIDS you taught, etc.
- Develop and administer pre-test and post-test questionnaires on HIV/AIDS. Then determine the success of your teaching by comparing the pre-test and post-test of each student. Questions should evaluate the students' understanding of the material that was covered. Good questions could be about things like HIV transmission, testing, risk behaviours, attitudes towards people living with HIV/AIDS (PLWHA), self-susceptibility to HIV

infection, using condoms and the negotiation/refusal of sexual intercourse.

- Appraise and review curricula. Use information offered by experts to determine the appropriateness and effectiveness of the curricula that are offered.
- Report your findings to colleagues and administrators. Data obtained by evaluating educational programmes on HIV/AIDS prevention is important for the further development of existing or future activities and for advocacy. Use verbal and written reports.

—Inon I. Schenker & Jenny M. Nyirenda: *Preventing HIV/AIDS in Schools*, International Bureau of Education, UNESCO, 2002, p. 27.

Gender issues in education have recently assumed great importance in teacher education. As the teacher is the life blood in the classroom, he/she cannot but address issues like teaching for women empowerment, equality, arresting all sensibilities of superstitions and narrowness to gender discrepancies, and absence of greater incentives and more advanced programmes of teacher training for the twenty-first century education for excellence in women's education packages. The role of the teacher as facilitator in this regard can hardly be averted. As the National Focus Group on "Gender Issues in Education "advocates:

> The teacher's role is to provide a safe space for children to express themselves and simultaneously to build in certain forms of interactions. While consolidating and constructively pushing the limits of the learner's understanding she needs to be conscious of how differences are expressed. An atmosphere of trust would make the classroom a safe space where children can share experiences, where conflict can be acknowledged and

> constructively questioned, and where resolutions, however tentative, can be mutually worked out. A space where they can practice democratic ways of interacting with each other and build skills to negotiate with conflicts outside the school. For girls I particular, schools and classrooms should be spaces to discuss processes of decision making, to interrogate the basis of their decisions and to make informed choices.
>
> The construction of the female learner as passive may act against her within participatory teaching and learning contexts. In our schools, where gender-based constructions underpin ideas of classroom discipline and strict divisions are maintained between girls and boys, a girl who is interactive is likely to be pulled up for transgressing the 'gender code'. Clearly, there needs to be a rethinking of the agency of the learner in the classroom context. This re-conceptualisation has to become an organic part of the way we think of education today and find a prominent place in the teacher training programmes.
>
> —"Position Paper: National Focus Group on Gender Issues in Education," *National Curriculum Framework,* National Council of Educational Research and Training, New Delhi, 2006, pp. 42-43.

Envisioning new possibilities of negotiating gender issues in education, teacher education needs to be of a very quality assured and evaluation effective programme of action. The life world of the learner in reality should always be under the careful and sympathetic scanner of the teacher. The innovative spirit of the teacher in close association with the learners requires a re-structuring of the essentials of excellence, and, for this end-in-view, some of the recommendations put forward by the National Focus Group as stated below deserve sincere attention:

A standard singular assessment is not desirable in the context of the differential needs and aptitudes of children. A variety of assessment strategies and multiple modes of assessment must be introduced that include the oral and the written, as well as objective, subjective, visual, narrative, abstract and concrete, arti-factual and symbolic, etc. these differential assessments should be designed to take into account the special aptitudes of different groups.

*Assessment Affirming a spirit of Critical Inquiry:* Assessment should affirm flexibility of mind, a questioning attitude, and scepticism towards some textbook writer's version of "eternal truth" rather than penalise learners for this.

Teacher Training to be more Self-Reflective, Participatory, and Research oriented.

Teachers' trainings, whether pre-service or in-service, need to have a vision of the teacher herself as a learner engaged in inquiry and reflection. A systemic study of gender theory should be combined with an engagement with their own position in society vis a vis gender roles.

Research skills need to be made part of the initial input given to teachers and research grants need to be provided to teachers to encourage to channelise their work into research material emerging from within the school to create an active situation of learning and energising the teacher.

Substantive support mechanisms need to be developed for teachers who are enthused to

> implement new ideas and pedagogies as part of their training, with the nurturing initiative emerging from within the school, rather perpetuate a top down approach.
>
> Mechanism for enhancing, evaluating and monitoring the quality, regularity and impact of teacher training programmes, specially in the rural areas, must be put in place.
>
> —*Ibid.*, pp. 52-53.

Good creative memory on the part of the twenty-first century teacher is not only a plus point for good teaching, but also a very important inspiring factor in a super computer conscious supersonic world of today signalling at every moment passive and artificial steps of the more engrossing and recapitulating brain power. If the teacher sets an example by judiciously displaying the role of good memory to the learners, it contributes a lot to self-assertion and self-dependence as adorning components of creativity rather than enslaving oneself to modern gadgets parasitically. As professor Highet characteristically comments:

> A display of good creative memory by a teacher helps the young in one of their most difficult jobs. Their attention is lively and their perception is keen, but they find it very hard to connect things. Many of the facts they learn merely drop into their minds like blocks of metal, and lie there. At examinations they take out the blocks, polish them, and show them to us. Then they put them back, or sometimes throw them away. If the facts simply remain on deposit, however neatly packed and highly polished, their possessors are not educated. The business of the teacher is to pass currents of interest and energy through the facts, while they are being learnt and afterwards, so that they melt, fuse, become

> interconnected, acquire life, and grow into vital parts of the minds which hold them.
>
> —Gilbert Highet: *The Art of Teaching,* Methuen, University Paperbacks, London, 1963, p. 58.

In the very first decade of the twenty-first century, teacher education has already welcome a series of challenges as above, and more challenges are yet to be encountered. Of these, overhauling teacher education in the light of inter-disciplinary approaches and cross-çounter nursling of scientific and humane values towards excellence and ascent of humans are beckoning every moment everywhere. In fact, teacher education has now been promoted to the culture of transparency and transcendence well crystallised in serenity and elegance, joy and poignance.

Meanwhile, let us envision ourselves in unison with the All Serene in the words of prayer:

> The poignant song is echoed through all the sky in many-coloured tears and smiles, alarms and hopes; waves rise uo and sink again, dreams break and form. In me is thy own defeat of self.
>
> This screen that thou hast raised is painted with innumerable figures with the brush of the night and the day. Behind it thy seat is woven in wondrous mysteries of curves, casting away all barren lines of straightness.
>
> The great pageant of thee and me has overspread the sky. Within the tune of thee and me all the air is vibrant, and all ages pass with the hiding and seeking of thee and me.
>
> —Rabindranath Tagore: *Gitanjali,* Macmillan India Limited, New Delhi, Macmillan Pocket Tagore Edition, 1983, No. LXXI, p. 48.

Are we prepared for the prayer?

# Index